CORRECTIONAL ADMINISTRATION AND CHANGE MANAGEMENT

CORRECTIONAL ADMINISTRATION AND CHANGE MANAGEMENT

MARTHA HENDERSON HURLEY
DENA HANLEY

CRC Press
Taylor & Francis Group
Boca Raton London New York

CRC Press is an imprint of the
Taylor & Francis Group, an **informa** business

CRC Press
Taylor & Francis Group
6000 Broken Sound Parkway NW, Suite 300
Boca Raton, FL 33487-2742

Printed in the United States of America on acid-free paper
10 9 8 7 6 5 4 3 2 1

International Standard Book Number: 978-1-4398-0392-9 (Hardback)

Library of Congress Cataloging-in-Publication Data

Hurley, Martha Henderson.
Correctional administration and change management / Martha Henderson Hurley, Dena Hanley.
p. cm.
Includes bibliographical references and index.
ISBN 978-1-4398-0392-9 (hardcover : alk. paper)
1. Correctional institutions--United States--Administration. 2. Correctional institutions--United States--Management. I. Hanley, Dena. II. Title.

HV9469.H87 2010
365.068--dc22 2010005448

Visit the Taylor & Francis Web site at
http://www.taylorandfrancis.com

and the CRC Press Web site at
http://www.crcpress.com

Dedication

This book is dedicated to those former and present correctional administrators who have been or are at the forefront of the "what works" and evidence-based practice movements in American corrections—administrators such as Reginald Wilkinson, Richard Seiter, and Edward Rhine, to name a few, who were fighting to change correctional organizations into more efficient, evidence-driven environments well before evidence-based decision making became fashionable.

Contents

Preface

Contemporary correctional administrators are faced with significant challenges. Correctional budgets have been reduced at a time when the offender population under supervision continues to grow. As a result, a constant refrain is sent to administrators and transmitted to staff: "Do more with less." This means that traditional modes of operation can no longer be sustained and that changing the way they do business is inevitable. Thus, it is imperative that correctional administrators understand how their agencies operate and identify the changes that can be successfully implemented within the organizational context.

The goal of this book is to provide both the student and the practitioner with a comprehensive examination of leadership, management, organizational culture, and results as they apply to correctional agencies. This work will introduce the correctional field to the concept of *organizational capacity*. Specifically, organizational capacity refers to the ability of the correctional agency to prepare, initiate, and successfully implement change within the organization. Thus, written for a broad audience, the book integrates leadership and management principles with organizational theory and assessment practices.

Organization of This Book

The organization of this book follows the order with which we believe change management should be addressed. The first chapter defines the construct of change management in corrections, reviews management theory, and discusses why change is so difficult in correctional environments. The chapter discusses why organizational capacity to implement change matters. Chapter 2 presents a description of the role of administration and guidance in driving and implementing change. Effective communication is a necessary ingredient for successful change initiatives. Chapter 3 reviews the literature on communication and discusses how correctional leaders can improve communication channels within their organizations. Next the book deals with information capital in Chapter 4. Information capital refers to the collection, access, and storage of the facts and figures necessary for informed data-driven decision making. Chapter 5 addresses the human element of change within the organizational context. Successful change initiatives are managed and implemented by staff with the requisite knowledge, skills, and abilities. The text then focuses on what we know "works" to improve correctional outcomes. Chapter 6 defines the concept of evidence-based practice and discusses its relevance within the correctional context. Managing for results is what legislative bodies and the public want to see correctional agencies accomplish. With this in mind, Chapter 7 describes the role of evaluation and outcome assessment in the process of improving correctional practice. Finally, the book ends with a call to action for correctional administrators seeking to initiate change.

Features

The outstanding feature of this book is the fact that it is not only a comprehensive text due to the range of topics, but it is presented in such a way that students and practitioners can easily grasp concepts and use the information quickly and efficiently. It is a working text, designed to allow students to roll up their sleeves and become enmeshed in the management decision-making process. The book is different from current texts in several important respects, including:

- It offers a thorough grounding in the foundational chapter about the nature of correctional organizations, organizational theory, and managing for change.
- Additionally, the chapters include learning objectives, a list of key terms, discussion questions, and suggestions for further reading. There is also a complete list of references and Web links.

Supplements

Several supplements are available for instructors and students to use with this book. The instructor resource includes access to PowerPoint lecture slides with graphics from the text. An accompanying solutions manual will allow correctional administrators to work through current issues that their agency is faced with in each topical area. At the same time, faculty teaching a correctional administration course can use the solutions manual as part of a management simulation program.

Acknowledgments

Thanks to our editor Carolyn Spence for your generous support and encouragement. We appreciate your sticking with us.

Thanks also to Kari Budyk, senior project coordinator, editorial project development, Taylor & Francis/CRC Press.

Thanks to my husband, David Christopher Hurley, for your love and continuous support on this publication journey. You know that I could not have done this without you.

Thanks to our children for providing us with amusement and distractions during our effort to complete this book.

About the Authors

Martha Hurley, Ph.D., received her doctorate in criminal justice from the University of Cincinnati in 2000, and has more than 10 years of experience working in the field. Dr. Hurley has conducted evaluability assessments and program evaluations in Ohio and Illinois. Specific areas of research experience include risk assessment and classification, analysis of performance measures, organizational change, and implementation of "best practices" in corrections. She has also conducted trainings on the use of the Level of Service Inventory-Revised (LSI-R) and "What Works" in corrections for state and local agencies.

Dr. Hurley is currently an associate professor at The Citadel in the Department of Political Science and Criminal Justice (Charleston, South Carolina). She has also worked as a senior researcher for the Ohio Department of Rehabilitation and Correction and served as a research analyst and facilitator of group sessions in a community-based juvenile program. She has conducted presentations and has published articles in the areas of evidence-based practice, organizational change, correctional attitudes, risk and needs assessment, and program implementation.

Dena Hanley, Ph.D., received her doctorate in criminal justice from the University of Cincinnati in 2002. She is currently employed as an associate professor in the Department of Political Science at the University of Akron, Ohio. Dr. Hanley joined Quest Consulting Network as a senior consultant in 2005. Her research interests include organizational capacity, delivery of effective services to offenders, and administrative and policy issues relating to corrections. Her primary focus lies in bridging the gap between quality research findings and the implementation of these findings into daily service delivery—the purpose being that research can help those who are in the trenches day-to-day, namely, offenders and the staff who work with them.

In addition to her degree, Dr. Hanley has worked in the field of corrections for more than 15 years. She has had the honor of being part of local community correctional organizations as well as larger federal agencies. She has served on a number of local, regional, state, and federal task forces for reentry, violence reduction, and community supervision.

Dr. Hanley lives in Akron, Ohio, with her two daughters.

Chapter 1

Introduction to Change Management in Correctional Organizations

> Change does not change tradition. It strengthens it. Change is a challenge and an opportunity, not a threat.
>
> **Prince Philip of England**

The field of corrections consistently fluctuates. External groups such as reform associations, legislatures, and the media, as well as internal influences such as employee unions and departments of corrections, are just a few examples of the sources that often need to be changed by correctional agencies and institutions (Stojkovic and Farkas 2003).

Too often, the correctional institution or organization rushes to implement the latest "fad" in corrections, in order to satisfy a demand from either external or internal stakeholders, without first considering how this may impact the organization or its members. One example of such a fad was the reliance on punishment-oriented community supervision during the mid-1980s and 1990s (Latessa, Cullen, and Gendreau 2002). This movement was led by the Intensive Supervision Program (ISP) demonstration projects, which were funded by the Bureau of Justice Assistance. Although the initial programs were evaluated and deemed somewhat successful (Petersilia and Turner 1993), replications of these programs failed to achieve the same results (Petersilia 1998). Further research showed that these replicated programs failed to implement the ISP model appropriately (Petersilia 1990a). In response to that discovery, researchers investigated the importance of program implementation in obtaining successful results (e.g., Byrne 1990; Gendreau, Goggin, and Smith 1999; Latessa, Cullen, and Gendreau 2002; Petersilia 1990a, 1990b).

ISPs are a prime example, but they are far from unique; the correctional field has fallen victim to many other fads as well. Such fads have included "three strikes" policies, prison construction, reentry, unproven treatment programs (such as acupuncture), and more. Indeed, any initiative can be termed a fad if it is not implemented appropriately (Hurley and Hanley 2006; Latessa, Cullen, and Gendreau 2002; Lawrence and Travis 2004; MacKenzie 2000; Seiter and Kadela 2003; Travis 2005). Often, programs are not successful due to improper implementation not design.

Change management is the key to effective, planned progress within the correctional milieu, both within institutions and among the community. The concept of change management should be incorporated into all aspects of correctional decision making.

Change Management

Change is an inevitable part of any correctional organization. Bureaucratic organizations, by their very nature, seek stability; hence, by design, they are resistant to change (Perrow 1970). Accordingly, correctional administrators hold the unenviable position of navigating between the need for stability and the forces that require change. All organizations must regularly address two issues: how to survive, grow, and adapt in the environment; and how to create internal structures that permit the organization to function (Schein 1992). Targeted, intentional changes can benefit the organization and its stakeholders. Improvements in the delivery of services, increased financial stability, and more positive outcomes for correctional clients are just a few of the benefits that can accompany changes in practice.

Change management for our purposes is defined as a systematic and planned process for utilizing internal and external resources to implement and monitor new initiatives in bureaucratic organizations. This process necessitates that organizations understand the driving forces of change and gather information about implementing the changes most efficiently. Change management includes developing a change management strategy; obtaining management and staff buy-in; developing the staff's knowledge, skills, and abilities; and monitoring the implementation so that adjustments can be made accordingly.

Correctional organizations frequently receive demands from external stakeholders to change or modify their processes. This type of change, when improperly executed, often creates a perpetual cycle of confusion (see Figure 1.1). In an attempt to institute changes within a system whose internal mechanisms are aligned against any threat to the status quo, correctional organizations are left in a constant state of uncertainty (Hanley 2007). A correctional organization's inability to successfully implement change decreases the confidence of external stakeholders while increasing the frustration of internal stakeholders who implement the organization's official mandate in the newly proscribed manner. This challenge often confuses

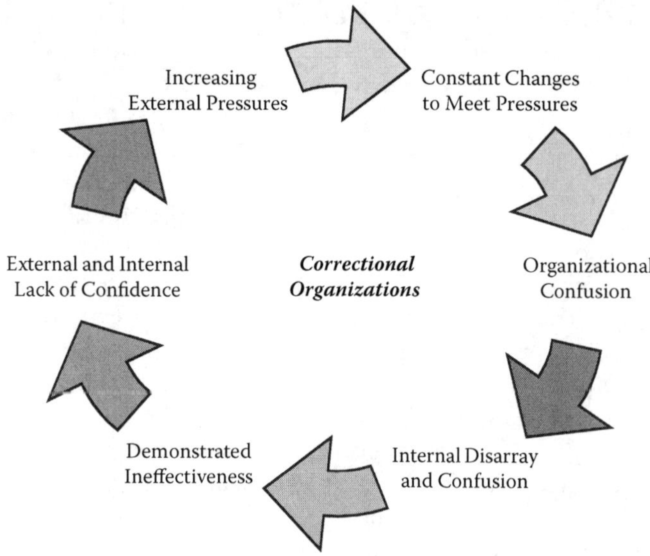

Figure 1.1 The perpetual cycle of confusion.

correctional staff, who are caught within the organizational crossfire and must choose between doing things the old, wrong way, which they understand, or the new, right way, which is incomprehensible. Thus, correctional staff members often become unsure of the organization's objectives and their role in achieving these goals. This uncertainty can lead to decreased organizational commitment as well as to the staff's failure to understand and perform their assigned duties.

External stakeholders, including legislators, judges, and the public, also experience confusion concerning negative consequences for the organization (Hanley 2007). External stakeholders habitually respond to correctional institutions' inability to implement legislative and judicial directives effectively by setting even more unrealistic demands. In response to the organization's inability to meet the new, unrealistic demands, the stakeholders' lack of confidence in the organization and its administrators increases even more. This doubt often undermines the organization's legitimacy, which results in reduced funding and other deficits in resources allocated to the organization.

Current correctional agencies will be forced to consider traditional policies and processes. This is evident based on the following external factors:

- Recent calls for reform in the wake of significant budget reductions.
- Requests from constituents for greater efficiency and accountability for correctional managers.
- Increasing demands for correctional agencies to implement evidence-based and best practices.

Correctional organizations can successfully answer such pleas only through effective change management. Numerous examples of failed correctional initiatives exist, where goals were not achieved, policies were not implemented, changes in service delivery were not observed, and overall confusion about the change management process plagued administrators, midlevel managers, and line staff. Correctional organizations that are unable to manage and successfully incorporate mandates for change become unsustainable, which frequently leads to a change of top-level correctional administrators.

The information presented in this book will introduce the correctional administrator to a variety of terms and concepts that are central to establishing a comprehensive change management process. The goal is not to provide the reader with a comprehensive examination of all aspects of change management; rather, this book presents a broad overview of the essential elements involved. Additionally, the book addresses issues that typically arise from change management procedures and describes potential remedies for these problems. The essential premise of this book is that correctional organizations must plan and manage change effectively in order to survive and grow.

This first chapter presents the concept of organizational capacity, which is the first step in developing a cohesive change management process and which has frequently been neglected as part of the process. Change management is essential for enhancing or limiting the ability of the correctional organization to successfully implement change.

Why Is Change Difficult in Corrections?

The management of correctional organizations is complex. Different institutions display wide variations in organizational structures, policies, and jurisdictions. Counties, cities, and all 50 states have their own individual ways of managing daily correctional operations. The correctional literature on the implementation of new initiatives in corrections reveals five issues that frequently block the success of correctional initiatives, in any type of institution:

1. A failure to engage in a strategic planning process for a new initiative.
2. A failure to consider current organizational functioning (or organizational capacity).
3. A failure to consider the organizational culture.
4. A failure to monitor and adjust the implementation of the new practice as time passes.
5. A failure to assess outcomes adequately.

Failure in Strategic Planning

In the field of corrections, when a new initiative is requested, it is usually instituted through a "one-size-fits-all" approach. Rather than engaging in a planned change process, the responsible managers try to force the new model to fit their specific organization. This is unwise; a carefully focused, specifically tailored change management process is required for full implementation of any new initiative. Several authors have supported the result of improved correctional outcomes when a strategic planning process is used (Stanton and Moultrie-Fierro 2004; Hurley and Hanley 2006). It is not realistic to assume that current deficits in organizational functioning would not affect the implementation of a new initiative; nevertheless, many (if not most) correctional organizations fail to assess organizational functioning prior to making significant changes. At a minimum, administrators must clearly understand what their organization is doing successfully or unsuccessfully, and why.

Failure to Assess Organizational Capacity for Change

Prior to implementing a targeted change process, organizations must conduct a frank internal self-assessment of functioning; this will identify the resources needed for the change, help build consensus, empower leadership with knowledge, and uncover potential areas of staff resistance. This type of assessment will reveal the organization's capacity to apply changes effectively. *Organizational capacity* refers to the ability of the correctional agency to prepare, initiate, and successfully implement change. To summarize, the analysis of organizational capacity provides four benefits for administrators, which increase the likelihood of success for new initiatives:

1. Discover staff resistance to change, prior to implementation so that issues can be addressed quickly.
2. Identify needed resources for change.
3. Build consensus among stakeholders.
4. Empowers leadership.

The assessment of organizational capacity is a process that addresses and evaluates the organization's strengths, weaknesses, opportunities, and threats that could hinder the implementation of the change initiative. This process allows the organization to assess its current situation, plan for the future, and capitalize on current successes.

Failure to Consider Organizational Culture

Significant organizational change coincides with a modification of organizational culture. Schein (1997) strongly suggests that before any change can occur, change agents must understand the organizational culture and environment.

As indicated below, many different characterizations can define *organizational culture*:

> A set of common understandings around which action is organized, . . . finding expression in language whose nuances are peculiar to the group. (Becker and Geer 1960, p. 29)

> A pattern of shared values and beliefs that help individuals understand organizational functioning and thus provide them with the norms for behavior in the organization. (Deshpandé and Webster 1989, p. 4)
>
> A pattern of shared basic assumptions that the group learned as it solved its problems of external adaptation and internal integration, that has worked well enough to be considered valid and, therefore, to be taught to new members as the correct way you perceive, think, and feel in relation to those problems. (Schein 1992, p. 12)

Regardless of which definition is selected, *culture* refers to an aspect of organizational life that indicates why workers do what they do. In a nutshell, organizational culture comprises the assumptions, values, and norms that are reflected by how the organization values resources, time, space, facilities, and people. More importantly, these basic beliefs that characterize the organization also impact behaviors, such as strategies utilized, technologies employed, services provided, and outcomes achieved.

Adei (2006) lists five areas in which organizational culture can be observed directly:

1. The general attitude toward leadership and leadership style
2. The general attitude toward time management
3. Work planning and performance
4. The propensity to consume resources
5. The manner in which people should be rewarded and controlled

Similarly, Schein (1985) reports that culture (1) determines what people pay attention to, (2) defines what things mean, (3) impacts how people react emotionally, and (4) informs about what actions should be taken at what times. Each area represents a practice that can be strategically influenced by management. This book fundamentally views organizational culture as a feature of an organization that is controllable by management and that impacts the organization's effectiveness. Good managers control and shape the culture to meet organizational goals (Schein 1997).

Researchers have long implicated organizational culture as a major culprit in the failure of new initiatives (Baker et al. 2003; Sherman, Milton, and Kelly 1973). This conclusion arises from the assumption that a correctional organization that possesses a strong culture, as evidenced by values, beliefs, and behaviors that support the new initiative, is more likely to meet organizational goals and to exhibit successful outcomes. As discussed by Deal and Kennedy (2000, p. 15), "A strong culture is a system of informal rules that spells out how people are to behave most of the time. In a weak culture, employees waste a good deal of time just trying to figure out what they should do and how they should do it." In a strong culture, managers take the lead and shape the atmosphere to support and meet organizational goals and demands (National Research Council Staff 1997).

Failure to Monitor Performance and Assess Outcomes

Even when correctional managers engage in a strategic planning process, some agencies fail to monitor, measure, and analyze performance and to adjust criteria accordingly (Hurley and Hanley 2006). In such cases, "The strategy realized often differs significantly from the strategy intended" (Boonstra 2004, p. 2). Good intentions do not always equal proper results unless they are carefully monitored. Far too often, the indications that an initiative was not properly implemented are discovered in an outcome evaluation that reveals failures, such as lack of savings, increased recidivism, and staff dissatisfaction.

Organizational Theory and Change

To understand the relationship between organizational theories and change, several concepts must be discussed. First, a definition of organization must be established. Next, this chapter will discuss the two dominant organizational models within the field of corrections as well as their inherent strengths and weaknesses amidst change.

Defining Organization

Organization can be defined in many ways. Minimally, an organization requires two or more people working in concert to accomplish some goal and objective. More complex definitions add an element of formal internal structure. Hence, an organization refers to any group or entity in which an administrative and functional structure act together to achieve common goals. Organizations can vary in size and length of time in operation. For the purpose of this book (which is to examine institutions of correction), *organization* will be defined as a group of individuals working together to achieve a set of goals or objectives within a framework of delineated administrative and functional processes that are overseen by management.

The Traditional or Classical Organizational Model for Corrections

Traditionally, correctional organizations tend to follow the classical organization model, and they typically operate as bureaucracies. Following the Weberian tradition, a *bureaucracy* is understood in terms of a hierarchical division of labor, regulatory procedural mechanisms, and impersonal relationships, and it is based on the need for legal or rational order (Weber 1947). According to this perspective, bureaucracies are characterized by:

- Fixed and official jurisdictional areas that are ordered by rules and administrative regulations
- Hierarchy and levels of graded authority, where the lower offices are supervised by the higher ones
- Management that is based on official policies
- Regular activities of workers that are distributed as official duties
- Set processes that are prescribed for the fulfillment of assigned duties
- Qualified employees

Weber views bureaucracies in a positive light due to the organization's rational approach and efficient methods used to achieve goals. According to Weber, bureaucracies were originally successful because they use a scientific approach to understanding and hence routinizing a process while reducing the number of exceptions in the raw material that will become the final product. In short, bureaucracies accomplish two things. First, bureaucratic management discovers the best method for producing something and then standardizes the process to ensure that it is conducted the same way each time. Second, management understands and engineers the raw materials in order to increase uniformity so that all materials can be processed identically. Hence, bureaucracies are financially successful because they radically decrease the unknown elements in the production process and therefore provide organizational stability.

If bureaucracies highlight the epitome of rational decision making and efficient processes, then why are they now viewed with disdain? *Bureaucracy* is often a pejorative term associated with inefficiency, waste, and the notion of "red tape." The strength of the bureaucratic process is its ability to function smoothly when the tasks are routine and the environment is stable; hence, the process works well when the organization's goal is to turn steel, plastic, and wiring into automobiles within the confines of a stable factory. When a bureaucratic model is utilized in an unstable environment or one in which tasks are not always routine, problems can result.

An organization's ability to implement change is constrained by its very structure. Not all methods of organization are equally conducive to managing change effectively. To explore this concept, this chapter will examine the two prevailing management theories that dominate the correctional literature: classical management (that is, bureaucratic) theory, which focuses on efficiency in the work process; and the human relations model, which tends to provide a more democratically oriented structure.

As already discussed, the strengths of classical organizations are the routinization of processes and the stability obtained by reducing exceptions in raw material. Not surprisingly, the original bureaucracies were found in manufacturing plants that produced tangible outputs. Weberian principles, coupled with classic engineering practices, dramatically increased the rate of production in industries, at least when the innovations were correctly applied.

Originally, the job of top management personnel was to design and maintain an engineering process that efficiently processed raw materials into tangible outputs within a milieu where administrators comprehended both the scientific process and the properties of the raw materials. The process of turning inputs into outputs could be logically subdivided into smaller functional components; in a sequential procedure, the raw material could be processed in specific stages. Correspondingly, labor could be divided. Each worker accomplished only one specialized task repeatedly, resulting in assembly line production.

When new advances in technology or technique were realized, management simply resigned to the process and then informed the factory workers of their new responsibilities. Successful top-down communication was enabled by the management's knowledge of the process and the raw material. Because of the unchanging nature of the materials, when exceptions did occur, they could be promptly investigated and understood. The solution to such problems would be recorded so that when future similar incidents occurred, the problems could be looked up in a manual and then solved by applying the prescribed, standardized solutions. Unsurprisingly, the favored organizational structure for such a business was a rule-bound institution with a hierarchical structure and centralized authority.

Proponents of classical bureaucratic theory advocated that all industries would benefit by conforming to a similar logical design. In response to such advice, top correctional administrators divided up their personnel, ranked them according to their areas of specialization, and then grouped them together according to their assigned tasks or roles. Each position within the correctional organization dealt with the execution of a specialized task. A clear division of labor resulted, and it is best illustrated by organizational compartmentalization of the competing correctional goals of treatment and security. Thus, the organizational structure reflects departmental or divisional subgroups with rigid boundaries that operate between specialized subgroups. Layers of management exist at each level of specialization, with higher positions controlling lower positions.

Within this structure, functions are well defined, and areas of responsibility are clearly delineated in a specific chain of command. A central goal within classically organized agencies is the creation of a compliant workforce whose members obediently follow the dictates of upper management. As a result, communication structures tend to be formal and are primarily vertical. Upper-level administrators form and transmit policies to lower-level staff members, who are expected to implement changes without providing input. Policy, procedure, and practices are designed to maintain the status quo. When problems occur within the system, it is assumed that the error lies with the raw materials or incorrectly applied procedures, not the process itself (i.e., organizational design errors or management flaws).

Classical management practices, however, face serious obstacles when applied to correctional organizations. The chief challenge is the assumption that engineering-based processes can be applied to the human condition effectively. There are two flaws in this concept. First, the raw material in the correctional process is human beings, most of whom are unhappy about their incarceration and who are merely compliant, at best, or openly hostile, at worst. Given the variability of human behavior and the difficulty of predicting it, the very material that provides the inputs into the correctional setting is not fully understood. Second, the same process does not always create the same results; even when inmates receive uniform treatments, the outputs will vary tremendously. Upon release, some inmates will stop offending, some will revert to their old pattern of offenses, and others will engage in greater deviances. Hence, the bureaucratic notion of a routine process performed in a stable environment is suspect when applied to a correctional setting.

Upon this shaky foundation, the ability to implement change within a correctional organization is also questionable. Top-down management in a bureaucratic setting implies that the managers, not the workers, have the best understanding of the effectiveness and efficiency of the organization's current daily processes. Because of the instability of the human condition, however, the first-line workers are generally first to notice changes in attitudes or issues within the prison population. By failing to include any staff other than senior managers when planning for change, bureaucratic management misses the insights, awareness, knowledge, and skills of those workers, which are necessary to successfully implement change. Consequently, initiatives often fail because they do not recognize the importance of staff support. Moreover, this lack of inclusion often increases the hostility of frontline and midlevel staff to upper management, which makes those employee layers even more resistant to implementing change.

The bureaucratic engineering approach also advocates the standardization of processes, which often translate into a one-size-fits-all approach. Because the offenders are perceived to be the raw materials, all experience the same process; if something goes wrong, the mistake is assumed to be defective raw materials, not processing errors or a failure to engage in a strategic implementation process. Moreover, these organizations fail to consider informal networks and the organizational culture, which hinders new initiatives by limiting the organization's ability to transmit the information, skills, and knowledge necessary to implement the change.

Lastly, classical management fails to consider any influences external to the organization. Through administrative, judicial, and legislative processes, external and internal stakeholders powerfully influence the inner workings of correctional institutions. Hence, the current fiscal crisis, the litigiousness of offenders, funding agencies' call for greater accountability, the greater participation of the public within correctional contexts, and the move toward evidence-based correctional practices are all dynamic features that highlight the constant state of flux in correctional environments. The top administrators' inability to control internal processes within their institutions undercuts the notion of stability, which is a central assumption of the bureaucratic model. Unfortunately, the majority of correctional organizations simply follow this classically structured but weak design because of tradition or inertia.

Human Relations

In contrast to the classical organizational model, which relies on formal hierarchical authority and rigid communication chains, the human relations management style is characterized by inclusion. The classical model is criticized because its highly bureaucraticized structures and organizational barriers limit the organization's ability to respond to change in a swift, certain, efficient, and timely manner. The human relations model, on the other hand, assumes that the workers, not the managers, have the greatest influence over the successful output of the product. It proposes that organizations do not operate strictly according to rule-bound authority; workers form their own norms that, at times, oppose those of the leadership (see Mayo 1949, for the initial formulation of this approach). In an organization driven by the human relations tradition, organizational structures are flexible; social relationships among workers matter; different sections of the organization interrelate; teamwork is emphasized; and all internal stakeholders, in addition to managers, are represented when establishing policy and implementing change.

The human relations model indicates that communication is essential for effective organizational functioning. Organizations do not change; people do. If the staff members do not trust the leaders, share the organization's vision, or support the reason for change, and if they are not included in the planning, then there will be no successful change, regardless of the strategy's brilliancy. Organizational success depends upon obtaining staff cooperation and maintaining open lines of communication. When managers develop relationships with their workers, both sides form more realistic expectations. This results in a management style that aligns the interests of the organization with those of its employees, allowing both to share both the risks and rewards of doing business.

The human relations model enables organizations to pursue new ideas, strategies, and target populations in order to sustain themselves and improve conditions for their workers. As a result, staffs can be compensated and treated fairly; they can develop professionally; and they can work within meaningful, challenging environments. Organizations can then expect their employees to engage in personal growth, idea development, quality service delivery, and organizational transformation.

The Management of Change

Regardless of the organizational management principle followed, change within correctional contexts should be achieved through a formalized process. When change is the result of predictable and unambiguous problems, then a planned change process can be utilized. This type of change is driven by senior managers. The upper levels of management initiate, guide, and monitor implementation, with limited input from staff (Boonstra 2004, p. 4). When the problems driving the change are ambiguous or when the direction of change lacks clarity, a developmental approach is more functionally appropriate (Boonstra 2004; Cummings and Worley 2001).

Planned Change Management

Planned change is a logical approach that is based on utilizing scientific knowledge in order to adapt, improve, and develop the organization (Bennis et al. 1976; Boonstra 2004). As described by Boonstra (2004, p. 5), "In order to achieve adaptations and improvements, managers and consultants take a rational approach: they analyse the surroundings, formulate goals, develop a strategy, and then implement change." Experts can educate upper management on practices and principles, but lower-level staff members are not incorporated into the change management process. Unfortunately, the approach still relies on a top-down implementation strategy. The changes are initiated, managed, and controlled by top management, and little emphasis is placed on transforming the organization into an environment in which learning and scientific knowledge are valued at all organizational levels.

Organizational Development

> *Organizational development* is defined as a systematic process for applying behavioural science principles and practices in organizations to increase individual and organizational effectiveness. The goal is to improve how organizations relate to their external environments and function internally to attain high performance and quality of work life. (Boonstra 2004, p. 7)

Organizational development refers to a transformative change management process in which input from all stakeholders is viewed as critical for the success of the initiative. This requires a shift away from a strictly hierarchical organizational model, in which only leaders know best, to an organization that values the opinions of all workers, seeks to educate workers in order to maximize efficiency, utilizes research literature in efforts to transform the organization, and ensures that employees can access the tools necessary to becoming lifelong learners of their trade. This type of organization engages in continuous quality improvement, uses data to inform practice, and institutes open directions for information flow. Leaders in this type of organization seek input from all internal stakeholders before initiating agency change.

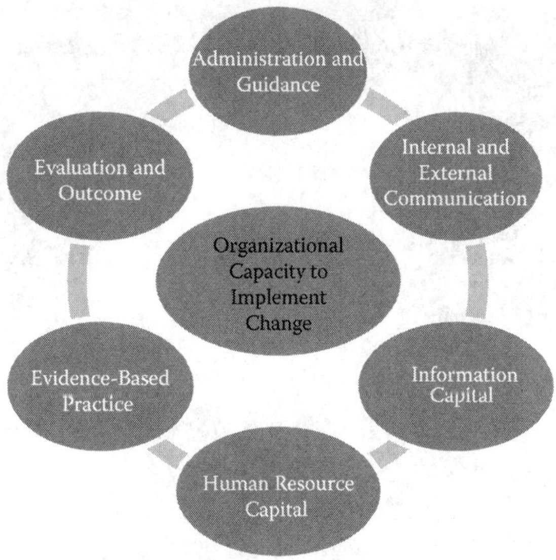

Figure 1.2 The change management process.

Managing for Results in Corrections

To improve correctional outcomes, correctional administrators need to create learning organizations that transcend traditional modes of operation and implement an administrative model that emphasizes cross-level collaboration, continuous quality improvement, and bridging the gap between research and practice. As seen in Figure 1.2, which depicts the change management process, correctional administrators need to examine several critical domains within their organizations in order to improve service delivery, enhance organizational performance, and remain sustainable. The full change management model includes six domains:

1. Administration and Guidance
2. Internal and External Communication
3. Information Capital
4. Human Resource Capital
5. Evidence-Based Practice
6. Evaluation and Outcome

When implemented effectively, these components reflect an organization that manages change efficiently and successfully.

Subsequent chapters will discuss each of these domains extensively. The overall goal of this text is to present administrators, middle managers, and other stakeholders with a model process for enhancing service delivery and improving change management processes. The change management process should always begin with a basic assessment of organizational capacity in the six critical areas.

Learning Objectives

After completing this chapter, you should be able to—

- Define *organization*
- Explain why change is an inevitable part of correctional organizational growth and development
- Discuss why change is difficult for correctional organizations
- Define organizational culture and its role in the change management process
- Explain the influence of management theory on organizational change in corrections
- Discuss the difference between planned change management and organizational development models
- Define *organizational capacity* to implement change

Key Terms

Bureaucracy
Change management
Classical organizational model
Human relations
Organization
Organizational capacity
Organizational culture
Organizational development
Planned change management

Discussion Questions

1. Select a local correctional agency (probation department, parole agency, treatment program, or prison), examine the organizational structure, and discuss the factors that might make change difficult to implement.
2. Using the same agency selected above, identify the specific areas within the organization that would need to be reviewed as part of an assessment of organizational capacity to implement change. Then develop a list of possible measurements for each area.

Suggested Reading

Kotter, J. 1996. *A force for change.* New York: Macmillan.

Perrow, C. 1961. The analysis of goals in complex organizations. *American Sociological Review* 26:194–208.

Stojkovic, S., and M.A. Farkas. 2003. *Correctional leadership: A cultural perspective.* Belmont, CA: Wadsworth Press.

References

Adei, S. 2006. The role of organizational culture and effectiveness of public organizations. Available at: http://www.public.iastate.edu/~fowusu/Accra%20Workshop/Wkshp_Appendix_A.pdf (accessed April 14, 2009).

Baker, G., H. King, J. L. MacDonald, and J. D. Horbar. 2003. Using organizational assessment surveys for improvement in neonatal intensive care. *Pediatrics* 111: 419–425.

Becker, H., and B. Geer. 1960. Participant observation: The analysis of qualitative field data. In *Human organization research: Field relations and techniques,* edited by R. N. Adams and J. J. Preiss. Homewood, IL: Dorsey Press.

Bennis, W. G., J. Van Maanen, E. J. Schein, and F. I. Steeles. 1979. *Essays in interpersonal dynamics.* Homewood, IL: Dorsey Press.

Boonstra, J. J. 2004. *Dynamics of organizational change and learning.* Hoboken, NJ: John Wiley & Sons. http://site.ebrary.com/lib/thecitadel/Doc?id=10113973&ppg=26 (accessed April 14, 2009).

Byrne, J. 1990. The future of intensive probation supervision and the new intermediate sanctions. *Crime & Delinquency* 36: 1–41.

Cummings, T. G., and C. Worley. 2001. *Essentials of organization development and change.* Cincinnati, Ohio: South-Western College Pub.

Deal, T. E., and A. A. Kennedy. 2000. *Corporate cultures: The rites and rituals of corporate life.* Cambridge, MA: Perseus Publishing.

Deschenes, E. P., S. Turner, and J. Petersilia. 1995. A dual experiment in intensive supervision: Minnesota's prison diversion and enhanced supervised release programs. *The Prison Journal* 75(3): 330–356.

Deshpandé, R., and F. E. Webster. 1989. Organizational culture and marketing: Defining the research agenda. *Journal of Marketing* 53: 3–15.

Deshpandé, R., J. Farley, and F. E. Webster, Jr. 1993. Corporate culture, customer orientation, and innovativeness in Japanese firms: A quadrad analysis. *Journal of Marketing* 57: 23–37.

Gendreau, P., C. Goggin, and P. Smith. 1999. The forgotten issue in effective correctional treatment: Program implementation. *International Journal of Offender Therapy and Comparative Criminology* 43: 180–187.

Hanley, D. 2007 Presentation. Organizational capacity: Establishing a baseline. Miami, Florida: American Association of Community Justice Professionals, June 2007.

Hurley, M., and D. Hanley. 2006. Planning for quality: A strategy for reentry initiatives. *Western Criminology Review* 7: 62–78.

Latessa, E. J., F. T. Cullen, and P. Gendreau. 2002. Beyond correctional quackery—Professionalism and the possibility of effective treatment. *Federal Probation* 66: 43–49.

Lawrence, S., and J. Travis. 2004. *The new landscape of imprisonment: Mapping America's prison expansion.* Washington, DC: The Urban Institute.

MacKenzie, D. L. 2000. Evidence-based corrections: Identifying what works. *Crime and Delinquency* 46: 457–471.

Mayo, E. 1947. *The political problem of industrial civilization.* Division of Research, Graduate School of Business Administration, Harvard University.

National Research Council Staff. 1997. Enhancing organizational performance. Washington, DC: National Academies Press. Available at: http://site.ebrary.com/lib/thecitadel/Doc?id=10041126&ppg=25 (accessed June 15, 2009).

Perrow, C. 1970. *Organizational analysis: A sociological view*, Belmont, CA: Wadsworth Publishing Co.
Petersilia, J. 1990a. Conditions that permit intensive supervision programs to survive. *Crime & Delinquency* 36(1): 126–145.
Petersilia, J. 1990b. When probation becomes more dreaded than prison. *Federal Probation* 1: 23–27.
Petersilia, J., and S. Turner. 1993. Intensive probation and parole. In *A Review of the Research*, edited by M. Tonry. Chicago: University of Chicago Press.
Schein, Edgar H. 1985. *Organizational culture and leadership*. San Francisco: Jossey-Bass.
Schein, Edgar H. 1991. What is culture? In *Reframing Organizational Cultures*, edited by P. J. Frost, L. Moore, M. R. Louis, C. C. Lundburg, and J. Martin, pp. 243–254. Newbury Park, CA: Sage.
Schein, Edgar. 1992. *Organizational culture and leadership* (2nd ed.). San Francisco: Jossey-Bass.
Schein, E. 1997. *Organizational culture and leadership* (3rd ed.). San Francisco: Jossey-Bass.
Seiter, R. P., and K. R. Kandela. 2003. Prisoner reentry: What works, what doesn't, and what is promising. *Crime and Delinquency* 49: 360–388.
Sherman, L. W. 1973. *Team policing: Seven case studies.* Washington, DC: Police Foundation.
Stanton, B. L., and B. J. Moultrie–Fierro. 2004. *Strategic planning: A 10-step approach.* Available at: http://nicic.org/Library/period264 (accessed June 29, 2009).
Stojkovic, S. and M. A. Farkas. 2003. *Correctional leadership: A cultural perspective.* Belmont, CA: Wadsworth Publishing.
Travis, J. 2005. *But they all come back: Facing the challenges of prisoner reentry.* Washington, DC: The Urban Institute.
Weber, M. 1947. *The theory of social and economic organizations.* Edited by T. Parsons. Translated by A. M. Henderson and T. Parsons. New York: Free Press.

Chapter 2

Administration and Guidance

You must be the change you wish to see in the world.

Mohandas K. Gandhi

Influences from virtually all directions impact the way an organization operates. Emery and Trist (1994) suggest that organizational change is difficult to study, primarily because of the constantly changing environment in which organizations exist. The driving forces of change vary often as a result of external influences (Dromgoole and Mullins 2000). Moreover, organizations while increasing their complexity are also under pressure to incorporate the latest management techniques and field practices (Emery and Trist 1994). This process of changing to meet the requirements of the external environment in order to receive funding, to meet legislative requirements, and other related issues forces the organization into a state of constant flux and confusion. The organization changes in terms of complexity to meet the demands of the environment, and the environment changes, which again impacts the organization. Therefore, organizations and the environment in which they operate are compelled into a continuous relationship of interdependence that Emery and Trist (1994) term *causal texture*.

The leadership and administration of an organization act as both liaison to the causal texture and a protective umbrella, shielding other members of the organization from the political and other forces that have influence over the operations of correctional institutions. This dual role of leadership requires that administrators serve multiple roles and functions within the organization. This chapter discusses how the various roles of administrators influence the organization more broadly and the characteristics associated with excellence in leadership. Furthermore, this chapter will discuss the impact leaders have on the organizational culture, and in turn, the operations of the correctional organizations. Finally, the role of leadership in the ever-changing environment will be presented. This chapter is not designed to be a comprehensive examination of leadership nor of the empirical findings related to leadership. However, this chapter will highlight some of the issues that are commonplace among correctional organizations and other agencies.

Distinguishing Leaders, Managers, and Administrators*

Administrators have many responsibilities in an organization. We use the word *administrator* because it implies both a leadership and a management function. Administrators will act as the gateway between the institution and funding sources, legislators, the media, the public, and other interested parties, as well as being responsible for the everyday running of their institution. Some distinction needs to be made between leadership and management. In the field, the terms *leader* and *manager* are at times used interchangeably, however, there are distinct differences between the two. Leadership has been defined as "a social process that involves determining the group's objectives, motivating behavior in pursuit of these objectives, and influencing group maintenance and culture" (Lewis, Goodman, and Fandt 1994, p. 425). This definition, while highlighting the visionary approach successful leaders incorporate, overlooks that leadership can and does occur within all levels of the organization. All too often leadership is thought of as simply the formal placement individuals into roles and positions within the organizational hierarchy. There are individuals outside the formal structure that have greater power to influence others in the institution than their position would normally dictate. This type of leadership is informal and can be found among the correctional staff or even the inmate population. So, the correctional administrators in order to successfully implement change must consider both formal and informal leaders at every level of the organization.

While leaders tend to focus on the vision or long-term positioning of the organization, managers maintain the status quo. As Stojkovic and Farkas (2003) point out, leaders establish the mission that managers execute or implement. Additionally, good leaders are good communicators, making sure their goals and objectives are well-formulated, coordinated, and understood. Good managers are efficiency-oriented, making sure these goals and objectives are translated into manageable tasks, that are completed smoothly and successfully by the line personnel (Hackman and Johnson 1991). Both positions contribute significantly to the organization's success. In corrections, due to public demand and legislative and judicial oversight,

* The terms *leader* and *administrator*, as well as *leadership* and *administration*, will be used interchangeably throughout this chapter.

administrators constantly have to restructure programs, services and, objectives while managers must ensure implementation of these changes are accomplished effectively within their limited pool of personnel, financial, and material resources. Hence, effective administrators must be constantly vigilant of the external environment and take this into account when making changes to or modifying the organization (McKevitt 2000).

The Need for Leaders to Emphasize Flexibility and Growth in Procedural Operations

Leaders may take different management approaches and must deal with various types of change initiators; effective leaders guide and prepare the organization for future events, despite these events being unknown. It is this role that leaders are most unfamiliar with and also that is the most important, from a causal texture point of view. Leadership is an "an essential ingredient in effective and successful management" (Adair 1984, p. ix.). In the criminal justice arena, particularly in the area of corrections, mandated changes will be enforced on the institution; and rigid, unprepared institutions will rush to accommodate the mandated changes. The rush to meet the new requirements or change will result in an organization that experiences continuous disorder and chaos. Most staff do not perform well under these conditions. Therefore, correctional organizations must be flexible to prepare for the unforeseen circumstances within an environment that is often described as "uncertain" (Hartley 2000). Strategic leadership is critical during times of major change (Dennis, Langley, and Cazale 1996).

To prepare the organization for unforeseen changes, leaders must integrate flexibility within the organization while maintaining a culture of efficiency and meeting the current demands set forth by the external and internal influences that impact the organization. In short, leaders are chiefly responsible for the vision of the organization and the establishment of an organizational culture that supports that vision (Gillen 2000; Stojkovic and Farkas 2003). Although this is a daunting task, correctional organizations, systems, and agencies are somewhat fortunate that the goals are already specified. A correctional agency or institution has two primary mandates: to protect society and reduce recidivism. There are various ways leaders can strive to achieve these goals and numerous delineations of the defining characteristics associated with quality leadership. However, one common theme among all of the typologies of leaders is that they must exhibit influence over others (Hackman and Johnson 1991).

While leaders are responsible for meeting specific goals set by external sources, leaders must also establish environments that are conducive to growth *within* the organization itself. It is critical that staff perceive the organization they work for to value them and have an interest in their well being. Staff need to perform at their optimum level, learn through their work, and put what they have learned where it can be most effective (Garratt 1990). The workplace should be a place where that process can occur (Manning 2001). If the organization is not conducive to this type of performance, leaders must develop a vision regarding where the organization should be in terms of environment and culture—a vision that enhances the ability to implement change (Stojkovic and Farkas 2003). The development of flexible, innovative, and growth-oriented correctional organizations requires administrators who are visionaries and who give priority to their role as change agent (Westley and Mintzberg 1989).

Roles of the Leader / Administrator

Correctional leaders vary in their perceptions of their primary role in the decision-making process. According to Farkas and Wetlaufer (1996), leaders assume one of five unique approaches in managing organization:

1. Strategic approach
2. Human-asset approach
3. Expertise approach
4. Box approach
5. Change approach

Farkas and Wetlaufer's essential premise is, No matter where a company is located or what it makes, its CEO must develop a guiding, over-arching philosophy about how he or she can best add value. The approach taken determines which aspects of the organization receive attention, such as strategic planning, research and development, recruiting, what kind of people and behaviors the CEO values in the organization, which decisions the CEO makes personally or delegates, and how he or she spends each day (Farkas and Wetlaufer 1996). Moreover, the approach indicates how the administrator responds to the winds of change.

Administrators who take the strategic approach believe that their primary job is to create, test, design, and implement long-term strategy and devote 80% of their time to issues external to the organization. The strategist is primarily concerned with changes driven by external stakeholders and would be less likely to address change driven by lower-level staff. Administrators who take the human-assets approach devote most of their time to the development of staff. They spend the majority of their time on personnel issues such as recruiting and conducting performance reviews. When change must occur, the human-asset administrator would be most concerned with staff satisfaction and performance over external stakeholder wishes. The expertise approach emphasizes the need for employees to develop specific expertise that will give the organization the competitive advantage. The expertise-oriented administrator would seek to provide advantages in change structures to upper-level, more educated staff rather than seeking to increase overall performance for all employees. An administrator who takes the box approach stresses stability and conformity in the delivery of services, the training of staff, and overall management of the organization. The box approach indicates an administrator who is least likely to innovate and change. This administrator is a traditionalist who must be forced to implement change. The majority of the box administrator's time is spent drafting policies and procedures, managing compliance, and dealing swiftly and quickly with exceptions to the rule. In marked contrast, the change approach administrator gives priority to the development of an organizational culture that supports innovation, flexibility, and growth.

Leaders as Change Agents

We focus in this chapter on those leaders who, in the current correctional environment, view their primary role to be that of change agent. The change that the leader is seeking might be driven by the need to innovate, such as through the introduction of new technology; the need to reduce costs; or the desire to imitate programs and practices that other organizations have found to be effective in meeting challenges (Freeman 1999).

Kania (2008) states that there are three types of natural change patterns that leaders must deal with: straight-line change, rise-plateau-crash change, and cyclic change. Correctional leaders, in particular, have a history of engaging in straight-line change. This type of change refers to the restructuring of organizational processes based on whatever is in fashion at the time, resulting in significant changes to practices and procedures every couple of years. Other times leaders serve as change agents for rise-plateau-crash innovations. This process refers to the implementation of specific technologies that become popular, are readily implemented, and are ultimately replaced by a newer version of the application. Most often, Kania suggests that correctional leaders must deal with cyclic change cycles where some aspect of the correctional organization experiences a problem, the problem is addressed and disappears for awhile, only to return again. This last type of change, cyclic in nature, is often a result of a failure of leadership to transform the organizational culture from one resistant to change to one supportive of change.

Characteristics of Effective Leaders

As evidenced from our discussion thus far, the concept of leadership effectiveness captures a plethora of often confusing characteristics and behaviors. To clarify the attributes of effective leadership, the National Institute of Corrections identified the core competencies—the key skills, knowledge, and attributes—that executive, senior-level, manager, and supervisory correctional leadership should possess (see Table 2.1). A review of the core competencies reveals that at a minimum, effective correctional leaders across all levels are ethical; think strategically and problem solve; reflect the mission, vision, and goals of the organization in

Table 2.1 Core Competencies of Correctional Leadership

Executives	*Senior Level*	*Managers*	*Supervisors*
Self-awareness	Self-awareness	Ethics and values	Ethics and values
Ethics and values	Ethics and values	Interpersonal relationships	Interpersonal relationships
Vision and mission	Vision and mission	Motivating others	Oral and written communication
Strategic thinking	Strategic thinking	Developing direct reports	Motivating others
Managing the external environment	Managing the external environment	Managing conflict	Developing direct reports
Power and influence	Power and influence	Team building	Managing conflict
Collaboration	Strategic planning and performance	Collaboration	Team building
Team building	Team building	Problem solving and decision making	Collaboration
	Collaboration	Strategic thinking	Problem solving and decision making
		Managing change	Criminal justice system
		Program planning and performance assessment	
		Criminal justice system	

Source: Campbell, N. M. (2005, p. 3). *Correctional Leadership Competencies for the 21st Century: Managers and Supervisors*. http://nicic.org/Downloads/PDF/Library/020475.pdf.

their interpersonal relationships with workers; take a collaborative approach; and engage in team building.

These competencies serve multiple purposes. Correctional organizations can use these characteristics to recruit and select leaders who have the greatest chance of improving service delivery and implementing change. Correctional administrators themselves may utilize these competencies for personal growth and professional development (Campbell 2005, p. xbvii). In the end the core competencies reflect the knowledge, skills, and abilities essential for effective leadership during times of instability and change.

What Is It That Effective Leaders Do When Trying to Initiate Change?

The core competencies reveal the individual characteristics associated with effective leadership, but it important that we also discuss what it is that effective leaders actually do (see Table 2.2). The field of corrections is a collaborative endeavor (Carter 2006). Thus, we present a description of what it is that an effective collaborative correctional leader does. Effective leaders are able to effectively communicate the mission and vision of the organization. The leader ensures that staff understand where the organization is heading and what it is trying to achieve, and informs them of their role in this process. A quality leader provides opportunities, incentives, and the tools for employees to excel in accomplishing organizational goals. Such leaders guide rather than criticize. They find the right people for the job. Effective leaders plan change and carry out the following activities:

- Engage in strategic thinking and planning activities.
- Conduct an assessment of organizational functioning.
- Develop a vision, mission, values, and goals for the organization.
- Address staff resistance and obtain commitment from staff for new initiatives.
- Communicate effectively.
- Implement and modify changes as necessary.

Strategic Planning

Correctional organizations exist in unstable environments as a result of fluctuations in funding, changes in the offender population, and other pressures from both external and internal stakeholders. Since the 1990s, organizations have focused on becoming more flexible and faster in response to environmental changes (Placet and Branch 2002). Environmental shifts have forced administrators to make decisions regarding complex issues under uncertain, volatile, and ambiguous situations and to

Table 2.2 What Is It That Effective Leaders Do?

Statement
They plan and think strategically.
They assess organizational functioning prior to considering and implementing change.
They develop changes consistent with the values, mission, vision, and goals of the organization.
They use data to aid in decision making.
They deal with organizational culture and address staff resistance.
They create learning organizations.
They motivate staff.
They are committed to full implementation of the new initiative.
They effectively communicate.
They implement the change in a manner consistent with the strategic plan.
They recognize that quality service delivery requires the utilization of quality assurance plans.
They are unafraid to admit that modification to strategic plans may be necessary.

create a culture and directives aimed toward multiple strategies that can be applied in changing environments, rather than focusing on one particular strategy designed to enhance the organization's success (National Defense University nd; Placet and Branch 2002). Organizations are expected to be adaptable in their operations and strategies but are burdened by large, bureaucratic policies, procedures, and operations that compel change to be a slow, daunting task (Placet and Branch 2002). Strategic planning and leadership must be examined within this context.

Strategic planning is described as follows:

> Systematic process of envisioning a desired future, and translating this vision into broadly defined goals or objectives and a sequence of steps to achieve them. In contrast to long-term planning (which begins with the current status and lays down a path to meet estimated future needs), strategic planning begins with the desired end and works backward to the current status. (*Business Dictionary*, nd)

More simply, strategic planning allows the organization to determine where it is going in the near future and identifies methods for the organization to reach its goals (McNamara nd).

The envisioning process is the cornerstone of strategic planning. The process facilitates strategic planning via an anticipatory decision-making process (Ackoff 1981). The envisioning process includes understanding and developing the necessary game plan in terms of the procedures and policies necessary to achieve the specific future outlined in the strategic plan. Proper envisioning includes input from all stakeholders and groups affected by the plan, to achieve proper buy-in and identify possible obstacles. While the process seems somewhat nebulous and future-oriented, effective administrators realize the future of their organization is not set, it is influenced by the steps and plans we make today. There are many potential benefits for those administrators who engage in the envisioning process including increasing teamwork, power over the organization's future destination, the capacity to obtain additional resources, the capability to better respond to crises, and the ability to exploit new opportunities.

A clear, comprehensive vision allows all subordinate managers and external stakeholders to understand where the organization is going and why senior administrators are pushing new policies, procedures and programs. Good administrators constantly analyze and monitor how well members are doing in terms of working together toward a common mission and vision. If the administrator has achieved proper buy-in for the vision, all elements of the organization should be able to effectively work together in this process, with each subunit understanding not only their role in the process but how their actions influence and affect other subunits. The process is somewhat tautological—a shared vision should bind the various components of correctional organizations together for a common purpose that can be achieved only through cooperation and teamwork.

Organizational futures will happen whether top administrators plan them or not, the strategic planner envisions where the organization needs to be in the future and works toward that goal. The correctional administrator can often be held hostage by the whims of the public as well those of the legislative, judicial, and executive branches of government. Moreover, the administrator is often held accountable for practices which fail and the flawed and often contradictory visions imposed on them by others. Smart administrators, through envisioning, prepare for such demands and requests by developing contingency plans for action via the strategic planning process. This allows the administrator to shape and guide these outside demands into realistic, achievable, and often more cost effective proposals.

Corrections often takes the largest share of the state budget every year. All too often, correctional institutions need and request additional funds to keep up with the growing, ever-changing offender population, and the increasing costs associated with maintenance of facilities. The strategic planning process can aid in such requests. First, it allows administrators to anticipate the need for requests in advance. Second, this additional time can be used to gather information and data to support the request, while giving the administrator the necessary time to garner support for funding. Finally, the plan will allow the administrator to show the stakeholder exactly how the money will be spent.

Unfortunately, the best laid plans devised by administrators do not always equate to a stable, smooth, running correctional environment. Issues of funding, problems with staff, and an unstable prison population consisting of drug abusers, sex offenders, and those suffering from mental illness ensure that a constant stream of problems and crises will occur. While many of the problems will be routine with regard to how staff should handle them in terms of policies and procedures, often nonroutine crises will occur that will not be adequately covered by the organization's standard operating procedures. When this happens, every level of decision making in the organization can benefit from a shared vision and a strategic plan. Low-level decision makers can use the plan to guide choices, particularly when decisions have to be made immediately and their next level supervisor is unavailable. Upper-level administrators benefit because they have provided adequate directions to aid decision making at all levels of the organization. Hence, a clear, concise plan and vision potentially brings order to crises.

Having a strategic plan allows administrators to exploit opportunities as they arise. Often grant and funding opportunities will occur that will coincide with the organization's strategic plan. The very essence of having a plan will assist in deciding what opportunities are in line with the organization's objectives. Moreover, having a plan will allow the agency to identify other organizations that have a similar vision and serve as an instrumental tool in the formation of valuable collaborative interagency partnerships. These partnerships, in turn, can be useful in acquiring additional grants and funding. For example, in order for community-based agencies to make full use of funding available from the Second Chance Act, agencies may need to collaborate with other agencies serving the needs of returning offenders. In one Southern state, the local prerelease center is currently looking to partner with community-based partners who listed prisoner reentry as a primary mission of their organization. The aim of the warden at the prerelease center is to develop a program with these partners and to apply for funding from the state, federal government, and nonprofit organizations to support the program for at least 3 years.

Senior leaders are responsible for making the final decisions about their organization's future. There are several perspectives relating to leaderships styles. The National Defense University presents five different categories of theories of leadership, two of these categories, strategic management and visionary theories, seem to provide the best context for discussing the envisioning process. Strategic management theories emphasize that successful leaders understand how the organization and the environment interact and affect each other. The leader is expected to analyze, create, and manage this fit. Characteristics associated with successful executives according to these theories include strategic leadership and the ability to make decisions, with demographic characteristics and personalities also playing a role in the level of success.

Visionary/inspirational leadership theories—this group of theories include those related to transformational and charismatic leadership. These leaders utilize vision to construct and encourage the organizational members to act in concert. Visionary/inspirational leaders focus on empowering and developing staff, especially those in lower positions. These leaders require cognitive abilities (such as creativity, verbal abilities, and intelligence), self-assurance, enthusiasm, and the ability to take risks and interact socially.

Regardless of the leadership style there are several different approaches administrators may want to consider in the envisioning process (Moore 2000). *Environmental scanning* allows the leadership and organization to examine the current state of the competitive environment and any changes that may be occurring or that are on the horizon. This approach examines various elements of the organizational process such as inputs and outputs, raw materials, and so forth. *Scenario planning and forecasting* allows leadership to develop possible scenarios, prepare various responses for the scenarios, and reach an agreement regarding the responses in advance. *Capital planning and budgeting* is a process in which each division or subunit submits a project-specific budget to the administration. Leaders then prioritize these projects and allocate funds. *Stakeholder analysis and engagement* recruits internal and external stakeholders to identify concerns and interests, and compares these to the goals of the organization. Typically, these strategies are coupled with relationship-building exercises and disclosure of information. *Decision science and analysis* was born from the engineering field and estimates the likelihood of outcomes. Probabilities and calculations are used to obtain the likelihoods (Plancet and Branch 2002).

Regardless of the envisioning approach used, there are certain fundamental organizational steps that must be addressed in order for this process to be developed into an effective strategic plan:

1. Assess current organizational functioning.
2. Develop the mission, vision, values, and goals of the organization.
3. Address staff-related issues and achieve staff buy-in.
4. Communicate effectively.
5. Implement the strategic plan.
6. Monitor, assess, and modify the implementation of the plan as necessary.

Each of these steps will be further developed in the following sections and chapters.

Assessment

Just as assessment is the first step in determining risk, needs, strengths, and weaknesses of offenders, assessment is the first step in ascertaining where an organization is in terms of function and status (Bertram 1991; Hanson, Melnyk, and

Calantone 2004). Effective correctional leaders make a concerted effort to know how their organization is functioning with regard to implementing the agency's objectives. These administrators understand that acquiring facts of an organization's history and present operations provides a wealth of information with which to begin conversations regarding the future of the organization (Greiner 1972). As suggested by Kania (2008), too often correctional administrators have engaged in straight-line change based on the current fashionable program, only to find that what worked for one jurisdiction or population could not work or was unnecessary for their own correctional population. Quality assessment of organizational functioning prior to implementation can help prevent the additional costs and the stigma associated with putting into practice a failed and unnecessary initiative.

Assessing the current state of the organization and identifying obstacles that could impede innovations that are necessary to ensure organizational growth (Baker et al. 2003; Hanna 2000). For example, leaders must be able to identify where underlying sources of power lie (whether formal or informal) and how these sources work. Determining who has the power within employee ranks is critical if resistance to the new initiative is expected. If these sources are identified, administrators can work to reduce or neutralize them in preparation for implementing strategies to improve practice (Eiring 1999). Although this type of assessment may be difficult for the organization, the advantages of this step far outweigh the temporary discomfort associated with its pursuit.

Aside from obtaining a starting point from which to begin planning and designing change (Kramer, Schmalenberg, and MacGuire 2004), communication channels begin to open as data from assessments are reviewed and integrated into implementation strategies. Baker et al. (2003) suggest that assessment provides an opportunity for effective teambuilding and identifying and opening communication channels between those individuals who are part of the strategic planning process. Additionally, assessment can identify and provide an opportunity to address problems with current operations (such as training or financial issues) that might hinder implementation efforts (Bertram 2003). Perceptual assessments conducted with staff are gauged to investigate the personal opinions, values, and attitudes of staff toward current and future operations to prepare administrators to address staff-related issues that may lie ahead (Gagan and Hewitt-Taylor 2004). The importance and benefits of an initial assessment cannot be understated. As Eiring (1999, p. 18) states, "accepting the reality of the environment will help minimize the frustration that can occur when dealing with political forces."

An initial assessment should be conducted to ascertain the current state of the organization, and subsequent assessments will also be required to determine the progress of the organization in reaching its goals, mission, and vision. Just as correctional organizations reassess offenders to determine their progress and identify areas that still need attention, correctional organizations must conduct similar processes on the organization itself. For correctional leaders seeking to implement organizational change, knowing where the organization is can be less troublesome than not knowing. Conducting an initial assessment can provide the organization with the knowledge (and data) to determine whether a change is truly needed.

Developing Vision, Mission, Values, and Goals

Correctional organizations are defined by their mission and vision, and it is the responsibility of effective leaders to establish goals, objectives, and performance criteria that reflect the purpose of the organization. The *mission* is the statement that describes the purposes and aims for the offender population within a particular agency; *vision* reflects the leaders' hopes for the future. Every aspect of an effective, efficient correctional organization is structured to reiterate the agency's mission and vision. Successful leaders analyze correctional operations and modify procedures constantly so that they are consistent with the purpose of the organization (McAlearney 2000). This process is especially important because correctional agency performance is assessed based on how well the organization does in meeting the performance standards associated with a particular mission (Gaes et al. 2004).

Borrill and Parker (2000) and McAlearney (2000) suggest that organizations should introduce changes only when the specific change is aligned with the vision and goals of the organization. "Jumping on the bandwagon" or changing practice to reflect the latest fad is not enough reason to turn the organization upside down (Borrill and Parker 2000). Any change initiated by the organization must be contemplated and investigated thoroughly. The realistic view ascertained from the assessment process (discussed earlier in this chapter) will offer a starting point for the organization to determine the appropriate strategies to utilize in order to achieve goals and objectives consistent with the organizational mission. Regardless of how the goals are formed or what they are designed to achieve, increasing quality for the organization requires that goals be relevant and planning be participative, inclusive of all members of the organization (Carroll 2000). Because all staff are responsible for the success of an organization, all staff should be able to contribute to the organization by contributing to decision making (Gagan and Hewitt-Taylor 2004; Perry, Wooten, and Crane 2004).

Staff

Staff support and staff motivation are key elements that must be considered when implementing any type of change (Kramer, Schmalenberg, and McGuire 2004). Thus, in thinking and planning for new initiatives, effective managers assess the attitudes and values of staff prior to beginning the correctional change process (Gagan and Hewitt-Taylor 2004). While identifying staff attitudes is often a difficult task, all too often the assumption by management of automatic staff support and motivation has led to the demise of many new initiatives at the outset (Graffam et al. 2004).

This process of successful innovation begins by establishing a clear mission and vision statement that are understood by the staff. To achieve staff buy-in, often the most effective way is to include staff representation from all sections of the organization in the development of these goals and objectives. The ability to have input into the new program, and the elicited buy-in from staff, reduces the amount of resistance from staff (Borrill and Parker 2000; Stojkovic and Farkas 2003). Obtaining staff input into the new strategy allows staff to perceive their importance to the organization. This includes not just giving staff a voice at the beginning of the process but accepting staff feedback at every step of the process. As with most types of new organizational initiatives, staff often take their cues from management. The perception of senior management's lack of commitment has been associated with failures in implementing organizational initiatives, hence, effective administrators lead by example (Bertram 1991). Commitment shapes organizational behavior at all levels (Camp, Saylor, and Gelman 1995), hence, in order for effective initiatives to be implemented, all levels of the organization must be committed to that change (Ma and MacMillian 1999; McGuire 2004; Tubman and Vento 2001). Often overlooked in the change process is the role of midlevel managers. According to Lipsky (1980), these managers are the gatekeepers of information, playing a key role—passing administrative directives to the staff and the workforce's feedback back to administrators—thus making the change process possible.

There are many ways to increase staff support and motivation for new initiatives, including giving staff a voice in the process, showing them that their opinions matter, soliciting staff feedback during each step of the change process, and providing them with incentives whenever possible. Research indicates that the success or failure of a correctional initiative is often associated with how well staff accept and implement the changes (Henderson, Mathias-Humphrey, and McDermott 2008; Wooten and Crane 2001; Stiles, 2000). One of the most salient factors distinguishing success and failure of new initiatives is the treatment of staff by administrators. Administrators, who demonstrated commitment and motivation, allowed staff to have a voice in the process while encouraging the staff to focus on the goals of the innovation, report higher rates of successful implementation (Carroll 2000; Gowdy, Carlson, and Rapp 2004). Moreover, once staff become accustomed to supporting initiatives, it becomes easier for them to accept other subsequent initiatives that the organization may pursue. This effort also sets a precedent for administrators and staff to work together, often benefiting the organization through increased interagency cooperation.

Communication

Hackman and Johnson (1991) emphasize that communication is the basis on which organizations are formed. Given that organizations are comprised of two or more people working toward the same goal or purpose, communication is the thread that holds the organization's members together. Communication is used by successful leaders as a tool to present the mission and/or vision in order to entice buy-in from staff (Stojkovic and Farkas 2003). Support of staff, quality communication, good practice, and patience lead to success (Thomas and Wellcoxson 1998).

Leaders should understand that buy-in to the new initiative or program is not immediate. Any major changes that affect the organization's daily processes and activities will be perceived by staff with a questioning glance. Once the initial destabilization occurs, time will pass and reveal those staff who were able to buy in to the new processes. Staff need time and should see that the organization is serious about the current change. The length of time of destabilization varies and is individual to the organization itself (Stojkovic and Farkas 2003). However, Gentry and Keilty (2004) suggest that an initial three-year implementation period should be expected before an organization's members take ownership of the plan and buy in.

Much work goes into the development of a strategic plan and the identification of goals for the organization. However, the development of the plan is only part of the effort that must be exercised for the organization to be successful. Once the mission and goals have been established, leaders must communicate these goals to the membership in the hopes of gaining identification and cooperation, as well as buy-in and support from organizational members.

A lack of vision and purpose contributes to dissatisfaction. Without leaders giving purpose to staff through vision, mission, values, and goals, staff must develop these on their own. This development can lead to further competing values between the organization and individual members (Stojkovic and Farkas 2003). However, if the organization is effective in delivering the strategic vision to staff, the result can be extremely beneficial. Increases in satisfaction and lower turnover rates result when values of the organization and individual staff coincide (Wooten and Crane 2003). Behavior of staff is guided by specifically defined mission statements and clearly outlined goals (Wooten and Crane 2003). Therefore, corresponding values between staff and the organization can significantly enhance the success of the organization.

One of the most salient issues relating to communication within organizations is the role of midlevel managers. Midlevel managers are important to an organization because they maintain a strong historical knowledge of the organization and identify with the organization itself. Further, they can provide a significant contribution for the formal and informal translation of information (Stiles 2000). Midlevel managers have traditionally been important in organizational planning—they provide information to the administration and receive plans from the administration (Stiles 2000).

Despite their importance to the organization, midlevel managers are often resistant to changes that threaten their self-interest or when changes are driven by the market. Most changes result in midmanagers losing authority, observing increases in their workloads, reduced job security, and lack of opportunities for advancement (Fenton-O'Creevy 2000). Midmanagers often undermine the goals of the organization, particularly when these goals are associated with change. Half of firms report that midmanagers are a barrier to implementation (Fenton-O'Creevy 2000).

Midlevel managers are not the only obstacle to implementation. Vertical management structures and individual perceptions and attitudes can impede implementation (Cameron and Wren 1999). Vertical management structures perpetuate an attitude of "us versus them" (Wicke, Coppin, and Payne 1997). Managers should be in the middle of the team, not on top (Wicke, Coppin, and Payne 2004). Changes must occur in the management structure for all to improve their job, share responsibilities, and develop interdependence (Bertram 1991). Structures of organizations must change. Older systems, based on vertical coordination, are no longer effective. Each division must be seen as a "subunit" in a horizontal formation. Each of these subunits come together to comprise a "community of communities" (Caroll 2000). Restructuring the organization will flatten the traditional hierarchical configuration (Rivard et al. 2004) and allow for more smooth communication channels.

Poor communication is also a major obstacle to initiate success (Tubman and Vento 2001; Wicke, Coppin, and Payne 2001). Too often there is a disconnect between those who develop the strategy and those who implement it (Gillen 2000). This separation impedes understanding and hence prevents buy-in and support from lower levels of the hierarchy. Lower levels of staff are most commonly responsible for the success of the organization and change initiatives (Cameron and Wren 1999; Flores et al. 2003; Gagan and Hewitt-Taylor 2004). Therefore, all levels of staff should be included in information-sharing sessions. The importance of participation may be the ability to communicate information (Hanna 2000) as well as lessen the negativity associated with a feeling of loss or autonomy associated with implementation (Gagan and Hewitt-Taylor 2004). Leaders must allow for constant open communication where management can share the vision and staff can express views on the changes and how those changes will impact their day-to-day operations (Cameron and Wren 2000).

Implementation

There is a difference between *strategic planning* and *strategic process.* Strategic planning is often like taking a photo of a moving object. It is only looking at the organization in one place and time (Dromgoole and Mullins 2000). Therefore, strategic planning is a continuous process. Strategic planning refers to the development of the vision, mission, goals, and strategies to reach those goals, while the strategic process refers to the implementation of that plan. Implementation includes the political and emotional processes, as well as the discussion and communication that are required for the plan to become a daily component of the organization (Fenton-O'Creevy 2000). However, the best-designed plans may not be implemented appropriately due to specific barriers to implementation. Effective programming means effective implementation (McGuire 2004).

One of the largest barriers to implementation is the culture of the organization (Baker et al. 2003). Once the strategy has been designed and implemented, it must be administered or led. Every strategy requires a learning component so that the strategy itself can become part of the organizational culture and be internalized by each staff member (Gillen 2000).

For administrators, implementation of the ideas (strategic vision, mission, and goals) is central to success. Without a quality implementation strategy and execution of that strategy, no plan will be effective. Therefore, leaders must (1) communicate and explain the mission, values, and strategies of the organization; (2) develop appropriate structure to support the strategy for implementation; (3) obtain and distribute resources appropriately to those who do the work; and (4) develop and manage a system of oversight and coordinate efforts as part of that system (Smith and Sims 2000).

Leaders are responsible for change within the organization. Once the organizational culture is conducive to changes, instituting change becomes a significantly smoother process. However, leadership is still ultimately responsible for adapting the organization to improve operations, meet external demands or expectations, or make any other necessary changes. Certain characteristics of leaders are especially pertinent to this situation. Leaders should be able to effectively communicate their own ideas. Organizational processes should be in place enough to function, regardless of who is in charge, yet flexible enough to adapt to the environment (Lappin 2008). In addition to being flexible, implementation strategies must be "defensible" (Gentry and Keilty 2004), meaning that leaders must be able to articulate why certain strategies were chosen over others.

One of the best predictors of success for any change is the amount of upper-management support for that change (Hanson, Melnyk, and Calantone 2004). Leadership has a strong influence on the success of a change strategy. Leadership needs to demonstrate enthusiasm and visibly show a strong diligence to the new idea for staff to follow suit (Redfern and Christian 2003). For staff to commit to a change, management must buy in to the strategy; the strategy must be successfully "sold" to senior management (specifically to IT) (Eiring 1999). If leader support for the initiative alters or fluctuates, staff will perceive the change to be questionable and therefore not buy in to the change completely (Rivard et al. 2004; Tubman and Vento 2001).

Often, management says one thing but does another. Line staff and midmanagers are left with the decision of what to follow. Line staff will follow the example set by the immediate supervisor (Stojkovic and Farkas 2003). Therefore, if midlevel managers are not clear on the goals and do not completely support the change, line staff will be lost in confusion. Changes and new initiatives cannot be "forced" (Gentry and Keilty 2004). Management must "walk the walk" (Koch, Cairnes, and Brunk 2000), meaning the words and behavior of administration must mesh (Stojkovic and Farkas 2003).

Conclusion

Anytime an organization is restructured, the organization is disrupted (Redfern and Christian 2003). Therefore, change should only be introduced when the change is deemed necessary and/or when the change will correspond with the vision and goals of the organization (Borrill and Parker 2000). Leaders are responsible for determining when change is necessary and for directing the process of that change. Leaders are different from managers in that managers are responsible for maintaining the status quo, while leaders are responsible for developing vision for the organization. Managers execute the vision that leaders formulate.

While executives may lead the way to a new strategy, they cannot do this alone. All stakeholders must be involved in the decision making of the strategy. Strategic planning involves a multitude of activities. The first step is assessing the organization and determining its current status. The organization must then develop the vision, mission, values, and goals; engage staff (motivate staff as well as reduce resistance); communicate effectively; and implement the plan. Without each of these elements, the strategic planning process will not be successful. Leaders are ultimately responsible for the success for the organization, as well as any initiatives, strategies, or programs the organization employs.

Learning Objectives

After completing this chapter, you should be able to—

- Define *causal texture*
- Distinguish leaders from managers
- Understand why strategic leadership is an important aspect of change management
- Explain the five roles that leaders take
- Explain what effective leaders do when trying to implement change
- Define *strategic planning*
- Describe the five schools of thought related to strategic management

Key Terms

Behavioral complexity theory
Box approach
Causal texture
Change agent
Change approach
Conceptual complexity theory
Expertise approach
Human-asset approach
Leader
Manager
Strategic approach
Strategic management theory

Strategic planning
Strategic process
Stratified systems theory
Visionary leadership

Discussion Questions

1. We have identified the characteristics of effective leaders. List and describe at least seven qualities a leader might possess that would limit their ability to be effective. For each characteristic, provide a current correctional example.
2. Review Table 2.1, which contains the core competencies of executives, senior-level leaders, managers, and supervisors. For each group, rank the competencies from most important to least important. Be prepared to provide a justification for your ranking. Compare rankings among students.
3. Leaders are responsible for determining when change is necessary. Describe two correctional situations where changing the correctional organization is necessary. For each scenario discuss the following:
   a. What type of change(s) would need to occur?
   b. How would the mission and vision statement for the organization need to be changed?
   c. What steps should the leader take, and in what order, to see the change implemented?

References

Adair, J. 1984. *The Skills of Leadership*. Aldershot, UK: Gower.

Baker, G., H. King, J. L. MacDonald, and J. D. Horbar. 2003. Using organizational assessment surveys for improvement in neonatal intensive care. *Pediatrics* 111: 419–425.

Bertram, D. 1991. Getting started in total quality management. *Total Quality Management* 2: 279–282.

Borrill, C., and S. K. Parker 2000. Change management and stress. *In Managing strategy implementation*, edited by P. C. Flood, T. Dromgoole, S. J. Carroll, L. Gorman, pp. 80–85. London: Blackwell Publishers.

Business Dictionary. (nd.). Fairfax, VA. Available at: http://www.businessdictionary.com/definition/strategic-planning.html.

Cameron, G., and A. M. Wren. 1999. Reconstructing organizational culture: A process using multiple perspectives. *Public Health Nursing* 16: 96–101.

Camp, S. D., W. G. Saylor, and E. Gilman. 1995. *Aggregate work environment measures and job separations at the Federal Bureau of Prisons*. Version of paper presented at the 1994 ACJS Meeting, Chicago, IL.

Campbell, N. M. 2005. Correctional leadership competencies for the 21st century: Managers and supervisors. Washington, DC: National Institute of Corrections. Available at: http://nicic.org/Downloads/PDF/Library/020475.pdf (accessed on June 15, 2009).

Carroll, S. J. 2000. Implementing strategic plans through formalised goal setting. In *Managing strategy implementation*, edited by P. C. Flood, T. Dromgoole, S. J. Carroll, L. Gorman, pp. 31–43. Oxford: Blackwell Publishers.

Connally, G. E. 1971. Training nursing management: How to develop a solid nursing management, given the tendency to be specialists first and managers second. *Training and Development Journal* 25(1): 11–17.

Carter, M. M. 2006. The importance of collaborative leadership in achieving effective criminal justice outcomes. Center for Effective Public Policy.

Craig, E., C. J. Russell, R. W. Beatty, and L. Baird (Editors). *The training and development sourcebook*, pp. 7–20. Amherst, MA: Human Resource Development, Inc.

Denis, J. L., A. Langley, and L. Cazale. 1996. Leadership and strategic change under ambiguity. *Organization Studies* 17: 673–697.

Droomgoole, T., and D. Mullins. 2000. Strategy implementation and polarity management. *In Managing strategy implementation*, edited by P. C. Flood, T. Dromgoole, S. J. Carroll, L. Gorman, pp. 57–68. Oxford: Blackwell Publishers.

Eiring, L. 1999. Dynamic office politics: Powering up for program success! *Information Management Journal* (January): 17–25.

Emery, F. E., and E. L. Trist. 1994. The causal texture of organization of environments. *Human Relations* 18:21–37.

Farkas, C. M., and Wetlaufer, S. 1996. The ways chief executive officers lead. *Harvard Business Review* 74(3), May–June: 110–122. http://hbr.harvardbusiness.org/1996/05/the-ways-chief-executive-officers-lead/ar/1 (accessed on August 12, 2009).

Fenton-O'Creevy, M. 2000. Middle managers resistance to strategic change initiatives. In *Managing strategy implementation*, edited by P. C. Flood, T. Dromgoole, S. J. Carroll, L. Gorman, pp. 152–167. Oxford: Blackwell Publishers.

Flores, A. W., C. T. Lowenkamp, A. H. Holsinger, and E. J. Latessa 2004. *Predicting outcome with the level of service inventory—Revised: The importance of quality assurance.* Unpublished manuscript.

Flores, A. W., A. Russell, E. J. Latessa, and L. T. Travis III. 2005. Evidence of professionalism or quackery: Measuring practitioner awareness of risk/need factors and effective treatment strategies. *Federal Probation* 69(2): 9–14.

Freeman, R. 1999. *Correctional organization and management: Public policy challenges, behavior, and structure.* Boston, MA: Butterworth and Heinemann.

Gaes, G. G., S. D. Camp, J. B. Nelson, and W. G. Saylor. 2004. *Measuring prison performance government privatization and accountability.* New York: Altamira Press.

Gagan, M., and J. Hewitt-Taylor. 2004. The issues for nurses involved in implementing evidence in practice. *British Journal of Nursing* 13: 1216–1220.

Garratt, B. 1990. *Creating a learning organization: A guide to leadership, learning and development.* Cambridge: Director Books.

Gentry, M., and Keilty, B. (2004). Rural and suburban cluster grouping: Reflections on staff development as a component of program success. *Roeper Review* 26(3): 147–155.

Gillen, D. 2000. The leadership of learning: The core process of strategy implementation. In *Managing strategy implementation*, edited by P. C. Flood, T. Dromgoole, S. J. Carroll, L. Gorman. London: Blackwell Publishers.

Gowdy, E., L. Carlson, and C. A. Rapp 2004. Organizational factors differentiating high performing from low performing supported employment programs. Psychiatric *Rehabilitation Journal* 28(2): 150–156.

Graffam, J., A. Shrinkfield, B. Lavelle, and W. McPherson. (2004). Variables affecting *successful reintegration as perceived by offenders and professionals. Journal of Offender Rehabilitation* 40: 147–171.

Greiner, L. E. (1972). Evolution and revolution as organizations grow. *Harvard Business Review*. Reprinted in *Family Business Review* (1997).

Hackman, M. Z., and C. E. Johnson. 1991. *Leadership: A communication perspective*. Prospect Heights, IL: Waveland.

Hanna, N. 2008. *Transforming government and empowering communities: The Sri Lankan experience with e-development*. World Bank.

Hanson, J. D., S. A. Melnyk, and R. J. Calantone. 2004. Core values and environmental management. *Greener Management International* (46): 29–46.

Hartley, J. 2000. Leading and managing the uncertainty of strategic change. In *Managing strategy implementation*, edited by P. C. Flood, T. Dromgoole, S. J. Carroll, L. Gorman, pp. 109–122. Oxford: Blackwell Publishers.

Henderson Hurley, M., A. Mathias-Humphrey, and M. J. McDermott. 2008. Barriers to effective program implementation: Rural school-based probation. *Federal Probation* 72(1): 28–36.

Kania, R. 2008. *Managing criminal justice organizations: An introduction to theory and practice*. Newark, NJ: LexisNexis.

Koch, R., M. J. Cairns, and M. Brunk. 2000. How to involve staff in developing an outcomes-oriented organization. *Education and Treatent of Children* 21(1): 41–47.

Kramer, M., C. Schmalenberg, and P. Maguire. 2004. Essentials of a magnetic work environment: Part 3. *Nursing 2005* 34: 44–47.

Lappin, H. 2008. Executive excellence. In *Prison and jail administration: Practice and theory*, edited by P. M. Carlson and J. S. Garrett, Chapter 19, pp. 213–224. Sudbury: MA.

Lewis, P. S., S. H. Goodman, and P. M. Fandt. 1994. *Management: Challenges in the 21st century*. Minneapolis/St. Paul, MN: West.

Ma, X., and R. B. Macmillan. 1999. Influences of workplace conditions on teachers' job satisfaction. *The Journal of Educational Research* 93(1): 34–47.

Manning, T. 2001. *Making sense of strategy*. Cape Town: Zebra Press.

McAlearney, A. S. 2000. Designing and developing effective disease management programmes. *Disease Management Outcomes* 7: 139–148.

McGuire, J. 2004. Minimizing harm in violence risk assessment: Practical solutions to ethical problems. *Health, Risk & Society* 6(4): 327–345.

McKevitt, D. 2000. Strategy implementation in public sector organizations. In *Managing strategy implementation,* edited by P. C. Flood, T. Dromgoole, S. J. Carroll, L. Gorman. Oxford: Blackwell.

McNamera, C. n.d. Basic guide to outcomes-based evaluation for nonprofit organization with very limited resources. Free Management Library. Available at: http://www.managementhelp.org/evaluatn/outcomes.htm (accessed February 21, 2009).

Moore, S. 2000. Analyzing strategic activity through narrative analysis. In *Managing Strategy Implementation,* edited by P. C. Flood, T. Dromgoole, S. J. Carroll, L. Gorman, pp. 44–56. Oxford: Blackwell.

Redfern, S., and S. Christian. 2003. Achieving change in health care practice. *Journal of Evaluation* in *Health Care Practice* 9(2): 225–238.

Rivard, J. C., D. McCorkle, M. Duncan, L. Pasquale, S. Bloom, and R. Abramovitz. 2004. Implementing a trauma recovery framework for youths in residential treatment. *Child and Adolescent Social Work Journal* 21(5): 529–550.

Smith, K., and H. Sims. 2000. Teams in strategy implementation: Some case examples. In *Managing strategy implementation*, edited by P. C. Flood, T. Dromgoole, S. J. Carroll, L. Gorman. London: Blackwell Publishers.

Stiles, 2000. Constraints on strategy implementation: The "problem" of middle managers. In *Managing strategy implementation*, edited by P. C. Flood, T. Dromgoole, S. J. Carroll, L. Gorman. London: Blackwell Publishers.

Stojkovic, S., and M. A. Farkas. 2003. *Correctional leadership: A cultural perspective*. Belmont, CA: Wadsworth Publishing.

Thomas, J., and L. Willcoxson. 1998. Developing teaching and changing organizational culture through grassroots leadership. *Higher Education* 36(4): 471–485.

Tubman, J. G., and R. S. Vento. 2001. Principal and teacher reports of strategies to enforce anti-tobacco. *Journal of School Health* 71: 229–235.

Westley, F., and H. Mintzberg. 1989. Visionary leadership and strategic management. *Strategic Management Journal* 10: 17–32.

Wicke, D., R., Coppin, and S. Payne. 2004. Teamworking in nursing home. *Journal of Advanced Nursing* 45(2): 197–204.

Wooten, L. P., and P. Crane. 2003. Nurses as implementers of organizational culture. *Nursing Economics* 21(6): 275–279.

Wooten, L. P., and P. Crane. 2004. Generating dynamic capabilities through a humanistic work ideology. *American Behavioral Scientist* 47: 848–866.

Chapter 3

Communication

Communication is one of the most important aspects of change management and serves as the foundation for every other change management domain. Often, organizations and their members *assume* that accurate information is effectively passed from one person to another. However, communication does not "just happen." Effective communication is a conscious effort that requires constant attention. Historically, communication was largely informal. Prior to 1920, small organizations passed information from one person to another (Baker 2003), typically in face-to-face or written person-to-person formats. As organizations increased in size, communication processes formalized, often following a top-down (for example, from administrators to line staff) mode of transmission (Baker 2003). Today, correctional leaders need to collaborate and coordinate more with internal and external stakeholders to accomplish their mission and to successfully implement change. Box 3.1 reveals what can happen when communication breaks down. Since correctional organizations are no longer closed, secret organizations, they are accountable to many different groups of stakeholders. Effective communication strategies are often individualized undertakings, based on the type and structure of the organization, as well as the goals of organizational leaders.

Communication structures within organizational contexts represent complicated and complex processes. Communication includes many different aspects, such as the type of audience, the content of the message, the format utilized to share the message, and so forth. This chapter will highlight some of the more common issues with communication and provide some topics to consider when altering a work environment and embarking on organizational change.

BOX 3.1 EXAMPLE OF MISCOMMUNICATION OF THE MISSION

We recently facilitated a vision and mission workshop for a community-based nonprofit organization in a small city. The purpose of the meeting was to determine how well the organization was doing at meeting its mission and defined objectives. The administrators also wanted to know why the organization had been losing many of its community partners. The session included stakeholders from all levels of the organization. The stated mission of the organization in its documentation was the reduction of recidivism for ex-offenders. During the session, the first thing we asked each participant to do was to write down the mission of the organization. When the group was asked to state the official mission of the organization, not a single person mentioned recidivism. There was no consensus regarding the mission, vision, and goals of the organization. Instead, we received the following types of responses:

The Top Executive of the Organization wrote: *Our mission is to serve as lobbyists for ex-offenders.*
An Executive Board Member wrote: *Our mission is to operate programs for ex-offenders.*
An Agency Partner wrote: *The mission of this organization is to help partners obtain grants.*
Another Executive Board Member wrote: *Our mission is to help find employment and housing.*
The Founder wrote: *Our mission is to serve as a group of interested citizens who work to change the system for ex-offenders.*

We also asked participants where they would go to find out the mission and vision for the organization. More than half of the participants could not recall ever receiving a document with the mission; consequently each individual determined for themselves the purpose of the organization.

When external stakeholders were asked about their departure from working with the organization, many replied that they could never figure out exactly what the organization was designed to do.

Defining Communication

There are numerous definitions of communication. At the interpersonal level, *communication* is defined as, "Any act by which one person gives to or receives from another person information about that person's needs, desires, perceptions, knowledge, or affective states. Communication may be intentional or unintentional, may involve conventional or unconventional signals, may take linguistic or nonlinguistic forms, and may occur through spoken or other modes" (National Joint Committee for the Communicative Needs of Persons with Severe Disabilities, 1992, p. 2). *Intrapersonal communication* is communication that we have with ourselves such as reflections about our day or working out a problem in our head (Dimbleby 1998). *Group communication* is communication within groups of people and by groups of people to others and exemplifies the type of communication that takes place in organizations where it is assumed that there is a common goal or purpose (Dimbleby 1998). If an organization is defined as two or more people working simultaneously to accomplish specific goals, communication then *becomes* the organization (Hackman and Johnson 1991). Organizations are formed through the process of communication and cannot exist without the transmission of information, signals, or messages between the people working together toward some goal. The translation of language and symbols must be associated with meaning. Without definition, symbols have no meanings. With predefined meanings, leaders can use the language and symbols to communicate with staff, thereby framing the structure of organizational culture (Hackman and Johnson 1991). The ability to shape organizational structure occurs because in the words of Dimbleby (1998, p. 22), communication can be used to warn, to advise, to inform, to persuade, to express opinions, and to amuse. Effective communication requires that administrators clearly define the audience and the message to be sent, and address staff interpretations of the message.

Audience

Audience refers to the recipients of organizational communication actions. Typically, there are two broad categories of audiences: internal and external stakeholders. *Internal stakeholders* refers to all administrators, management, staff, employee unions, department of correction employees, or volunteers working in unison with the purpose of achieving the same or similar goals. External stakeholders, however, are more difficult to identify because they can come from virtually an infinite number of sources. For example, external stakeholders can include clients, community partners, government agencies (Cameron and Wren 1999); and community stakeholders such as key legislators, governors, media, courts, private interest groups, and other criminal justice system agencies (Stojkovic and Farkas 2003), as well as other agencies and groups. However, some stakeholders, internal and external, are more "in tune" with the organization and may need to be prioritized based on their proximity to and influence over the organization (Stojkovic and Farkas 2003). Organizations must be ready to answer to any of these groups when asked for a specific piece of information.

Audiences or stakeholders can also be classified based on the types of roles they play for the organization (Manning 2001). First, *company actors* are people who work for the company (insiders). *Customers* are individuals who purchase or obtain the organization's goods or services. *Competitors* are organizations that are separate from the organization but may offer the same or similar services as the organization. *Suppliers* provide elements that are necessary for the organization to function, such as financial resources, supplies, utilities, and so forth. Any organization, group, or individual who could make things easier or more difficult for the organization at hand can be termed an *influence*. Influences can also be external stakeholders who have a vested interest in the organization. Finally, *facilitators* are those agencies or organizations that allow the organization to operate, such as pertinent government agencies, licensing authorities, accreditation granting organizations, and so forth.

The most common and largest group of internal stakeholders is the staff. Without staff and employees, the organization does not exist. The greatest asset to any organization is staff, particularly in labor-intensive organizations such as correctional agencies (Borrill and Parker 2000). For an organization to offer quality services, the organization must show that staff are important (Bertram 1991). Chapter 5 discusses the importance of *investing* in an organization's human resources.

Messages

Open lines of communication are a requirement for any type of message to flow through the organization. Messages convey organizational values, mission, vision, norms, and expectations. Overall, the values of the organization, even if newly introduced, must permeate the entire organization, from the highest levels of administration down to line staff. Core values are the important, shared beliefs of the members of the organization that direct decisions and actions of members of the organization. These particular values reflect and define the organizational culture (Hackman and Johnson 2000). The values of customer care, quality service delivery, staff and organizational development, as well as performance management, are a few of the values common among successful organizations (Moon and Swaffin-Smith 1998). High-performing organizations have been found to be more value centered, thereby reinforcing the belief that successful outcomes can be achieved for clients and that staff are critical for this success (Gowdy, Carlson, and Rapp 2004).

The pressing need for new methods to express ideas and sentiment is evident in virtually every organization. For example, although a specific goal of the vision may have multiple meanings or interpretations (which could be problematic), the vision must be communicated (McAlearney 2000). When a new employee is hired, he or she should be enmeshed in the new culture, language, and climate of the organization. While it may be easier to introduce the new concepts and strategies to employees who have not been indoctrinated into the previous way of doing things, existing staff must accept and internalize a new common language that expresses the new concepts and processes (Thomas and Wellcoxson 1996). In order for staff to be given the opportunity to accept new approaches, staff must be provided with a clear, concise message regarding why the change is needed, how their daily routine will be changed, and what outcomes are expected.

To effectively communicate messages a common language must be instituted within the organization to perpetuate a universal understanding of the values, even to new or incoming staff (Thomas and Wellcoxson 1996). Instituting language and symbols can assist in the development of *synthesis* throughout the organization. Synthesis is commonly underrated but essential for success of an organization. Organizations that utilize synthesis, or commonly agreed-upon processes and practices, are more successful in implementing necessary changes. This level of operations is achieved by having constant, creative, and constructive conversations about appropriate topics related to planned changes in practice (Manning 2001). Despite the best efforts of organizational leaders to develop synthesis and specify messages as much as possible, individuals will process information through their own interpretation.

Interpretation

While it is not possible to determine how each individual member within an organization will perceive information, communication strategies should be deployed to reduce staff misconceptions. Every person has their own experiences, values, attitudes, beliefs, and perceptions that form a "lens" through which information enters the five senses to the brain for processing. All information is processed through this lens. Depending on the individual, information sent by different sources and through different media will have differing effects. It is the individual's influence, not the influence of the individual's position, that impacts how information is received (Hackman and Johnson 1991). Individuals can interpret messages sent from executives and managers in a manner different from what was intended (Stiles 2000). Consequently, differential interpretations of information by staff can lead to differential application or problems with service delivery, despite the fact that the same information was transmitted to all staff. In this manner, implementation of policy can be "context sensitive" (Hanna 2000).

To reduce the negative interpretations of messages sent from administrators to staff:

1. Clarify the content of the message.
2. Ensure that the message is sent to the right audience within the organization.
3. Provide opportunities for stakeholder voices to be heard.
4. After providing an opportunity for stakeholders to be heard, create feedback loops.

Methods of Communicating

There are numerous mechanisms used by organizations to convey messages to employees. Formal communication within organizations typically involves the distribution of written material via a top-down circulation process. Staff meetings, agency-sponsored videos, bulletin boards, and newsletters are examples of formal communication. It should be recognized, however, that much of what staff know and understand about vision, goals, and drives of the organization comes through informal, nonadministratively sanctioned communication processes. As discussed by Corrado (1994, p. viii) in many organizations the real way employees find out what is going on might include the grapevine, conversations overheard in restrooms or elevators, a memo left on a desk, or the business section of a daily newspaper.

Regardless of where the information comes from, Corrado (1994, p. 13) suggests that employees have very simple communication needs—they want to know:

- What the problems are
- How the company is going to deal with them
- What their role as an employee is
- How they can become empowered to assume more responsibility

Team Building

One approach utilized to improve the transmission of messages within organizations and to reduce staff misinterpretations of information is teambuilding. A major component of teamwork is effective communication. Quality communication is essential for the transfer of clinical and organizational information and improving working relationships. Team meetings and case conferences offer a way for staff to communicate (Rivard et al. 2004). Scheduled meetings also provide an opportunity for staff development (Gentry and Keilty 2004). However, scheduled meetings regarding case plans or documentation of cases is not an adequate substitute for verbal communication (Wicke, Coppin, and Payne 2004).

Moreover, commitment also assists in the development of a collaborative problem-solving approach (Ma and MacMillan 1999). All staff need to be committed and motivated (Bertram 1991). One of the most effective methods to instill commitment in an organization is through the establishment of teams. Aside from modeling commitment for the organization, teams are beneficial because they can clarify objectives, provide opportunities for learning, and increase the flexibility of communication by offering alternative means of information sharing (Smith and Sims 2000). Establishing consistent team meetings provides opportunities to participate in *managed conversations*. Most daily conversation that occurs within organizations does not serve a purpose. However, managed conversations are intentional and have a specific purpose. When discussing strategies and policies, managed conversations can become nourishing conversations (those that relate to success) or toxic conversations (those that relate to failure) (Manning 2001). The organizational culture can dictate which type of conversations occur within the organization.

In a study comparing high-performing organizations with low-performing organizations, team meetings were utilized to enhance communication, which in turn allowed for the operation of the program to run more smoothly (Gowdy, Carlson, and Rapp 2004). Teams can maintain open communication pathways for organizations that are in fast-changing environments so that the organization's plan is constantly flexible (Smith and Sims 2000), allowing for the adaption of the plan to modifications within the environment and, subsequently, information flow regarding these plans throughout the organization.

Teams can also scan the external environment for changes or anticipated changes. This scanning technique (conducted at various levels of the organization) can provide information to the organization for the purpose of proactively responding to change and modifying the strategic plan and/or process (Smith and Sims 2000). In addition to providing the organization with a competitive edge to competition, this process also allows for change to occur more smoothly within the organization, reducing the negative impact of change on staff and organizational operations as a whole.

Despite the benefit of teams to the organization and its operations, obstacles can still present themselves. Regardless of how diligent an organization is about to initiate and maintain open communication strategies, these strategies can be blocked by various obstructions.

Communication and Change Management Success

Organizations must adapt to change constantly. Without a strong organizational capacity to adapt to change, the organization cannot adjust to an ever-changing environment and thereby eventually becomes obsolete and ineffectual. However, the process of building the organizational capacity to adapt and change can be tedious, time-consuming, and chaotic, especially for staff within the organization. Strategic plans may be complete, with agreed-upon vision and mission statements, as well as goals, but the process of implementing that plan may compromise the intent and quality of the plan. Therefore, communication of the plan is essential to its implementation.

The manner in which communication is delivered will vary. Communication strategies must consider the message, the audience to which the information is being delivered, the originator of the information, and the context in which the information is delivered (Stiles 2000). However, the ultimate effect of the information is based on the information itself, not on the context in which it is delivered (Hanna 2000). For this reason, information must be constantly repeated. Although the mission statement and goals deserve special attention during their development, repetition and reinforcement are crucial components of effective communication and implementation, but these are often overlooked and forgotten (Bertram 1991; Gentry and Keilty 2004).

Change Management and Communication with Internal and External Stakeholders

Both internal and external stakeholders must perceive change as a credible, worthwhile endeavor and the individuals in charge of the change capable of effectively conducting and managing the changes (McKevitt 2000). Communication has a negative relationship with chaos (Rivard et al. 2004). As communication strategies become more efficient and successful, chaos and confusion decrease. Effectively communicating the plan and its related information to all stakeholders is crucial to maintaining balance within the organization and legitimacy with outside sources. Stakeholders must be made continuously aware of the status of the change process.

Communicating effectively to both internal and external stakeholders is an important element to success of the initiative (Borrill and Parker 2000; Ford and Ford 1995). Providing specific, accessible, and desirable information to stakeholders regarding the change process (Stiles 2000) is the foundation that will maintain the organization's credibility among all parties involved. Additionally, educating the community about a new program or initiative will allow those groups to make better, more informed decisions related to the change (Lim and Fortaleza 2000).

Internal stakeholders (for example, staff) have a vested interested in the success of an organization. Administrators have several tools at their disposal, but communication is one of the most powerful (Hackman and Johnson 1991). Effective communication can perpetuate success, while ineffective communication can impede not only success but also organizational functioning. All members of the organization must be clear on the goals they are working toward as well as how those goals are to be reached. Therefore, communication channels must be open throughout the entire organization. When communication channels between administration and midlevel managers improve, the communication and the synchronization of the entire organization increase (Stiles 2000). Moreover, daily communication between staff and administrators more strongly enhances the quality of communication within an organization (Gentry and Keilty 2004).

Another element of communication important to success is the concept of consensus. Consensus is the agreement of organizational members on goals, as well as the methods to obtain those goals. Communicating effectively can provide information that could build consensus (Hanna 2000), thereby providing support for the new plan and/or initiative of the organization. The effectiveness and efficiency of communication can improve implementation processes and therefore strengthen the change being executed (Stiles 2000). While the process of communication can be enhanced, the intended message must still progress through the system.

Management Views of Communication

According to Peter Hartley (2000), administrators typically use one of three different approaches to communicate with employees: the "arrow," the "circuit," and the "dance."

> *Arrow managers* believe that communication operates one way, as in shooting an arrow. If your aim is good, then you will hit the target. If you have a clear message, then you will communicate.
>
> In contrast, *circuit managers* concentrate on communication as a two-way process, emphasizing the importance of feedback. They usually emphasize the importance of good listening and trust in relationships. (p. 13)

"…*dance* is the most appropriate way of describing communication" (Hartley 2000, p. 14). To support this metaphor, he discusses a number of similarities between communication and dance, including the following:

- Both are used for multiple purposes. You can dance to entertain others, to impress your partner, to express yourself, and so on. In the same way, you can communicate for different reasons: to inform, to persuade, to impress, and so forth.
- Both involve the coordination of meanings. The importance of coordination is an obvious feature of dance. You have to know what your partner thinks is the best way of doing the dance—you have to know what they are going to do next! When we communicate we also have to recognize how other people see the situation, recognize what they are doing, and respond accordingly.
- Both are governed by rules. There are sets of rules that apply to different types of dance: what sort of steps to use, how these steps are organized in sequence, what dress is appropriate.

The view that administrators take influences how they behave and how they will communicate with employees during times of change. Arrow managers tend to view employees as passive consumers of messages. They assume that their message is clear and unambiguous. Such administrators are less likely to implement feedback loops because they assume that their instructions have been made clear and will be carried out. "Circuit managers may assume that disagreement is simply a matter of poor communication and that more communication will almost automatically lead to agreement. It may be that more communication is necessary to work out how and why we have different opinions and values" (Hartley 2000, p. 13). Administrators who commit to the dance approach are the most flexible. Dance administrators tend to have larger communication toolboxes. They pick and choose among options.

Obstacles to Effective Communication

Although effective communication is a key component of establishing and maintaining organizational capacity, obstacles can present themselves and make it difficult for an organization to instill quality communication. One of the most common obstacles relates to an organization's size. Communication and coordination can be difficult for larger organizations (Greiner 1972). A large number of employees can confuse information and have a high potential for mixed messages. Multiple methods of communication only aggravate this problem (Stiles 2000). Large organizations typically also have complicated hierarchies and vertical leadership structures. These types of leadership styles tend to block communication channels, thereby rendering communication ineffective (Redfern and Christian 2000). Also, larger organizations must pay more attention to commitment. Establishing feedback loops can connect administration, midlevel managers, and staff (Stiles 2000). Second, poor communication can be an obstacle for implementation of new strategies, programs, and initiatives (Tubman and Vento 1991; Wicke, Coppin, and Payne 2004). However, obstacles can be used as negotiation tools (Gowdy, Carlson, and Rapp 2004). Organizations that learn how to overcome obstacles can not only overcome the obstacle itself but also build confidence and the ability to internally collaborate.

Organizational Culture

Another major obstacle for the organization can be the organizational culture. Organizational culture can be a benefit or an impediment of any desired change. Every organization "looks" different from the outside. Each organization has a history and a culture. Culture allows for the interpretation of reality and provides guidance for appropriate behavior from organizational members. Organizational culture is related to organizational identity.

Organizational culture encompasses many elements. Typical behavior, norms and values of the group, formal philosophy, operational "rules," operational climate, necessary skills, forms of thinking behavior, thinking patterns, and shared meanings or rhetoric (Stojkovic and Farkas 2003) are just a few of the elements that are addressed under the umbrella concept of organizational culture. Two major components included under organizational culture are *shared values* and *shared norms.* Shared values are those principles and ideals that organizational members hold as central to their work. These values significantly contribute to the way in which a group member acts and thinks. Shared norms are passed from established members to new members of the organization. These norms dictate appropriate ways to act and influence behavior (Kramer, Schmalenberg, and Maguire 2004).

Organizational culture dictates the behavior and knowledge of staff for what is of value to the organization (Wooten and Crane 2003). An individual's personality and individual work performance are influenced by organizational culture and cultural factors (Hatton et al. 1999). The culture of an organization impacts many daily practices of the organization, including service delivery (Kramer, Schmalenberg, and Maguire 2004). In short, the organizational culture should be recognized as the defining factor in how staff relate to the administration, to clients, and to each other (Wooten and Crane 2003). The future of an organization is highly dependent upon how well the leadership of an organization deals with the difficulties and obstacles within the current culture (Stojkovic and Farkas 2003).

Additionally, visions of the future—the variations and agreement—between managers and leadership will also determine how well the organization succeeds in the future (Stojkovic and Farkas 2003). The culture of an organization, on a more broad scale, forms a context that outlines rules of organizational change (Stiles 2000). When an organization makes a change, the culture of the organization produces unintended or unseen consequences experienced by both staff and other interested parties (Wooten and Crane 2003). Changes in the culture of the organization must follow the development of vision and goals. Modifications to the culture of an organization should focus on the thoughts, knowledge, and behaviors of staff to form a culture that enhances the experience of all members and groups affiliated with the organization (Gillen 2000), as well as dictates the behavior and knowledge regarding what is valued in the organization (Wooten and Crane 2003). One way in which this culture can be formulated is to facilitate ownership by staff of the vision and mission of the organization. Clearly defined goals and a widely accepted mission statement guide employee behavior (Wooten and Crane 2003). Further, staff should be persuaded to make the vision, mission, and goals of the organization their own (Gillen 2000). However, in a correctional setting, officers and staff must adhere to the policies and procedures of the facility, while still being encouraged to achieve the organization's goals in their own ways (Stojkovic and Farkas 2003). Redfern and Christian (2003, p. 228) note that change requires "organizational commitment; active support from key stakeholders; recognition of the importance of change; a credible change agent; enthusiasm; ensuring target staff have ownership of change and are empowered to change."

Any change in an organization must consider the organizational culture as a context in which this change can occur. Despite the most diligent planning, an organization's culture can significantly hinder or enhance the success of the change. Staff and client attitudes are based on the organizational culture (Baker et al. 2003). Staff and client attitudes based on organizational culture (Bond 2004). A negative organizational culture can permeate staff attitudes, values, and beliefs, perpetuating a negative environment that is a breeding ground for staff resistance. Staff resistance is an obstacle (Bertram 1991); however, individual staff attitudes do not have to be changed in order to alter the culture. Demonstrating and providing staff information so that the organization is productive and successful can alter the organizational culture, without focusing on individuals (Hatton et al. 1999). The demonstration of success allows staff ownership and pride in the organization, allowing for a "grassroots" basis of collaboration and cooperation toward similar goals (Hatton et al. 1999). A consistent focus on client-directed outcomes should be the foundation of the organization's culture (Wooten and Crane 2003).

However, change—even when recognized as positive—can produce negative feelings. Administration's recognition of the disturbing feelings that change perpetuates among staff may reduce the negative emotions experienced by the members of the organization. While administrators may not identify staff anxiety and disruption as problematic, research has shown that increases in stress can produce poor communication, increased uncertainty, and lack of clarity of goals (Borrill and Parker 2000). Stress is also a common reason for absences from work, which can lead to turnover and poor employee performance, even accidents. Organizations should focus efforts on preventing rather than fixing stress (Borrill and Parker 2000). Assessing the organizational culture (including staff attitudes) prior to initiating an organizational change can shed light on the state of the organization. This knowledge provides administrators with a starting point from which to improve the organizational culture, assist staff with accepting changes, and reduce the likelihood of failure.

Table 3.1 Characteristics of Effective Communication

Effective Communication
Is accurate, concise, and timely.
Answers the who, what, when, where, and why associated with change.
Eases staff and stakeholder concerns.
Provides guidance on how the change process will be applied.
Uses consistent names and terms for all aspects of the change.
Provides evidence and not just anecdotes.
Acknowledges the risks associated with change.
Is repeated frequently during the change process.
Incorporates feedback channels.
Sends communication in a manner consistent with the presence of different learning styles among staff and stakeholders.
Includes checks to see if the communication has been received and understood as intended.

Conclusion

As Hackman and Johnson (1991) observe, communication is an ongoing dialogue that constantly changes and is a dynamic process. It is complex, irreversible, and based on personalities of the individuals involved. Communication is considered to be the essence of an organization. Without effective communication strategies, an organization cannot function. Communication should be deliberate and purposive, providing all members (internal and external) with valuable, quality, appropriate information, particularly during times of change. Table 3.1 presents the characteristics of effective communication.

Communication strategies must consider the audience that is to receive the information, the message being delivered, and how that message is being delivered. Further, strategies, such as teams, can facilitate information sharing, while elements such as organizational culture may hamper the ability of organizational members to communicate. Change is difficult for any organization. Necessary resources and effective organizational structures (including effective communication channels) are imperative to successful change (Stiles 2000).

Learning Objectives

After completing this chapter, you should be able to—

Define *communication*
Know and define the elements of communication: audience, message, and interpretation
Discuss categories of audience
Explain how team building can enhance communication
Discuss the role of communication in change management
Discuss obstacles to effective communication

Key Terms

"Arrow"
Audience
"Circuit"
Communication
Competitors
Customers
"Dance"
Interpretation
Message
Suppliers
Team building

References

Baker, G. R., H. King, J. L. MacDonald, and J. D. Horbar. 2003. Using organizational assessment surveys for improvement in neonatal intensive care. *Pediatrics* 111(4): e419–e425.

Bertram, D. 1991. Getting started in total quality management. *Total Quality Management* 2: 279–282.

Bond, M. H. 2004. Culture level dimensions of social axioms and their correlates across 41 cultures. *Journal of Cross-Cultural Psychology* 35: 548–570.

Borrill, C., and S. K. Parker 2000. Change management and stress. In *Managing strategy implementation,* edited by P. C. Flood, T. Dromgoole, S. J. Carroll, L. Gorman, pp. 80–85. London: Blackwell Publishers.

Cameron, G., and A. M. Wren. 1999. Reconstructing organizational culture: A process using multiple perspectives. *Public Health Nursing* 16: 96–101.

Cheney, G. 1983. The rhetoric of identification and organizational communication. *Quarterly Journal of Speech.* 69: 143–158.

Dimbleby, R. 1998. *More than words: An introduction to communication.* Florence, KY: Routledge. Available at: http://site.ebrary.com/lib/thecitadel/Doc?id=5002862&ppg=26.

Ford, J. D., and L. W. Ford. 1995. The role of conversations in producing intentional change in organizations. *Academy of Management Review* 20: 541–570.

Gentry, M., and B. Keilty. 2004. Rural and suburban cluster grouping: Reflections on staff development as a component of program success. *Roeper Review* 26(3): 147–155.

Gillen, D. 2000. The leadership of learning: The core process of strategy implementation. In *Managing strategy implementation,* edited by P. C. Flood, T. Dromgoole, S. J. Carroll, L. Gorman, pp. 138–151. London: Blackwell Publishers.

Gowdy, E., L. Carlson, and C. A. Rapp. 2004. Organizational factors differentiating high performing from low performing supported employment programs. *Psychiatric Rehabilitation Journal* 28(2): 150–156.

Greiner, L. E. 1972. Evolution and revolution as organizations grow. *Harvard Business Review,* Reprinted in *Family Business Review* 1997, 10: 397.

Hackman, M. Z., and C. E. Johnson. 1991. *Leadership: A communication perspective.* Prospect Heights, IL: Waveland.

Hanna, N. 2008. *Transforming government and empowering communities: The Sri Lankan experience with e-development.* World Bank.

Hartley, P. 2000. *Business communication: An introduction.* Florence, KY: Routledge. Available at: http://site.ebrary.com/lib/thecitadel/Doc?id=10016928&ppg=29.

Hatton, C., M. Rivers, H. Mason, L. Mason, E. Emerson, C. Kiernan, D. Reeves, and A. Alborz. 1999. Organizational culture and staff outcomes in services for people with intellectual disabilities. *Journal of Intellectual Disability Research* 43: 206–218.

Kramer, M., C. Schmalenberg, and P. Maguire. 2004. Essentials of a magnetic work environment: Part 3. *Nursing* 2005, 34: 44–7.

Lim, G., and K. Fortaleza, K. 2000. Overcoming challenges in newborn hearing screening. *Journal of Perinatology: Official Journal of the California Perinatal Association* 20: 138–42.

Ma, X., and R. B. MacMillan. 1999. Influences of workplace conditions on teachers' job satisfaction. *The Journal of Educational Research* 93(1): 34–47.

Manning, T. 2001. *Making Sense of Strategy.* Cape Town: Zebra Press.

McAlearney, A. S. 2000. Designing and developing effective disease management programmes. *Disease Management Outcomes* 7: 139–148.

McKevitt, D. 2000. Strategy implementation in public sector organizations. In *Managing strategy implementation,* edited by P. C. Flood, T. Dromgoole, S. J. Carroll, L. Gorman, pp. 96–108. London: Blackwell Publishers.

Moon, C., and C. Swaffin-Smith. 1998. Total quality management and new patterns of work: Is there life beyond empowerment? *Total Quality Management* 9: 301–310.

National Joint Committee for the Communicative Needs of Persons with Severe Disabilities. 1992. Available at: http://www.unm.edu/~devalenzuela/handouts/defcinn.html (accessed May 15, 2010).

Redfern, S., and S. Christian. 2003. Achieving change in health care practice. *Journal of Evaluation in Clinical Practice* 9: 225–238.

Rivard, J. C., D. McCorkle, M. Duncan, L. Pasquale, S. Bloom, and R. Abramovitz. 2004. Implementing a trauma recovery framework for youths in residential treatment. *Child and Adolescent Social Work Journal* 21(5): 529–550.

Smith, K., and H. Sims. 2000. Teams in strategy implementation: Some case examples. In *Managing strategy implementation,* edited by P. C. Flood, T. Dromgoole, S. J. Carroll, L. Gorman, pp. 224–235. London: Blackwell Publishers.

Stiles, P. 2000. Constraints on strategy implementation: The "problem" of middle managers. In *Managing strategy implementation,* edited by P. C. Flood, T. Dromgoole, S. J. Carroll, L. Gorman, pp. 168–180. London: Blackwell Publishers.

Stojkovic, S., and M. A. Farkas. 2003. *Correctional Leadership: A Cultural Perspective.* Belmont, CA: Wadsworth Publishing.

Thomas, J., and L. Willcoxson. 1998. Developing teaching and changing organizational culture through grassroots leadership. *Higher Education* 36(4): 471–485.

Tubman, J. G., and R. S. Vento. 2001. Principal and teacher reports of strategies to enforce anti-tobacco. *Journal of School Health* 71: 229–235.

Wicke, D., R. Coppin, and S. Payne. 2004. Teamworking in nursing home. *Journal of Advanced Nursing* 45(2): 197–204.

Wooten, L. P., and P. Crane. 2003. Nurses as implementers of organizational culture. *Nursing Economics* 21(6): 275–279.

Chapter 4

Information Capital

The importance of information technology for organizations has significantly increased over the past few decades. Cash and Konsynski (1985) provide several reasons for this increase. First, organizations often exist in fast-paced environments. These environments demand that organizations respond to information requests quickly and automated systems allow these requests to be filled. Second, guidelines, polices, and procedures have changed, prompting more uniform collection, analysis, and distribution of data. Third, the cost and capabilities of computers have engrained technology into everyday life. Fourth, technology has advanced and become more reliable. Organizations have developed trust in these systems and the information produced from them. Finally, organizations are able to separate activities, which provides for a more in-depth examination of organizational functioning. Distinguishing between those activities that support the organization and those activities that service clients is essential for documentation and appeasement of funding sources.

For these reasons, information has become a cornerstone of organizational success. However, information capital includes much more than simply placing a desktop computer on desks. Introducing computers or any technology into an organization cannot solve the organization's problems alone (Somagyi and Galliers 1994; Zachman 1981). Systems can provide the organization with information, but *how* this information is used is dependent upon the recipients of this information. Investing in the development of an organization's information can help the organization in many ways, including demonstrating the success or failure of initiatives and the organization itself. This chapter examines some of the issues surrounding information capital, including definitions, types of automated systems, issues with implementation of these systems, and examples for how organizations can use information to expand and develop.

Definitions

One of the first distinctions that should be made in any discussion regarding information is the difference between *data* and *information. Data* refers to the recorded elements of events, business contracts, and so forth. Data are the raw materials from which information is gleaned. *Information* refers to the useful outcome of processing data. Information that is useful to the beneficiary is obtained from processing data (Rowley 1994). Organizations are constantly required to produce information from collected data. There are many ways in which organizations can collect and store data, from handwritten notes to sophisticated automated systems. However, the decision to invest in data collection methods rests heavily on the intended use of the information produced. Information capital, knowledge capital, and intellectual capital are a few of the terms used to present intended uses of information.

Building information capital is a complicated process that takes time and effort (Fahey 1989). However, utilizing the information system as a strategic resource can be extremely beneficial. Rowley (1994, p. 2) states, "MIS [management information system], is then, any system that provides information for the management activities carried out within an organization." She further explains, "All information systems should be strategic; that is, they should all have an effect on the organization's competitive position" (Rowley 1994, p. 3). The importance of the link between information systems and the overall vision, mission, and goals of the organization cannot be overstated.

"*Information capital* (IC) is the original or unique understanding developed by a person or company about its business" (Gupta 1997, p. 1, emphasis added). The ability of an organization to understand itself and the work it does is considered as important as other capital, such as buildings or staff (Snyder and Pierce 2002). Often, information capital is confused with *knowledge capital* and/or *intellectual capital. Knowledge capital* is the accumulation of experience, information, learning, and skills of staff (Business Dictionary nd). Knowledge capital is applied by individuals who are using information to make the organization successful and in the content (typically written) that is available (McGovern 2001). *Intellectual capital* is the aggregation of individual staff-member knowledge (Business Dictionary nd). Intellectual capital includes intangible assets (such as historical organizational knowledge) that provide the ability to manage knowledge throughout the organization (Synder and Pierce 2002). Although each of these concepts is separate, together they all contribute to the same outcome: the organization's ability to obtain, analyze, report, and use information. However, this chapter will focus primarily on information capital and the resources and processes necessary to gain it.

Information capital encompasses access to data, information storage capacities, and dissemination capabilities. Thus, *information capital,* as defined in this text, refers to the ability of an organization to collect, access, and analyze data readily, typically through an automated management information system.

Components of Information Capital

Information capital can be broadly divided into four components (see Table 4.1). The first component is the support and maintenance function and refers to the information necessary to operate the facility. The second component of interest, concerning personnel, is human resource-staff management information. The third area concerns correctional clients. The final area includes the processes, procedures, and programs managed by the correctional agency.

Table 4.1 Information Capital Components and Type of Information Collected

Data Element	*Type of Information*
Logistics, Support, Maintenance	Number of beds, population projections, equipment counts and expenditures, etc.
Human Resource-Staff Management	Number of staff, staff training, professional development, staff attitudes and perceptions, staff competencies, assessments of staff performance, etc.
Profiling and Describing Correctional Clients	Demographic characteristics of offenders, socioeconomic status, family characteristics, living arrangements
	Committing Offenders: Characteristics of the criminal incident, conviction offense, criminal history, sentence imposed, current commitment, expected time to be served, risk assessment, needs assessment, classification documents, confinement characteristics
	Managing Offenders in Correctional Facilities: Postcommitment movements, offender program participation and outcomes, drug testing, medical care, good time and other adjustments to sentences, releases from custody, misconduct and infractions, responses to misconduct, proceedings against offenders
	Supervising Offenders in the Community: Employment information, residence information, behavior on supervision, response to violations of conditions of supervision, new crimes, victims of new crimes
Facility/Program Management	Assessment of treatment programs, assessment of program or institutional management, review of services

Logistics, Support, and Maintenance

Correctional administrators have long understood correctional information requirements in terms of logistics, support, and maintenance functions of the correctional facility. This includes tangible information such as the number of beds needed to house inmates, the current status of the food pantry, and projected space available. This type of information can be further developed to project trends such as numbers of incoming inmates as well the accoutrements necessary to house them.

Human Resource–Staff Management

Human resource-staff management information increases management awareness of personnel status such as training, professional development, and deficiencies, particularly in large state systems where personnel frequently transfer. Such information can be aggregated to track staffing requirements and highlight staff training needs, resulting in improved service delivery.

Profiling and Describing Correctional Clients

Correctional administrators are charged with the supervision and delivery of services to offenders from vastly different backgrounds, with different needs and different criminal justice backgrounds. To carry out their mission and have a greater chance of optimal functioning, information on offender characteristics is necessary for improved monitoring and planning. Thus, the profiling and describing component includes the input of information such as offender demographics, criminal background data, offender movement through the system, and participation in treatment programs.

Facility / Program Management

The facility/program management component refers to the information and knowledge needed to assess organizational processes, implementation, and outcomes. The purpose is to collect information and conduct research to indicate how well the organization is doing in terms of achieving organizational goals and its mission. As will be discussed in greater detail in Chapter 7, this would include the collection of data to assess organizational, programmatic, and managerial successes and failures.

The logistical and personnel functions of corrections are somewhat unique in their specifics, but the overall manner in which they are carried out is not much different from any well-run businesses. Correctional organizations are distinct, however, in their mandate to rehabilitate, to secure those convicted of major deviance from each other as well as from the larger community, and to protect the public. While logistical and personnel functions are important to the continued operation of correctional agencies and require mention in terms of information management, the scope of these functions falls outside the parameters of this book; therefore, they will not be further developed.

Types of Automated Management Information Systems

Multiple terms have been applied to automated data and/or information systems. Management information system (MIS), information management system (IMS), strategic information system (SIS), and other terms are commonly used to refer to an organization's data management system. Although there are slight technical differences between each of these terms, the primary difference lies in the purpose of the system itself. That is, what does the organization intend to do with the data stored in the system?

One of the key components of information capital is its link to the strategy of the organization. By linking information to the strategic plan of the organization, a *strategic management information system* (SMIS) is produced (Fahey 1989; Rackoff, Ullrich, and Wiseman 1989; Rowley 1994). Information capital serves as an enhancer of strategic management by providing better and more information quickly and at less cost for decision makers.

Basically, organizations can choose to employ an information system for strategic or nonstrategic purposes. Research has suggested various definitions for strategic management information systems. For example, Rackoff, Ullrich, and Wiseman (1989, p. 413) suggest that "Strategic Information Systems (SIS) is an information system needed to support or shape an organization's competitive strategy, its plan for gaining and/or maintaining advantage." Most of the definitions relating to SISs refer to the systems' impacting or increasing the organization's *competitive* advantage within its industry. Since correctional agencies rarely fit the traditional concept of *competitive* organizations, the definition of a strategic management system must be modified for this text. Therefore, our definition of a *strategic management system* is as follows:

> Any information system that allows the organization to collect, store, and analyze data for the purpose of providing the organization comprehensive information relating to its activities. An information system that provides the organization with information relating to its functioning and to adherence to best practices, and that assists in enhancing services can be considered strategic.

Advantages of Strategic Information Systems

There are many advantages to investing in a strategic management system and an organization's information capital. One of the most evident advantages of strategic information systems is the ability of an organization to make resource distribution decisions based on the objectives and goals of the organization rather than on what is most beneficial for one or two groups (Zachman 1981). Additionally, investing in a quality strategic information system is crucial to identifying what is working within the organization and what is not working. The ability to modify services, treatment, classification strategies, and so forth is invaluable to correctional organizations.

Once information systems are in place, benefits of the system can be actualized. Porter and Miller (1985) suggest that information technology has far exceeded the traditional accounting and recordkeeping responsibilities once expected of computers. Information systems will change the way an organization operates (Cash and Konsynski 1985; Porter and Miller 1985). By allowing the organization to review its activities on a wide scale, the organization can assess strengths and weaknesses on a continual basis (Anderson 2009; McFarlan 1985). The constant and consistent examination of organizational practices can increase the level of efficiency within the organization. Organizations that participate in collaborative efforts may also experience changes within these collaborations due to information technology. With the introduction of information technology in collaborations, specific concerns must be addressed. For example: What organization will be responsible for maintaining a shared information system? What elements of information can be legally, ethically, and comfortably shared with other organizations? (Cash and Konsynski 1985).

Information systems can also increase the use of physical processing, allowing for a faster response time in obtaining necessary reports. While the information system will impact individual staff members and how they perform their job duties, it also impacts how these individuals relate to others in the organization (Porter and Miller 1985). E-mail, intranet, Internet, and other types of technology have significantly increased the amount of information provided to staff, in a more precise and swift manner. Furthermore, technology can be utilized to include all levels of staff in decision-making processes, increasing support for changes and cohesion within the organization (Palmquist 1992). Anderson (2009) also explains that information systems can promote individual staff interest in organizational change and aid in developing relationships. However, there are disadvantages to technology that are often experienced by staff.

Disadvantages of Information Technology

To use information systems effectively, data must be entered, software must be developed, and the network or storage system must be managed (Cash and Konsynski 1985). Hardware,* software,† and creativity are required to accomplish

* The actual computer, monitor, keyboard, etc.

† The applications or programs contained in the computer. Software is often referred to as anything other than hardware. Examples include word processing programs, databases, Internet, etc.

these tasks (McFarlan 1985). Additionally, information systems require communication between the end users (people who enter data) and the technological resources of the organization (those who design the databases and storage, and assist with computers). Often, the communication between these two groups is difficult. Language barriers, lack of understanding of job responsibilities, and hesitation to define measures prevent the effective communication between programmers and end users.

Information systems are not as accurate as they could be for other reasons as well. Often, management is hesitant to define measures—of success, failure, effectiveness—because once those measures are defined, the organization is held accountable by them (Rowley 1994; Zachman 1981). Accountability may be one reason why administrators are reluctant to support or be involved in the development of information systems (Rowley 1994). This lack of support and involvement, however, significantly impedes the ability of the information system to provide the type of reports needed by the administration. Organizational success is determined by how closely the organization reaches benchmarks or measures as outlined in the strategic plan. In order to ascertain organizational success, consistent data must be available (Zachman 1981).

One of the primary difficulties in developing effective information systems is the lack of understanding of management and management responsibilities. Different levels of management are associated with different responsibilities and therefore have different information needs (Rowley 1994; Zachman 1981). Moreover, correctional organizations exist in constantly changing environments, regardless if the impetus for the change comes from internal or external sources. These constantly changing environments also demand changes in the types of information needed by administrators (Rowley 1994). Further, correctional organizations are influenced by how decisions are made (typically related to the personality and leadership style of individual administrators) and level of prediction required at various times (Rowley 1994). Failing to consider these idiosyncrasies when developing and maintaining an information system can have detrimental effects on the information relayed to staff and released to the public. For example, administrators may generalize statements as applying to the entire organization, when in reality the statements apply to only one segment of the organization (Zachman 1981). Inaccurate statements such as these can cause significant difficulties both inside and outside of the organization.

Differing Levels of Management and Information

Varying levels of management require different types of information (Rowley 1994; Zachman 1981). Table 4.2 provides examples of the types of information that may be needed by different levels of administrators in correctional organizations. The following describes some of the differences in the types of information needed by

Table 4.2 Level of Administration and Type of Information Needed

Type of Manager	*Level of Management*	*Example of Responsibilities*	*Type of Information Needed*	*Type of Reports Needed*
Warden or Chief	Administrative	Develop mission, vision, goals, objectives	Broad, industry level Preliminary baseline information regarding organization	• Estimates (and projections) of offenders being released to the community for the next 5 years • Changes in standards and/or requirements for accreditation • Crime trends
Assistant Warden or Division Head	Midlevel Manager	Assess current resources and determine necessary resources to meet goals and objectives Distribute resources	Somewhat broad Continual status reports on resources needed and gaps in resources Status reports once objectives are defined	• Budget information for the past 5 years and estimates for the upcoming 5 years • Workload and caseload analyses • Organizational capacity assessments
Supervisor	Operational Manager	Assure resources are being used efficiently and effectively	Specific service delivery and resource allocation	• Number of cases per officer • Number of beds available • Number of contacts made • Number of clients/offenders by risk/need level

the different types of management that are typically present in a traditional correctional system hierarchy.

Administration

High-level administrators are responsible for developing vision and mission goals for the organization, as well as coordinating the development and execution of the strategic plan to meet such goals. Through this process, objectives are selected, tools may be altered, and policies that determine behavior and the use and disposition of resources are decided (Reinhart 1981; Rockoff, Ullrich, and Wiseman 1989; Zachman 1981). The information needed by high-level administrators is often broad because the information will be utilized to answer unstructured or undetermined questions (Rowley 1994). Accomplishing this task requires information to be broad and less detailed because it relates to the organization itself. Typically, upper-level administrators focus on goals that are to be reached within the next decade, with a very small amount of time spent on short-term accomplishments (Reinhart 1981; Rockoff et al. 1989). The types of information needed for this level of analysis include current resources, state of the industry or field, and data elements that will be useful in predicting upcoming events or changes in the external environment (Reinhart 1981; Rockoff et al. 1989; Rowley 1994; Zachman 1981).

Midlevel Management

Midlevel managers have a less vague responsibility in terms of organizational functioning. These individuals are most commonly tasked with obtaining and analyzing information regarding the achievement of goals (Rackoff et al. 1981). Specifically, midlevel managers are often tasked with reporting on the efficient and effective use of resources, sometimes termed *management control* (Zachman 1981). These managers are preoccupied with decisions that may impact the organization within 3 to 6 months, but at times may participate in decision making or information that will impact the organization 1 to 5 years in the future (Reinhart 1981; Rockoff et al. 1981). Rowley (1994) suggests that these managers utilize decision support systems to solve unstructured and semistructured problems facing this level of management.

Operational Management

Operational management (commonly termed *supervisors* in corrections) is the level of management closest to the line staff or staff with direct contact with clients/offenders. These managers are responsible for ensuring that goals are attained in the most efficient and effective manner (Reinhart 1981; Rockoff et al. 1981). Operational managers are focused on current activities, most often what is happening today and in the very near future (i.e., a few weeks ahead). Operational managers or supervisors ensure that specific activities are performed so the objectives and goals of the organization can be met (Zachman 1981). Distribution of specific resources, such as line staff time, scheduling, and so forth, is a large part of this activity. These managers utilize management information systems to assist in answering well-structured and defined questions (Rowley 1994).

In summary, the level of detail required for the specific level of management increases as one moves down the hierarchy (Hayes and Radosevich 1974). Operational managers will need more detailed information than administrators. However, the level of detail is not the only issue that changes with the different levels of management. Other issues also impact the quality of information between information technology and those who need it to make strategic decisions.

What Constitutes "Good" Information?

There are many elements that constitute "good" information. According to Rowley (1994), there are two characteristics of information: function and content. Function relates to the specific type of information needed, and content refers to the message within the information. However, much of what constitutes good information is specific to the purpose of the information, which often leads to more questions than answers. For example, Fahey (1989) discusses how information must be examined in terms of accessibility and the ease of that accessibility. Additionally, information obtained is often not sufficient (whether it be invalid, unreliable, too broad, inappropriate, etc.). Quality information is reliable, timely, relevant, and complete, see Table 4.3 for clarification. Organizations must then ask whether the cost of obtaining or collecting more information is ultimately worth the benefit of that

Table 4.3 Characteristics of Quality Data

Characteristic	*Questions to Ask*
Validity	Do the data measure what they are supposed to measure?
Reliability	Are the data collected in a consistent manner?
Timeliness	Are the data collected quickly and efficiently?
Relevance	Do the data captured address relevant issues? Are the data collected used for the purpose intended?
Completeness	Are the data elements completely filled out? Is there only a limited amount of missing, incomplete, or invalid information?

information. Finally, once information is collected and obtained, organizations must determine the audience for that information. Will the report or information be disseminated to all staff, internal and external stakeholders, or a select group of individuals such as board members (Fahey 1989; McFarlan 1985)?

Despite these questions, there are several characteristics common to good information. De Carbonnel and Dorrance (1981) describe five characteristics of information that should be included in any strategic management system:

1. *Variables must be interactive*—Organizational members must be able to enter and modify information as needed.
2. *Answers to questions must be accurate and reflect the values of the organization*—One of the primary issues with many automated information systems, particularly in the area of corrections, is inaccuracy. Inaccurate data can be especially problematic in terms of obtaining resource-level data (e.g., caseload and workload analyses, numbers of offenders under the custody/supervision of the organization). Furthermore, the information must reflect the values of the organization. Relevance to the values of the organization will allow necessary data elements to be included in the database and therefore analyzed to report on the status and progress of the organization toward the broader goals.
3. *Respond to questions from management quickly*—Often, many automated systems are "black holes" of information. Data continues to go in, but nothing ever comes back out. Managers (if not all members of the organization) must have access to reports that analyze the data entered. Reports should be relevant to the questions asked by specific managers at varying levels and apply directly to their individual management responsibilities (see Section 4.6, Differing Levels of Management and Information). Although all reports should not be available to all staff, all staff should have access to some reports. Ideally, these reports would allow the user to select appropriate variables and produce an interactive report.
4. *Frequency of tasks included in data*—Consideration must be given to how often specific tasks are conducted within the organization. Reports for semi-annual budget audits, for example, do not need to be produced on a monthly basis. In the ever-changing world of corrections, more erratic trends should be tracked, such as population changes, specific needs levels, treatment completion rates, and so forth.
5. *Amount of information*—The amount of information requested by management as a whole can be daunting. In a perfect world, all questions to all answers would be available at one's fingertips. However, this is simply not realistic. Necessary data elements, analyses, and reporting should be prioritized while considering the amount of information technology resources. Constant revisions and modifications to existing reports can absorb resources

and lengthen the amount of time required for new reporting requirements to be achieved.

For good information to be assembled, the system itself must be appropriate for the organization. The following discusses some of the ways in which organizations can design or evaluate effective automated strategic management information systems.

Designing a Quality System

As with the organization as a whole, information systems should be evaluated to determine what data are currently available and how the data are collected, stored, analyzed, and reported (Porter and Miller 1989). This initial assessment will provide the organization with a baseline from which to develop a plan to increase the effectiveness and usefulness of an information system. Second, the organization should investigate how information systems and, more broadly, technology, can assist the organization in measuring, reporting, and achieving the goals and objectives established in the strategic plan (Porter and Miller 1989). Ideally, the system should specifically reflect the goals and objectives of the broader organization (Rowley 1994). Typically, the next step involves the organization's examining this assistance in terms of competitive advantage (Porter and Miller 1989). However, as discussed previously, correctional organizations are not commonly placed in "competitive" positions within the field. Therefore, the third step for correctional agencies would be to determine how information technology can assist the organization in becoming more effective. Often, this effectiveness can be examined within the context of effective case management. Automation of risk/needs assessments, case plans, treatment placements, security levels, and other case management functions can significantly enhance the organization's ability to effectively use resources. Additionally, automation can support the organization in not only implementing but also monitoring the implementation of evidence-based practices. Information systems should support and influence, but not determine, the daily operations of the organization (Rowley 1994). Collecting and storing appropriate data through automated systems can also accelerate the evaluation process many organizations so desperately need.

Identifying the benefits of the system is the next step in the initial assessment process (Porter and Miller 1989). While closely related to the second and third steps, this step is distinctive in that it provides a long-term analysis of how information technology can be beneficial for the organization. Moreover, the organization must be able to determine when the information system is not effective or needs modification to improve its function (Rowley 1994). The organization must have the capability to plan, measure, and evaluate the system. If any of these are not available, the system is not effective (Zachman 1981). Simultaneously, the organization should examine the resources required to maintain the system in its current state as well as in the future. Identifying how far into the future expectations should focus is individual to the organization. However, these expectations should fit closely with the elements contained in and timelines outlined in the broader strategic plan of the organization.

The final step in assessing the technology status of the organization is to develop a plan for taking advantage of and reaching all of the goals outlined in the above steps (Porter and Miller 1989). Similar to developing a strategic plan, this step summarizes all of the decisions and work contained in the above steps and puts into place a workable, realistic plan of action. Within this plan, techniques for monitoring and evaluating the effectiveness of the system should be included. Benefits of the system will be unveiled with continuous monitoring (Rowley 1994).

What Does Quality Information Provide to Leaders?

Information capital provides organizational leadership with critical insight into the inner workings of the organization. However, efforts to obtain quality information are often complicated by the fact that correctional organizations do not exist in a vacuum. Administrators must be responsive to requests for information from external and internal stakeholders and often lack the infrastructure to satisfy stakeholder desire for knowledge. This being said, although there are numerous benefits to having quality information capital, six primary advantages will be discussed here.

The Assessment of Performance Advantage

Information capital serves as a source of data for assessment of performance. In recent years there has been a movement to tie correctional organizational sustainability to performance (Gaes, Camp, Nelson, and Saylor 2004; Logan 1993). *Assessment of performance* refers to an analysis of current organizational functioning compared with a set of predetermined criteria related to economy, cost-efficiency, and the effectiveness with which the correctional organization carries out its mission. In correctional environments assessment of performance typically refers to how successful correctional organizations are in their primary mission. It should be noted that the primary mission varies depending on the type of correctional organization. For some agencies performance could deal with such issues as reducing recidivism, changing offender thinking patterns, finding offenders employment, or protecting the public from harm. Correctional administrators themselves have admitted that they needed a better set of "...performance indicators that could be used to describe, measure, and compare management outcomes" (U.S. Department of Justice, 1998, p. 3). The implementation of quality information protocol significantly enhances the ability of the agency to assess performance at all levels of the organization.

The Financial Advantage

Measuring correctional organization performance has become a mainstay as legislative bodies have paired correctional funding with successful outcomes and the implementation of evidence-based practices. Such stakeholders want a guarantee that their dollars are being invested wisely in correctional organizations that are increasing public safety in the most cost-efficient manner possible. Legislators in Oregon, for example, passed Senate Bill 267 in 2003, which mandated that programs and interventions receiving state funding be based on practices that had been tested and proven through research to be effective (State of Oregon 2003). "Without data indicating efficiency, performance, and quality assurance, new initiatives cannot be evaluated and ultimately run the risk of losing funding" (Henderson, Mathias-Humphrey, and McDermott 2008, p. 30).

With this in mind information capital may provide direct financial gains for correctional organizations. Quality information allows administrators to ensure that organizational structures are aligned with the mission and vision of the agency, resulting in a more streamlined and cost-efficient system. Correctional agencies have a long history of funding programs that are not necessarily advancing correctional goals. Such programs could be eliminated or reduced with resulting cost-savings returned to the system. Improved accounting is also likely to reduce costs by stopping or limiting program cost overruns. The better the data, the better correctional managers will be able to allocate resources in a manner that improves service delivery and satisfaction among correctional stakeholders.

The Advantage of Improved Motivation among Staff

Additionally, information capital can be utilized to create a more motivated workforce. Information gathered as part of individual employee performance evaluations and regular feedback mechanisms can do more than simply assess whether the employee is doing his/her job. Gathering higher-quality information on staff attitudes can be used to motivate staff to carry out the mission of the agency more effectively. As will be discussed in Chapter 5, negative staff attitudes have a negative impact on the operational successes of correctional organizations (Fulton et al. 1997; Latessa 2004; Lehman, Greener, and Simpson 2002). When gathered and used by administrators to address staff concerns, the result is that the information can:

- Improve communication between line staff, middle managers, and executives.
- Improve motivation, as staff feel they are an integral part of the organization because their opinions matter.
- Create transparency in the achievement of goals so that staff are less likely to perceive upper-level administrators to be trying to "pull one over" on them.

- Improve staff engagement because employees understand how their jobs contribute to organizational goals.
- Develop initiatives that can be directly aligned with organizational needs and designed to address deficits of staff knowledge, skills, and abilities.
- Better incentivize staff, therefore motivating staff to do more than simply "business as usual," often with fewer resources.

The research reveals that properly motivated staff perform better, are more satisfied, and are less likely to call in sick or transfer. In the end a highly motivated staff saves administrators time and money.

The Advantage of Improved Strategic Thinking and Planning Processes

To have higher-quality strategic thinking and planning processes, it is essential to have more accurate and diversified data to aid in formulating and implementing organizational change and innovations. According to Tavakoli and Lawton (2005, p. 156) "... strategic thinking is the cognitive process...that precedes strategic planning whereby an individual contemplates the future development of the organization while considering its attributes, its past and present and the external realities within which it operates." Thus, strategic decision making requires the utilization of a more expedient and efficient process for the transference of knowledge within the agency between top management, middle management, and line staff. However, the inability of correctional organizations to generate beneficial data and to ultimately transfer that knowledge is well established in the literature (Henderson, Mathias-Humphrey, and McDermott 2008; Miller, Koons-Witt, and Ventura 2004). The goal is to improve the organization's ability to engage in strategic thinking regarding any proposed change. Prior to any targeted organizational change being implemented to improve functioning, correctional agencies need to know (a) how they are currently functioning with regard to the agency's mission, (b) whether they are ready to implement change, and (c) whether they have the capacity to implement proposed changes. These assessments allow the organization to gauge any daily operational problems that might prevent the agency from fulfilling its mission. Good information capital decreases the time it takes to develop and implement operational changes. Thus, a strategic decision-making process mandates that the correctional organization have the ability to retrieve, gather, and disseminate information for analysis and quality improvement of service delivery.

The Defensive Advantage When Practices Are Challenged

Better information capital provides administrators with data that can be used to defend existing practices when challenged by stakeholders. Correctional administrators are responsible for providing information to numerous stakeholders—the public, the legislature, the press, nonprofit organizations, and other funders to name a few. Such stakeholders are often critical of correctional agency policy, procedure, and responses to critical incidents. The provision of valid and reliable data addressing stakeholder concerns can help to allay fears, prevent litigation, and enhance the overall performance of the organization.

The Enhanced Leadership Advantage

Finally, good information capital enhances leadership and the ability of correctional managers to achieve an agency's mission. A manager who has access to high-quality information is able to simplify communication by having a well-documented process for obtaining and disseminating information within the organization. This process allows leadership to clearly display relationships using data and consequently makes it easier to comply with legislative mandates. Further, leadership is able to respond to critical incidents more rapidly. The data on who, what, when, where, and why are readily available to leadership with only limited restrictions.

Examples from the Field

Correctional facilities typically operate with two primary, competing goals. The first is to change the behavior of the inmate, that is, to treat or rehabilitate the detainee so upon their release they desist from their deviant ways. A second mandate is to secure those incarcerated primarily from the larger community and prison staff and subsequently from each other. The security function includes the requirement that correctional agencies monitor and supervise offenders. Automated information management systems can assist in both endeavors.

Treatment

The provision of treatment to correctional clients is a dynamic process. New ideas, methods, and programs are constantly being developed and advocated; and whether voluntarily or officially mandated, these innovations become part of the correctional process. Moreover, correctional administrators armed with the correct data can be the first to discover and understand new trends or needs within the correctional community. Beyond developing new programs, correctional administrators are responsible for the maintenance and success of already established programs. Both old and new treatment programs fall within the staffing and budgetary constraints that all correctional facilities operate within. With so many mandates and requirements it becomes essential that correctional treatment resources are allocated through well-organized, economical, and impactful processes.

Good information capital on effective treatment can be derived with the use of an automated information system. Automated information systems provide correctional management with insight into the overall treatment needs of a correctional agency. For example, many correctional facilities have established GED programs designed to educate their incarcerated population. At the basic level, information capital can tell officials how many individuals are currently enrolled and the ratio of enrollment to successful completion. If the ratio is low, the problem might be improper implementation. Alternatively, data might reveal a hidden problem of a high illiteracy rate among those enrolled, so providing high school level courses to those who have difficulty reading might prove to be somewhat incongruous. By collecting the data, prison officials might enhance the success of a program by understanding the obstacles to its success.

To continue with our GED example, let's suppose the opposite: the success level is very high. This could be the reflection of a well-implemented, well-run program, or the data might reveal inconsistencies in the program administration. Is the program accepting those in need, or is it selectively only choosing those candidates with proven educational success ("stacking the deck," so to speak)?

Often correctional agencies will collect information in offender files but lack electronic access to results. By automating the in-processing data of each inmate, prison officials can track the needs and the progression of each individual inmate. This ensures that the inmate does not get lost in the system. Moreover, this information can be aggregated to project the treatment needs for the inmate population; thus, prison officials can allocate resources and staffing based on the current and projected needs.

With proper intake instruments, treatment programs can be tailor-made to fit the needs of specific inmates rather than the one-size-fits-all approach of many institutions. Mandatory treatment, although bureaucratically appealing, typically wastes resources by treating those who don't need treatment and not providing enough to those who do. For example, all too often, inmates with drug charges are enrolled in mandatory drug and alcohol programs whether they have a history of substance abuse or not. While bemoaning the evils of addiction to all, might those resources be better used selectively for those with an addiction problem? The lack of information capital is often the reason for such a ubiquitous approach: Prison officials do not know who has a substance abuse problem and who does not.

Once the proper treatment is connected with the proper offender population, the question of scope arises. How much treatment will each offender need, and how will program managers know if or when the treatment is effective? All treatment programs need stated goals and objectives; moreover, these goals and objectives must be quantifiable, that is, measurable with real numbers that correctly reflect the successes and failures of the program.

Automated information systems can greatly assist the treatment process. First, automated information systems and data collection will allow prison officials to administer the correct treatment to the correct target population. Second, automated information systems will allow program mangers to track the progress of targeted inmates. Third, automated information systems will give prison officials an overview of each program in terms of resources, staffing, and successful outcomes.

Custody and Supervision

The competing goals of treatment are custody and supervision. Custody in terms of information capital can be examined regarding the security of three groups: correctional staff, offenders, and the outside community. Supervision, confinement, and guardianship must be maintained and understood within the context of an ever-changing environment. Automated information processes can assist with these issues.

Prison Example

Within the correctional milieu, often the personnel requirements for both staff and management are constantly changing. While much of the administrative tracking for correctional personnel is managed by the human resource department, larger issues such as changes in the workforce can frequently be overlooked. Within the prison ecosystem changes in the guard force may be reflected in prisoner behavior either positively or negatively. For example, an increase of inmate and guard altercations might be the result of improper communication skills stemming from a new guard force exasperating instead of calming potentially volatile situations through an improper verbal approach. By examining automated records of intervention training, correctional supervisors might determine that the new guards were not adequately trained in crisis intervention and hence remedy this oversight.

Automated information systems can track job performance and the career development of employees. They might also uncover more specific trends among informal employee groups within the correctional facility. For example, perhaps the increase in altercations is due to particular subgroups of employees who have "a beef" with a particular group of inmates or inmates in general. The subcultural norms of this particular group of employees may supersede the goals and objectives of correctional management. Automated information systems could assist in identifying and tracking such employee groups as well as arming the correctional manager with appropriate information capital to be able to take action.

Often worse than correctional officers being at odds with the inmate population is when correctional staff are either negligent or in cahoots with those they are mandated to treat and secure. Problems within the prison population such as an influx of prohibited items may be more of a reflection of the staff than inmates. Automated information can be valuable to correctional management because once a problem arises, automated systems can give managers critical insight into which events and personnel changes preceded the influx.

Characteristics of the inmate population like those of the guard force are not static. Changes in the incarcerated population may be reflected in changing needs for both treatment and custodial issues. New trends can emerge suddenly or slowly over time. As in the previous example the unexpected increase in altercations between guards and inmates could be a result of overall changes within the inmate population. At the general level the incarcerated population is reacting to a change in policy that has broken the status quo and increased the number of potential situations where guards and prisoners are at odds with one another. More specifically, the increase in incidents may be due to a more general trend that the incarcerated population is experiencing such as an influx of first-time, younger inmates. Younger inmates are more likely to seek out confrontations with correctional staff as a means of enhancing their status or reputation among the other inmates. It may be that is a change in subgroup behavior as a new gang attempts to emerge in the facilities by establishing its bona fides. It may be that a few specific individuals are involved in most of the increased altercations. Automated information concerning characteristics of the prisoners, guards, and events could provide key insight. While all of the above situations are plausible explanations, aggregated indicators and data, compiled by an automated system, would greatly assist prison officials in understanding the nature of the problem so the proper solution could be implemented.

External stakeholders such as lobbying groups concerned with safety, funding agents, and legislative mandates will also affect how correctional organizations operate. These influences are often reflected in the programs and policies implemented by top-level administrators to counter, change, or improve custodial, supervision, or treatment processes. Many of these programs and policies will be successful, but how is that success quantified? There is a significant amount of evidence indicating that programs or policies do not always have their intended effect. The key to any program or policy is to understand how successes and failures are measured. This is why it is of critical importance to determine the desired outcomes when such programs and policies are administrated. The simple answer is to monitor indicators of the success or failure of these programs and policies via an automated information system.

Broad changes in laws and policies in the larger criminal justice system can have a major impact on correctional facilities. For example, mandatory sentencing laws might increase the number of younger offenders, while three-strike laws may have the opposite effect of increasing the overall age of the incarcerated population. Both will impact the medical needs of the inmate population in perhaps different manners. Moreover, both can have an impact on custodial and treatment programs.

Information capital gathered through automated information systems can give correctional officials keen insight into the status of treatment, custodial, and supervision issues. This type of information is critical for understanding the status of the staff, inmates, and external influences and will be of assistance to correctional officials in navigating an ever-changing environment.

Conclusion

The addition of information technology can be a great benefit to any organization. However, if the system is not appropriate, efficient, and effective, it can be an enormous misuse of resources. An organization must be clear on the intent and purpose of the information system before investing time and money into development. Multiple types of data systems exist, and each organization must decide which system best suits its individual needs. Regardless of the system used, information systems must be strategic (Rowley 1994). That is, data elements and information obtained from the system must assist the organization in making decisions that align with the broader strategic plan.

Within the organization itself, different levels of managers will have different needs for data. As the hierarchy of organizations descends, the detail of information needed increases (Hayes and Radosevich 1974). Therefore, there is an inverse relationship between administrative management levels and information detail. Although the level of detail may vary by level of management, indicators of quality information and the elements of a system that can produce that information do not. Common themes exist between the information needed for each level.

Organizations must manage the information capital process. This requires the oversight of what is needed to be effective, while allowing staff the flexibility to be creative in reaching these requirements. Further, quality information systems take time. Administrators specifically, and organizations more broadly, must understand that the design and development of a quality, appropriate, effective system will take patience and collaboration. It is not enough to simply provide staff and external stakeholders with information. Strategic support systems must be created and supported on a continual basis (Fahey 1981). With the proper effort and resources, investing in information capital can significantly increase the organization's effectiveness and its ability to demonstrate that effectiveness.

Learning Objectives

After completing this chapter you should be able to—

- Describe why data are important for correctional agencies
- Define *information capital*
- Learn the components of information capital
- Learn how information capital is related to organizational goals
- Learn about the importance of automation
- Describe major concerns associated with correctional data collection and access
- Define *quality assurance*
- Understand why quality assurance plans are important
- Learn the four principles guiding quality assurance
- Learn about the basic components of quality assurance plans

Key Terms

Automated management system
Data
"Good" information
Information capital
Quality data system
Strategic information system

Discussion Questions

1. Examine the mission statements for three correctional agencies. Discuss what types of data would be needed to determine whether the agencies are effectively implementing their mission.
2. Interview three executives of criminal justice agencies, three midlevel line staff within those agencies, and three line staff about the quality of information capital. Compare and contrast the responses.

References

Anderson, D. L. 2009. *Organization development and the process of leading organizational change.* Thousand Oaks, CA: Sage.

Business Dictionary. n.d. http://www.businessdictionary.com/definition/knowledge-capital.html (accessed February 2009).

Cash, J. I., B. R. Konsynski. 1985. Information systems redraw competitive boundaries. In *Harvard Business Review: Strategic planning comes of age.* Boston: Harvard.

deCarbonnel, F. E., and R. G. Dorrance. 1981. Information sources for planning decioins. In *The practice of planning: Strategic, administrative, and operational,* edited by L. H. Reinharth, H. J. Shapiro, E. A. Kallman. New York: Van Nostrand Reinhold.

Fahey, L. 1989. Applications in strategic management: Don't let data collection bring down your strategic analyses. In *The strategic planning management reader*, edited by L. Fahey, pp. 141–144. New Jersey: Prentice Hall.

Fulton, B., A. Stichman, L. Travis, and E. Latessa. 1997. Moderating probation and parole officer attitudes to achieve desired outcomes. *The Prison Journal* 77(3): 295–312.

Gaes, G. G., S. D. Camp, J. B. Nelson, and W. G. Saylor. 2004. *Measuring prison performance government privatization and accountability*. New York: Altamira Press.

Gupta, R. n.d. Maximizing information capital: Successful business development in the information age. Available at: http://www.fiveoclockclub.comarticles/1997/09-97-informationcapital (accessed May 2009).

Hatton, C., M. Rivers, H. Mason, L. Mason, E. Emerson, C. Kiernan, D. Reeves, and A. Alborz. 1999. Organizational culture and staff outcomes in services for people with intellectual disabilities. *Journal Intellectual Disabilities Research* 43: 206–218.

Hayes, R. L., and R. Radosevich. 1974. Designing information systems for strategic decisions. *Long Range Planning* 7(1974): 45–48.

Henderson, M., A. Mathias-Humphrey, and M. J. McDermott. 2008. Barriers to effective program implementation: Rural school-based probation. *Federal Probation* (June) 72(1): 28–36.

Latessa, E. 2004. The challenge of change: Correctional programs and evidence-based practices. *Criminology and Public Policy* 3(4): 547–560.

Lehman, W. E. K., J. M. Greener, and D. D. Simpson 2002. Assessing organizational readiness for change. *Journal of Substance Abuse Treatment* 22: 197–209.

Logan, C. H. 1993. Criminal justice performance measures for prisons. In *Performance measures for the criminal justice system*, edited by L. Greenfield, pp. 1–18. Washington, DC: Bureau of Justice Statistics.

McFarlan, F. W. 1985. Information technology as the way you compete. In *Harvard Business Review: Strategic planning comes of age.* Boston: Harvard.

Miller, J. M., B. Koons-Witt, and H. Ventura. 2004. Barriers to evaluating the effectiveness of drug treatment behind bars. *Journal of Criminal Justice* 32: 75–83.

Palmquist, R. A. 1992. The impact of information technology on the individual. In *Annual review of information science and technology*, edited by M. E. Williams, pp. 3–42. Medford, NJ: Learned Info, Inc.

Porter, M. E. and V. E. Miller. 1985. How influence gives you competitive advantage. In *Harvard Business Review: Strategic planning comes of age.* Boston: Harvard.

Rackoff N., C. Wiseman, and W. A. Ullrich. 1985. Information systems for competitive advantage: Implementation of a planning process. *MIS Qtly* 9: 285–294.

Reinharth, L., H. J. Shapiro, and E. A. Kallman. 1981. *The practice of planning: Strategic, administrative and operational.* New York: Van Nostrand Reinhold.

Rowley, J. 1994. *Strategic management, information systems, and technology.* Oxford: Blackwell Publishing.

Snyder, H., and J. B. Pierce. 2002. Intellectual capital. In *Annual review of information science and technology,* edited by B. Cronin, pp. 467–500. Medford, NJ: Information Today.

Somagyi, E. K., and R. D. Galliers. 1994. Information technology in business: From data processing to strategic information system. In *Strategic information management: Challenges and strategies in managing information systems*, edited by R. D. Galliers, B. S. H. Baker, pp. 9–27. Oxford: Butterworth-Heinemann.

State of Oregon. 2003. 72nd Oregon legislative assembly—2003 regular session. Available at: http://www.leg.state.or.us/03reg/measures/sb0200.dir/sb0267.a.html (accessed on April 16, 2009).

Tavakoli, I., and J. Lawton. 2005. Strategic thinking and knowledge management. *Handbook of Business Strategy* 6(1): 155–160. Available at: http://www.emeraldinsight.com/Insight/ViewContentServlet?Filename=Published/EmeraldFullTextArticle/Articles/2890060122.html (accessed on April 16, 2009).

U.S. Department of Justice. 1998. *State and federal corrections information systems: An inventory of data elements and an assessment of reporting capabilities.* Washington, DC: Bureau of Justice Statistics.

Zachman, J. A. 1981. Control and planning of information systems. In *The practice of planning: Strategic, administrative, and operational,* edited by L. H. Reinharth, H. J. Shapiro, E. A. Kallman, pp. 283–295. New York: Van Nostrand Reinhold.

Chapter 5

Human Resource Capital

All organizations must invest in and expand resources to remain efficient. Production and generation of outputs require resources. These resources must be replenished once they have been expended to produce outputs, regardless of how outputs are defined. Human resources are no exception. Staff are one of the most valuable resources of any organization (Wooten and Crane 2003). Staff hold the keys to implementation and the focus for administrators must be on getting the right people in the right positions, motivating them to perform, maintaining and upgrading skills, and providing leadership (Fogg 1999). As depicted in Table 5.1, human resources has a role at all levels of planning and initiating change.

Typically in corrections, front-line staff are responsible for most of the contact with offenders. Often, this contact is the sole representation of the quality of the organization or agency, the activities of the agency, and the organizational culture. The type and quality of these contacts can impact the success of the client (Hanley 2002). Staff attitudes can transfer to clients very quickly and intensely. Therefore, staff attitudes become essential to establishing and maintaining prosocial attitudes among clients and offenders. When a client perceives staff to have professional, fair, and helpful attitudes, the client's performance improves (Dowden and Andrews 2004). Improvement in performance can lead to success for the participating client, for the program in which the client is participating, or both, which in turn demonstrates the program's effectiveness. Staff attitudes improve when individuals feel that they are making a difference and what they are doing is successful. Figure 5.1 demonstrates how this process works and how staff attitudes impact client success.

Given the importance of staff attitudes and the impact staff can have on clients, it is essential that the agency or organization conduct an assessment to ascertain a baseline of staff attitudes, values, and beliefs. This assessment refers to a process where the organization continually analyzes its human resources needs under

Table. 5.1 The Role of Human Resources in Change Management Processes

Role of Human Resources in Change
Provide internal diagnosis.
Help create future leadership for the initiative.
Leverage their current skills.
Participate in strategic planning.
Help plan implementation.
Help train, facilitate, and prepare teams.
Serve as a general sounding board.
Help institute an accountability system design and implementation.
Help recruit for the initiative.
Help develop incentive plans for staff.
Participate in new skills training and education to support the initiative.
Participate in plan monitoring and modification efforts when necessary.

Source: This is a modified version of the table entitled "The Role of Human Resources Change" that appeared in Fogg, C. D., 1999, *Implementing Your Strategic Plan*. Atlanta: American Management Association, p. 418. (Reproduced with permission from Amacom Publishers.)

Figure 5.1 Staff attitudes and client success.

changing conditions and develops the structures necessary to satisfy those needs (see Walker 1980, for a discussion of this idea).

Assessment

Just as assessment of offenders is the first step to uncovering strengths and weaknesses of the offender, the organization must undertake a comprehensive assessment of itself to identify organizational strengths and weaknesses. The area of human resource capital is an especially important component in this endeavor. Staff are assets of the organization (Perry Wooten and Crane 2003) and must be perceived as such. The organization must make every conscious effort to ensure that staff are valued and developed. If not, staff can have a significant negative impact on the success of the organization. High staff turnover (Redfern and Christian 2003), impeding implementation of processes (Koch, Cairns, and Brunk 2000), and resistance to organizational change (Greiner 1972), just to name a few issues, can hamper the success of any organization.

Since staff are so critical to both individual client and organizational success, assessing their attitudes, values, and beliefs is an important factor in investing in the success of an agency. One of the primary differences between the traditional approach of identifying issues with staff and investing in human resource capital is that this investment outwardly recognizes that staff are important to the agency (Bertram 1991). Conscious steps must be taken to show staff they are not only important to the organization but also valued as assets.

Assessing staff attitudes toward the organization, their jobs individually, and offenders is particularly important for correctional agencies. Table 5.2 shows the types of questions that might be asked of staff to determine their perceptions of current organizational functioning and support for change. Staff attitudes may be different from what administrators assume (Graffam et al. 2004). Administrators may perceive staff as appropriately trained and supporting the mission and vision of the organization. However, in reality, staff may be adhering to policies and procedures without completely supporting the mission or vision. The lack of agreement, support, or confidence in the mission will be revealed in the contacts with clients. Information is given and interpreted within a specific context. As Hanna (2000) explains, the context in which information is given provides meaning to that information. Further, personal attitudes and values typically establish the context in which information is disseminated (Hanna 2000). Therefore, negative attitudes or values will set a negative context for which information is delivered and interpreted. Hence, staff with negative attitudes or values or those contrary to the mission and vision of the organization could alter, hinder, or reduce the importance of the information directed toward clients.

Communication between staff and clients is not the only area in which staff attitudes play a part in processing information. The interpretation of information

Table. 5.2 Sample of Questions Administrators Might Want to Ask

Discussion Questions You Might Ask Staff to Assess Perceptions Prior to Implementation
Describe the organization's current mission in three sentences.
Explain how your job helps to fill the agency's current mission.
We are considering making the following changes in the organization, how do you think your job will be impacted by this change?
We are considering making changes in the organization, what are the most significant barriers which must be overcome?
What skills do you feel are necessary for you to do your current job well?
What new skills would you need in order to do your job if we implement proposed changes?
Given the description of the changes that are being considered, where do you see your job fitting in?
In your opinion, what other organizational structures would need to be changed for this initiative to be successful?

Note: This is a sample of the types of questions the authors have administered to staff during focus groups in organizations planning to implement evidence-based practice.

is very much the result of differential staff attitudes, values, and beliefs. Wicke, Coppin, and Payne (2004) cite poor communication as one of the primary issues to implementing evidence-based practice, while resistance to change is cited by McAlearney (2000) as another concern for organizations. Support for the organizations' mission or vision can reduce the amount of resistance staff exhibit toward organizational changes. In order to make changes to an organization, that organization or agency must provide various types and amounts of information to staff. The information must follow a trail—beginning with the administration, flowing through middle managers, to line staff (i.e., those who work with clients on a daily basis). The processing of this information can become complicated at best, chaotic at worst. Given the multiple levels of information processing, the information can get distorted and diluted, resulting in confusion, lack of buy-in from staff, and ultimately lack of support for organizational policies, procedures, and changes. The end goal is to achieve successful staff buy-in; for if new initiatives are seen by staff as mandates from above, seldom will these initiatives be effectively implemented.

This type of situation is particularly critical when considering how conditions of program participation are delivered. Typically, line staff are responsible for the type and quality of services provided to clients (Cameron and Wren 1999; Flores et al. 2005). For example, a custody- or surveillance-oriented community supervision officer (pretrial, probation, or parole) may deliver conditions of successful completion differently from a rehabilitation- or treatment-oriented officer. The surveillance-oriented officer will emphasize the custodial requirements of supervision (e.g., appearing for supervision meetings, drug tests, adherence to curfews), while the treatment-oriented officer will emphasize and hold the offender accountable to make treatment-oriented requirements such as 12-Step program meetings, completion of treatment programs, and so forth. The reality of this differential emphasis not only impacts the way in which information is delivered, but also what types of conditions are enforced on each caseload. These correctional personnel have considerable discretion that can be used to sanction or even revoke an offender's community supervision for violating one condition. Using the example above, what this means is that the offender under the supervision of the surveillance-oriented officer could end up being revoked for violating conditions, while another under the supervision of the treatment-oriented officer may not be revoked or sanctioned for the same violation. If the goal of the community-based agency is treatment, then the actions of the surveillance-oriented officer are undermining the organizational goals. This differential response is especially problematic in organizations that have little to no specific direction (e.g., policies or procedures) for the enforcement of supervision conditions, revocations, or even explanations of conditions to offenders. The basic concepts of justice and fairness are significantly compromised by the lack of consistent enforcement of conditions.

Further, negative attitudes among staff can extend beyond individual interactions between staff and clients. In organizations such as corrections that are constantly in a state of flux and change, negative attitudes toward change in general may impact job performance. For example, a study examining staff attitudes toward a statewide reentry initiative showed that more than 30% of staff never used the LSI-R in a policy-mandated prescriptive case management system to assess treatment progress, determine risk for recidivism, or set conditions of supervision (Haas, Hamilton, and Hanley 2006). This same study also found great variation in the length of time staff took to complete an LSI-R (from less than 15 minutes to more than 2 hours) (Haas, Hamilton, and Hanley 2006).

Negative staff attitudes are also problematic in the progression of information within and between levels of management and staff. All organizations are subject to both external and internal political forces. Internal political forces, if identified and understood, can be used in a positive or negative manner. Underlying power structures or informal social controls can be reduced or neutralized if the administration focuses on utilizing data obtained from staff assessment (Eiring 1999). The ability to honestly examine itself is the organization's first step in understanding the inner workings of the organization (Bertram 1991; Hanson, Melnyk, and Calantone 2004). This self-assessment is essential prior to implementing any changes within the organization (Kramer, Schmalenberg, and MacGuire 2004). Obtaining a baseline of the perceived investment in human resources is crucial for understanding where the organization currently stands with staff, identifying a plan for future activities or undertakings, and having the ability to measure improvements in human resource capital. Since resistance to change is prevalent in any organization, identifying where the sources of the resistance lie and any obstacles to advancing the organization can provide the organization with a roadmap on how to overcome these issues (Baker et al. 2003). Further, understanding staff attitudes, values, and beliefs can provide great insight into the culture of the organization.

Organizational Culture

Historically, correctional organizations have been evaluated using process measures, such as number of contacts with offenders, number of drug screens conducted, or the infamous recidivism rate of participants. However, these outcomes have failed to consider much of what occurs within the agency. Moreover, these outcomes hold the organization accountable for results that may simply be beyond the organization's control. For example, participants may recidivate for many reasons—relapse in substance abuse, lack of employment, mental health issues, and so forth. Often, these situations occur after the offenders have left the program or are off of supervision. Yet, the organization is still held accountable for the rate at which offenders "fail."

Alternative measures of outcome may be more applicable to correctional organizations. One of the most overlooked issues in any organization is its organizational culture. This has a great influence on how the organization operates and how successful the organization is in accomplishing its goals. Although empirically based best practices can be designed for implementation in an organization, the implementation of these initiatives can be hampered by the organizational culture (Baker et al. 2003).

A consensus on the definition of organizational culture has not been reached by academics (Anderson 2009). However, a simple definition of organizational culture, provided by Walter (1985, p. 301), is: "the shared attitudes, values, beliefs and customs of members of a social unit or organization." While staff do not constitute all of the members of an organization, front-line staff often make up a large number of these members and can significantly influence a correctional agency's culture. The definition of the concept of organizational culture may not be as important as the impact that organizational culture can have on staff, outcomes, and the values of the organization.

Research on how organizational culture impacts staff has been conducted and shows that organizational culture can increase or decrease stress in the job environment. Further, organizational culture is linked to job satisfaction and turnover (Gillet and Stenfert-Kroese 2003). Job satisfaction, stress, staff support, and communication have all been found to be significantly related to officers' intentions to leave their job (Mitchell et al. 2000). Multiple problems result from high staff-turnover rates, which can impede continuity of care, disorient cognitively impaired individuals, and challenge established relationships between staff and clients (Cohen-Mansfield 1997). Additionally, high staff turnover increases recruitment, hiring, and training costs and limits the quality of service delivery provided to clients (Aarons and Sawitzky 2006). Therefore, attention to the organizational culture is of great importance to any organization.

A salient component of organizational culture is the concept of values. Values of staff, as well as the organization as a whole, emphasize what is important to the organization. Success of the organization should be measured based on its unique value system. Organizations that perform more efficiently are value centered and more likely to encourage client success (Gowdy, Carlson, and Rapp 2004). However, individual staff values may contradict the values of the organization, which can pose great obstacles in multiple areas, including service delivery (Kramer et al. 2004) and the implementation of evidence-based practice (Hanson et al. 2004). Changing the organization means changing values (Hanson et al. 2004). Changing values includes such initiatives as a strong commitment to training, modifying language, and daily practice to reflect the emphasis on new values, among others. Although traditional values may be entrenched in the organization and very difficult to change (Baker et al. 2003), modifications to the organizational culture, which in turn will produce changes in daily practice (Wooten and Crane 2003) can be made. All stakeholders, including staff, must be able to have input into the values of the organization, and these values should reflect at least some of the individual values of staff (Wooten and Crane 2003). Once these changes have been made, the organization can be proactive in dealing with the internal and external politics that introduce change to the organization (Kramer et al. 2004).

Methods for Investing in Staff

Multiple methods can be utilized to demonstrate to staff that the organization values their work and staff as individuals. First, as previously discussed, assessment of staff attitudes is a valuable tool for the organization to determine the current status of staff and how to proceed with investment in human resource capital (Baker et al. 2003; Bertram 1991; Bond 2000; Eiring 1999; Hanson et al. 2004; Kramer et al. 2004). Second, leadership must determine what avenues to take to increase the organization's human resource assets. Participatory decision making (Perry Wooten and Crane 2003) can improve staff empowerment and responsibility for the organization's success. Including line staff (and junior staff) in decision making and implementation of new policies, procedures, and programs can increase staff buy-in (Thomas and Wellcoxson 1999). Contrarily, lack of input into decision making can increase job dissatisfaction (Stojkovic and Farkas 2003). Allowing staff to participate in decision making increases their ability to provide feedback to the administration and the rest of the organization (Koch, Cairns, and Brunk 2000). This feedback can include issues with implementation, difficulties in applying values of the mission and vision statements, and unrealistic expectations the administration may place on line staff. Possibly more importantly, these staff can assist administrators in disseminating information and implementing the necessary changes by answering questions from peers and explaining specific decision-making processes (such as the reasons behind the changes). Recognizing these issues early in the process can assist organizations in avoiding major downfalls—and ultimately, failure.

In addition to including staff in decision making to the extent possible, the manner in which information is provided to staff can also increase their commitment and buy-in to change. For example, assessing the workload of staff to determine whether cross-training into other areas of the organization can be a benefit not only to the individual, but also to the organization (Gentry and Keilty 2004). Cross-training can provide staff with more information on how the organization works, an understanding of the constraints and responsibilities of other members, as well as an opportunity for advancement within the current structure of the organization. For the broader organization, having staff that can perform multiple tasks and are knowledgeable in multiple job positions increases the organization's ability to promote from within and maintain a cohesive organizational culture.

Consultants or outside experts can also be helpful for investing in staff (Baker et al. 2003; Gentry and Keilty 2004). Consultants can assist with dissemination of information and explanations of why change must occur, and they can answer any questions that staff might have related to the implementation of the new initiative. While outside experts can provide training sessions, direct (often one-on-one) contact with these experts can often give staff a more intimate understanding of the changes being made. This understanding promotes buy-in and allows staff an opportunity for ownership of the change since their questions are being answered by experts in the field. However, an organization must carefully consider the consultants contracted for this type of work. Frequently, consultants or experts are hesitant, for whatever reason, to work directly with front-line staff outside of a training context. Personalities of consultants must also be considered prior to any contact with line staff. For example, a consultant that is perceived by line staff as patronizing will only push staff further from ownership and buy-in so important to successful change.

Staff development is another area where the organization can invest in staff (Gentry and Keilty 2004). Training provides staff with the skills and conceptualizations to perform their current job role. Development of staff invests in their future and offers them an opportunity to professionally grow. Development can focus on skills but, often, staff development focuses on behaviors, values, and beliefs. Similar to cognitive behavioral treatments for offenders, development programs include role modeling, practice in simulated situations, and monitoring evaluation. Staff development is not a one-time activity. It is a process that takes time but can be extremely beneficial to all involved.

Changing behavior, attitudes, and values can also be accomplished through attention to the organizational culture. As Hatton et al. (1999) explain, organizational culture can mediate an individual's personality, thereby reducing discontent and increasing team cohesiveness among staff. Further, organizational culture can increase staff morale (Hatton et al. 1999), decrease individual subjective interpretation of policies and procedures (Hanna 2000), and impact service delivery to clients

(Kramer et al. 2004). Organizational culture is a difficult concept to grasp because it is different for every organization. If an organization has multiple locations or field sites, the culture can vary between these sites. Although it is difficult to grasp and comprehend, acknowledging the culture and respecting the influence it can have on all staff, stakeholders, and even clients is crucial for an organization that is subjected to internal and external change.

Conclusion

Investment in human resource capital is a crucial component to effective organizational performance. Most often, staff are the greatest expenditure for organizations. This expenditure should be viewed as an investment, not as a liability.

Learning Objectives

After completing this chapter, you should be able to—

- Discuss how staff attitudes impact client success
- Explain the role of assessment
- Discuss why staff attitudes may differ from what administrators expect
- Discuss how staff attitudes negatively impact implementation of new initiatives
- Explain how organizational culture impacts implementation of new initiatives
- Describe ways to invest in staff

Key Terms

Assessment of staff
Impact of staff attitudes
Investing in staff
Organizational culture

Discussion Questions

1. How does staff attitude impact the ability to implement change within correctional contexts?
2. What steps can an administrator take to address staff concerns surrounding a change initiative?

References

Aarons, G. A., and A. C. Sawitzky. 2006. Organizational climate partially mediates the effect of culture on work attitudes and staff turnover in mental health services. *Administration and Policy in Mental Health and Mental Health Services Research* 33(3): 289–301.

Anderson, D. L. 2009. *Organizational development: The process of leading organizational change.* Thousand Oaks, CA: Sage Publications.

Baker, G., H. King, J. L. MacDonald, and J. D. Horbar. 2003. Using organizational assessment surveys for improvement in neonatal intensive care. *Pediatrics* 111: 419–425.

Bertram, D. 1991. Getting started in total quality management. *Total Quality Management* 2: 279–282.

Bond, M. H. 2004. Culture level dimensions of social axioms and their correlates across 41 cultures. *Journal of Cross-Cultural Psychology* 35: 548–570.

Cameron, G., and A. M. Wren. 1999. Reconstructing organizational culture: A process using multiple perspectives. *Public Health Nursing* 16: 96–101.

Cohen-Mansfield, J.1997. Turnover among nursing home staff: A review. *Nursing Management* 28(5): 59–64.

Dowden, C., and D. A. Andrews. 2004. The importance of staff practice in delivering effective correctional treatment: A meta-analytic review of core correctional practice. *International Journal of Offender Therapy and Comparative Criminology* 48(2): 203–214.

Eiring, L. 1999. Dynamic office politics: Powering up for program success! *Information Management Journal* (January): 17–25.

Flores, A. W., A. Russell, E. J. Latessa, and L. F. Travis III. 2005. Evidence of professionalism or quackery: Measuring practitioner awareness of risk/need factors and effective treatment strategies. *Federal Probation* 69(2): 9–14.

Fogg, C. 1999. *Implementing your strategic plan.* Atlanta: American Management Association.

Gentry, M., and B. Keilty. 2004. Rural and suburban cluster grouping: Reflections on staff development as a component of program success. *Roeper Review* 26(3): 147–155.

Gillett, E., and B. Stenfert Kroese. 2003. Investigating organisational culture: A comparison of a "high"- and a "low"-performing residential unit for people with intellectual disabilities. *Journal of Applied Research in Intellectual Disabilities* 16: 279–284.

Gowdy, E., L. Carlson, and C. A. Rapp 2004. Organizational factors differentiating high performing from low performing supported employment programs. *Psychiatric Rehabilitation Journal* 28(2): 150–156.

Graffam, J., A. Shrinkfield, B. Lavelle, and W. McPherson. 2004. Variables affecting successful reintegration as perceived by offenders and professionals. *Journal of Offender Rehabilitation* 40: 147–171.

Greiner, L. E. 1972. Evolution and revolution as organizations grow. *Harvard Business Review.* Reprinted in *Family Business Review* (1997) 10: 397.

Haas, S. M., C. A. Hamilton, and D. Hanley. 2006 (July). Implementation of the West Virginia Offender Reentry Initiative: An examination of staff attitudes and the application of the LSI-R. Charleston, WV: Mountain State Criminal Justice Research Services.

Hanley, D. 2002. Risk differentiation and appropriate supervision: A meaningful union? Dissertation presented July 2002, University of Cincinnati. Available at: http://criminaljustice.cech.uc.edu/docs/dissertations/Hanley.pdf (accessed April 2, 2009).

Hanna, N. 2008. *Transforming government and empower communities: The Sri Lankan experience with e-development.* World Bank.

Hanson, J. D., S. A. Melnyk, and R. J. Calantone. 2004. *Core values and environmental management: A strong inference approach.* Greenleaf Publishing.

Hatton, C., M. Rivers, H. Mason, L. Mason, E. Emerson, C. Kiernan, D. Reeves, and A. Alborz. 1999. Organizational culture and staff outcomes in services for people with intellectual disabilities. *Journal Intellectual Disabilities Research* 43: 206–218.

Koch, R., J. M. Cairns, and M. Brunk. 2000. How to involve staff in developing an outcomes-oriented organization. *Education and Treatment of Children* 21(1): 41–47.

Kramer, M., C. Schmalenberg, and P. Maguire. 2004. Essentials of a magnetic work environment: Part 3. *Nursing 2005* 34: 44–7.

McAlearney, A. S. 2000. Designing and developing effective disease management programmes. *Disease Management Outcomes* 7: 139–148.

Mitchell, O., D. L. Mackenzie, G. J. Styve, and A. R. Gover 2000. The impact of individual, organizational, and environmental attributes on voluntary turnover among juvenile correctional staff members. *Justice Quarterly* 17(2): 333–357.

Redfern, S., and S. Christian. 2003. Achieving change in health care practice. *Journal of Evaluation in Health Care Practice* 9(2): 225–238.

Stojkovic, S., and M. A. Farkas. 2003. *Correctional leadership: A cultural perspective.* Belmont, CA: Wadsworth Publishing.

Thomas, J., and L. Willcoxson. 1998. Developing teaching and changing organizational culture through grassroots leadership. *Higher Education* 36(4): 471–485.

Tubman, J. G., and R. S. Vento. 2001. Principal and teacher reports of strategies to enforce anti-tobacco. *Journal of School Health* 71: 229–235.

Walker, J. W. 1980. *Human resource planning.* New York: McGraw Hill.

Walter, G. A. 1985. Culture collisions in mergers and acquisitions. In *Organizational culture,* edited by P. J. Frost, L. F. Moore, M. R. Louis, C. C. Lundberg, and J. Martin, pp. 301–314. Beverly Hills, CA: Sage.

Wicke, D., R. Coppin, and S. Payne. 2004. Teamworking in nursing home. *Journal of Advanced Nursing* 45(2): 197–204.

Wooten, L. P., and P. Crane. 2003. Nurses as implementers of organizational culture. *Nursing Economics* 21(6): 275–279.

Chapter 6

Evidence-Based Practice

There are many types of *evidence-based practice* (EBP) that apply to correctional organizations. The past 30 years have provided the field with a wealth of information under the title of "what works." However, the field has failed to identify exactly how to make "what works" work. This chapter focuses on outlining principles for effectively disseminating and implementing EBPs.

Defining Evidence-Based Practice

An understanding of the role of EBP in shaping and managing correctional organizations should begin by deriving a definition of just what EBP means. In the literature EBP has been defined in multiple ways depending on whether one is dealing with an academic or practitioner audience. Academics such as Petersilia (2005) refer to evidence-based *policy* rather than evidence-based *practice*. Evidence-based policy is "an approach that helps people make well-informed decisions about policies and programs by putting the best available evidence from research at the heart of policy development and implementation" (Petersilia 2005, p. 2). Practitioners define EBP as programs, services, or practices that integrate the best research evidence with clinical expertise, cultural competence, and the values of the clients receiving the services (AMH 2007). Most commonly, EBP definitions utilize the approach taken by medical professionals and define EBP as the use of the best available evidence from systematic research, combined with professional expertise and judgment in making decisions about service delivery (Dollaghan 2004; Prendergast, Schinke, and Sachwald 2006; Sackett et al. 1996). EBP is a lifelong learning process that involves a constant posing of "questions of direct practical importance to clients, searching objectively and efficiently for the current best evidence relative to each question, and taking appropriate action guided by the evidence" (Gibbs et al. 2007).

The limitation associated with the majority of the definitions is that most fail to consider criminal justice organizational constraints. Some organizations may not have the organizational capacity to implement an evidence-based approach. Consistent with the Council for Training in Evidence-based Practice, we take an ecological approach in defining EBP (Spring 2007). This approach recognizes that for EBP to be implemented, interpersonal contexts, organizational contexts, and the external environment should all be contemplated as part of the implementation process. Thus, as depicted in Figure 6.1, *evidence-based correctional practice* "entails making decisions about how to promote definable and measurable correctional outcomes by integrating the best available evidence with practitioner expertise and other resources, and with client characteristics, state, needs, values and preferences of those who will be affected" (Spring 2007).

According to Campbell (2008), the correctional organizations that are successful at implementing EBP have addressed three critical areas within their organizational contexts. They have created an organizational environment that stresses

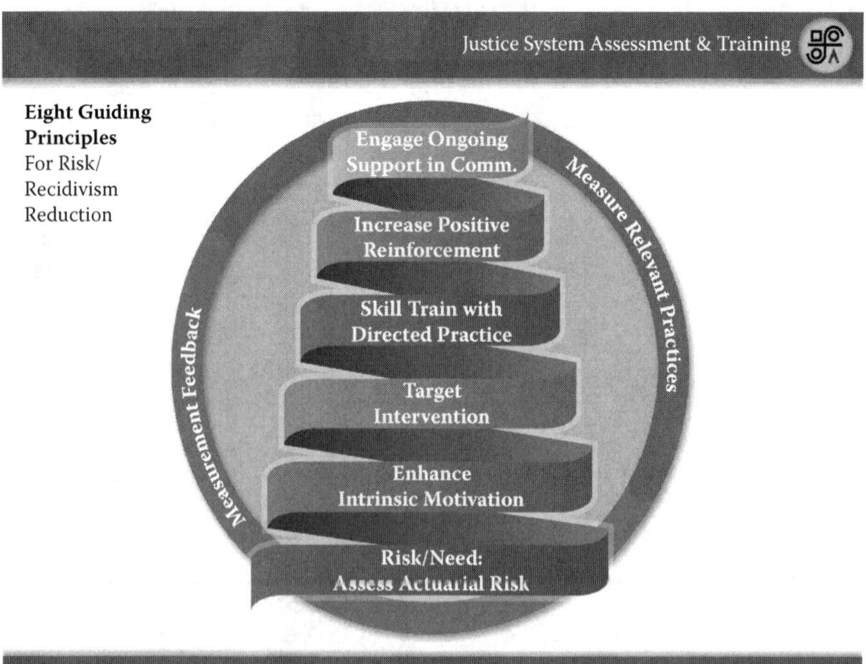

Figure 6.1 Guiding principles of evidence-base practice.

putting in place the technology, tools, and systems necessary to help agencies learn about implementing EBPs. These correctional agencies have focused on creating organizational structures and cultures supportive of EBP. Finally, they emphasize cross-agency collaboration.

Advantages of Evidence-Based Practice (EBP) in Corrections

There are several benefits to implementing EBP in corrections. First, a direct advantage of evidence-based corrections is that it integrates criminal justice research with practice (Sperber, Henderson-Hurley, and Hanley 2005). EBP is a process that serves to bridge the significant gap between research and practice, a gap that has long been considered a causal factor for programmatic failures. EBPs typically have well-described service components and often provide detailed implementation manuals allowing for a guided, more efficient implementation process (Center for Substance Abuse Treatment 2006).

Second, EBPs have been shown in the literature to improve client outcomes, leading to recidivism reductions, improvement in the chances for recovery from drug addictions, and increased social capital (Warren 2007). " …A large body of rigorous research conducted over the last 20 years has proven that well-implemented rehabilitation and treatment programs carefully targeted with the assistance of validated risk/needs assessment tools at the right offenders can reduce recidivism by 10% to 20%" (Warren 2007, p. 2).

A third benefit is that when EBPs are effectively implemented they can and often do lead to significant improvements in organizational functioning (Bogue, Campbell, and Clawson 2004; Davidson, Crawford, and Kerwood 2009; Joplin et al. 2004). EBP has the potential for helping correctional organizations make better use of limited resources by enabling them to evaluate the effectiveness of the services the organization provides to correctional clients. For example, a Washington State Institute for Public Policy study revealed that if the state of Washington implemented a "…moderate-to-aggressive portfolio of evidence-based options, a significant level of future prison construction can be avoided, taxpayers can save about two billion dollars, and crime rates can be reduced" (Aos, Miller, and Drake 2006).

Fourth, EBP can be learned by people from different backgrounds, at different stages of their career, and who work in diverse areas of corrections. This means that you do not have to be a statistician to understand the evidence. In most cases summaries of the research are readily available through organizations such as the National Institute of Corrections, The Campbell Collaboration and the Washington Policy Center, to name a few. Moreover, EBP provides a common framework for problem solving within complex correctional organizations. It is a framework that uses evidence to help drive decision making.

Disadvantages of EBP in Corrections

While EBP has the potential for improving practice in corrections, it is not without drawbacks. First, the decision to implement EBP requires a long-term commitment from correctional organizations. Implementing EBP is not a quick process to put in place. It takes time to learn what EBP is, time to assess which practices are relevant, and time to implement.

Second, establishing the infrastructure within a correctional organization for practicing EBP is not without cost. EBP requires a significant commitment of staff resources. Dedicated staff are necessary to do the following:

- Research EBPs appropriate for agency needs.
- Modify EBPs to fit the organizational context.
- Implement the practice within programs.
- Train others within the agency on the practice.
- Gather data, and monitor and assess outcomes.
- Engage in continuous quality management.

EBP requires at a minimum that dedicated staff members within the correctional organization are computer literate, have keyboarding skills, and have the ability to conduct basic research reviews and appraisals.

Third, EBP may require additional expenditures in the area of information capital. EBP is data driven and consequently may require more sophisticated technology than that currently utilized within the agency. For example, organizations may need to buy computer hardware and software.

Additionally, it is possible that no research evidence would be available to answer the question of interest. If such a circumstance occurs, the organization is left without an EBP to consider. We have assessed a very limited number of programs described as evidence-based. There are a growing number of promising practices that will need to wait several years for enough evidence to be compiled for a program model to be considered evidence-based. A significant portion of what we do in corrections remains unproven, untested, and in place simply because we have always done things a certain way (Latessa, Cullen, and Gendreau 2002).

Finally, while EBP has received widespread support among academics and increased use by practitioners, the greatest challenge to implementing EBP is staff resistance. Why wouldn't staff want to implement EBP? Staff have relayed several myths as justifications for why they do not want to implement EBP:

1. We are already doing EBP.
2. This is just another excuse for cutting costs, staff, or content.
3. Research is irrelevant. Expert opinion is what matters.
4. One man's evidence is another one's quackery.

5. EBP still constitutes a one-size-fits-all approach.
6. This is just another fad. The only difference is that this time we have a manual.

Bridging the gap between research and practice may require administrators to confront the myths that have come to be associated with EBPs in criminal justice. These myths are inconsistent with the intentions of EBP. First, the idea that "we are already doing it" does not fit with the extensive body of evidence indicating that what some correctional organizations are in fact currently doing in their organization is what some academics have referred to as "correctional quackery" rather than EBP (Latessa, Cullen, and Gendreau 2002). Correctional quackery refers to the implementation "of treatment interventions that are based on neither (1) existing knowledge of the causes of crime nor (2) existing knowledge of what programs have been shown to change offender behavior" (Latessa, Cullen, and Gendreau 2002, p. 43). Often what correctional organizations are doing for their clients is not based on sound research but instead represents a continuation of outdated policies and procedures (Campbell 2008). Numerous examples exist of correctional programs that were implemented with good intentions but turned out to be failures (Henderson Hurley and Hanley 2005; Petersilia 1993).

Second, suggesting that EBP is an excuse for cutting costs and downsizing reveals a fundamental misunderstanding of EBP. EBPs seek to maximize correctional service delivery using the best available evidence to improve quality. Improving correctional service may require that organizations devote more resources for services, not necessarily less.

Third, EBP does not exclude the role of expert opinion and is not prescriptive in nature. EBP seeks to enhance decision making by incorporating evidence of success to produce practices that are more powerful, more accurate, and more efficacious. Thus, a carefully designed EBP monitors for results, modifies structures as necessary, and emphasizes the continuous development of quality service delivery. Finally, EBP does not constitute a one-size-fits-all approach. Instead, as we define EBP, it is an approach that joins together the best available evidence, professional expertise, and organizational needs and gives consideration to environmental constraints. EBP recognizes that the best evidence may be inapplicable or inappropriate within some correctional contexts. The challenge is for correctional organizations to continuously seek to implement approaches that are supported by evidence and fit with the correctional context—and not to implement an approach simply because it worked elsewhere.

Key Steps to Implementing EBP

As indicated earlier, correctional agencies have a long history of implementing the latest fad only to find that what should work doesn't upon empirical evaluation. Such failures can be attributed to several factors, but two seem directly related to management issues. The first is that some correctional administrators implement programs, practices, and procedures that are not based on research evidence. Such administrators have based decisions on out-of-date policies, simply do something because another state agency has taken that approach, or overinterpret results from their individual experiences on the job (Campbell 2008). Consequently, these administrators fail to consider implementing EBP even when dramatically positive results from rigorous studies are reported.

The second problem occurs when a correctional administrator actually would like to implement EBP but (a) does not know which question to ask; (b) does not know where to go to find information that answers a question; (c) is unable to distinguish whether a selected practice is in fact an EBP; or (d) does not know how best to implement a practice that is found to be evidence-based within their correctional context. Evidence-based corrections, just as EBPs in other fields, are about asking questions, finding and appraising the evidence, and utilizing the evidence to improve daily practice and client outcomes. The key steps for implementing EBPs are outlined below:

1. Formulate an answerable question:
   The question that initiates EBP in corrections can pertain to the offender population, the services your agency provides, or an organizational issue that needs to be changed.

2. Acquire the best available evidence regarding the correctional question(s) asked:
   Conduct literature searches of criminal justice bibliographic databases and review criminal justice practice journals. Collect evidence from published systematic reviews, well-designed randomized studies, controlled trials without randomization, case studies, and so forth.

3. Critically appraise the evidence gathered:
   Evaluate the evidence for its validity and usefulness. Determine whether the results are valid, reliable, and applicable to your organizational needs.

4. Make a decision on applying the evidence:
   Consider whether the practice can be effectively implemented within your organizational context. This involves an assessment of organizational capacity to implement the EBP.

5. If a decision is made to implement the practice, engage in a strategic planned management process:
   Follow a change management plan that ensures you have the resources, staff support, and external support for the EBP.

6. Implement the practice.
7. Reevaluate implementation of the EBP and make changes appropriately.

Although recognizing the need to implement EBP is an important step, many managers struggle with how to identify and implement EBP within their correctional organization. Several issues must be addressed in order to effectively implement EBP. First, correctional organizations should restrict the question to be answered in Step 1 to a topic directly related to the organization's primary mission. Second, the question to be answered in Step 2 and Step 3 is, What is the strength of the evidence that indicates a particular practice will achieve a desired correctional goal? Consequently, Steps 2 and 3 require that the organization dedicate resources either to providing staff with the knowledge, skills, and abilities to gather and assess the research literature or to hiring an external consultant to do this work for the agency. Furthermore, it should be noted that the criteria for identifying individual treatment modalities that are evidence-based will vary depending on the correctional context. As depicted in Table 6.1, multiple criteria for determining which practices are evidence-based are widely available.*

Correctional organizations have often been accused of rushing to implement new programs without fully considering "organizational fit" (see Step 4). A central requirement for effectively doing EBP is that organizations engage in a careful assessment of their capacity to implement any new EBP initiative. By *organizational capacity* we are referring to an analysis of current organizational functioning regarding the ability of the organization to carry out its current mission and a review of the structures in place to implement the EBP. The failure to consider the organization's capacity to implement an EBP could lead to negative outcomes for what otherwise would have been an effective practice. For example, as discussed by Henderson and Hanley (2006, p. 64) with regard to the implementation of reentry programs, the failure of correctional organizations to consider how reentry programming fit within the larger criminal justice system in their jurisdiction and to coordinate efforts with community agencies resulted in an initiative that lacked program integrity and ultimately failed to reduce the barriers offenders face when returning to the community.

Once the decision has been made to implement a particular EBP, a strategic management planning (SMP) process significantly increases the likelihood of success (Step 5). SMP generally refers to a set of procedures that guide the organization through the implementation of a new initiative (Berman 1998). This planned change process ensures that you have the resources, staff support, and external support for the EBP. The utilization of a strategic management process for implementing EBP is strongly supported by the National Institute of Corrections, which makes available technical assistance to correctional organizations interested in implementing EBPs.

* A detailed discussion of the criteria for determining whether a practice is evidence-based is beyond the scope of this book. Interested readers should review the resources available on the Web sites listed in Table 6.1 for a more extensive discussion.

Table 6.1 Methods for Ranking Research as Evidence-Based

Maryland Scientific Methods Scale *Five-Level System: 1 = weak / 5 = strong*	*Blueprint Program Model and Promising Programs*	*Oregon EBPs* *Levels I, II, and III Are EBPs; Levels IV, V, and VI Are Nonevidence-Based*	*OJJDP*
http://www.ncjrs.gov/pdffiles/171676.pdf	http://www.colorado.edu/cspv/blueprints/criteria.html	http://www.oregon.gov/DHS/mentalhealth/ebp/ebp-definition.pdf	http://www2.dsgonline.com/mpg/ratings.aspx
Level 1 Weak practice Practice reveals correlation between a prevention program and a measure of crime at single point in time.	Model programs Evidence of deterrent effect w/ strong experimental design (e.g., experimental designs with random assignment or quasi-experimental designs with matched control groups). Sustained effect of program at least 1 year beyond treatment, with no subsequent evidence that this effect is lost. Practices must have replicated success in diverse settings and with diverse populations.	Level I Prevention or treatment practice supported by randomized, controlled studies showing consistently positive results and whose outcomes have been achieved in scientifically controlled and routine care settings.	Exemplary programs have demonstrated program integrity, provide robust empirical findings, and use an experimental evaluation design.

Level 2 Measures before-and-after program crime effects but no comparable comparison group used.	Promising programs Show evidence of deterrent effects via the use of a strong experimental design. Do not need to meet sustained effect and replication criteria.	Level II Prevention or treatment practice supported by sound experimental studies showing consistently positive outcomes that have been achieved in scientifically controlled or routine care settings.	Effective programs provide positive outcome support obtained via a control or matched comparison group but without randomization.
Level 3 Measures before-and-after program crime effects with experimental and comparable control comparison group.		Level III A prevention or treatment practice derived from Level I or Level II but modified in practice and applied in a setting or population that differs from the original.	Promising programs have demonstrated effectiveness using a more limited evaluation design and require causal confirmation using other evaluation techniques and more sophisticated methodology.
Level 4 Measures of crime before-and-after program with comparable experimental and control groups, controlling for other variables that influence crime.		Level IV A practice not yet sufficiently documented or examined using scientifically sound research; however, the practice is in the process of building evidence.	

(*Continued*)

Table 6.1 Methods for Ranking Research as Evidence-Based (Continued)

Maryland Scientific Methods Scale *Five-Level System: 1 = weak / 5 = strong*	*Blueprint Program Model and Promising Programs*	*Oregon EBPs* *Levels I, II, and III Are EBPs; Levels IV, V, and VI Are Nonevidence-Based*	*OJJDP*
Level 5 Research uses random assignment of program and control conditions.		Level V A practice based solely on clinical judgment and/or noncontrolled studies without comparison groups. Practice is not research based.	
		Level VI A practice with consistently poor outcomes as revealed by research evidence.	

What Works to Reduce Crime

A central tenet of EBP is taking "what we know works" to reduce or prevent crime and implementing it in various correctional contexts while eliminating ineffective correctional practices. EBP is concerned with improving the success rates of correctional interventions. Correctional interventions are considered successful when they reduce offender risk, prevent future crime, reduce substance use, change offender attitudes, reduce prison misconduct, and/or lead to significant reductions in cost (Welsh 2007).

"What Works" and Does Not Work to Reduce Recidivism

The research literature has produced a wealth of information on the factors that predict offender recidivism, community supervision misconduct, and prison misconduct. "These include, most importantly: (1) antisocial values, (2) antisocial peers, (3) poor self-control, self-management, and prosocial problem-solving skills, (4) family dysfunction, and (5) past criminality. This information is critical, because interventions that ignore these factors are doomed to fail" (Latessa, Cullen, and Gendreau 2002, p. 44). The factors referred to above are what we in corrections refer to as *criminogenic needs*. Criminogenic needs are those characteristics of individual offenders that when addressed reduce recidivism and misconduct. Thus, at a programmatic level we have been provided with clear direction regarding the programmatic components to include at the treatment level.

Treatment program evaluations and systematic reviews of the literature reveal that treatment modalities incorporating criminogenic needs are most effective in improving correctional outcomes. Some examples of treatment models that are supported by evidence are cognitive behavioral therapies, aggression replacement training, moral reconation therapy, motivational enhancement therapy, interpersonal communication, and skills training (White 2005). Positive outcomes from these approaches are significantly increased when targeting high-risk offenders.

Conversely, a growing body of literature continues to specify "what does not work" in offender treatment. Incorporated in the list of failed treatment programs are intensive supervision programs, boot camps, "scared straight" programs, shock probation, wilderness programs, insight-oriented programming, and nondirective counseling treatments (Aos, Miller, and Drake 2006; Lipsey and Wilson 1998; White 2005). These programs have failed primarily because they are not based on nor do they incorporate what we know based on evidence works to improve correctional outcomes.

The Washington State Institute for Public Policy has published the most recent literature review of programs that work to reduce recidivism. Appendix A contains a list of the studies used in their analysis. As seen in Figure 6.1, there are effective correctional programs that reduce recidivism. The goal of EBP is to increase the number of correctional organizations implementing "what we know works" to reduce recidivism.

What Works to Prevent Crime

This section has focused on "what works" to reduce recidivism, a primary concern for correctional agencies, but it is important for the reader to understand that we now have some idea of "what works" to prevent crime as well.* Systematic reviews of the literature on crime prevention suggest that there are effective family-based, community-based, school-based, and place-focused crime prevention models (Sherman et al. 2006; Welsh 2007). Family-based crime prevention programs aim to address family risk factors related to supervision, discipline, and poor parenting. Parent training, preschool, social skills training, and multisystemic therapy are examples of family-based programs with evidence of success (Borduin et al. 1995; Welsh 2007). Community-based programs found to be effective in preventing crime are gang intervention programs targeting cohesion, mentoring, and afterschool recreation (Braga et al. 2001; Welsh 2007). According to Welsh (2007), school-based initiatives significantly impact the likelihood of future criminality. The most effective programs address disciplinary issues, establish norms and expectations for behavior, and teach self-control skills. Evaluations of programs targeting locations reveal that nuisance abatement, improving lighting, and the placement of closed-circuit television surveillance cameras have all effectively reduced crime in various locations.

Eight Evidence-Based Principles of Effective Interventions

While the preceding section identified programs with evidence of effectiveness, realistically speaking, academics and practitioners recognize that there is diversity in correctional programming, meaning that organizations have different target populations, offenders with different needs, and different external and internal organizational constraints. Rather than focusing on specific programs, evidence-based corrections has proceeded by identifying eight evidence-based principles that have the potential to create successful outcomes for correctional clients within various correctional contexts (see Figure 6.1). These principles apply regardless of whether you are discussing institutional or community corrections populations (Bogue et al. 2004; Serrin 2005). According to Serrin (2005, p. 2), "The same principles that are successful in reducing prison misconduct (that is, dynamic assessment of criminal risk; correctional programming) also generalize to yield reductions in recidivism (French and Gendreau, 2003)."

* The focus of this book is "what works" to reduce correctional population outcomes. We recognize that some correctional agencies may in fact provide services aimed toward crime prevention. A detailed review of such programs, however, is beyond the scope of this book.

This section provides a brief explanation of each of the principles found in Clawson, Bogue, and Joplin's (2005, pp. 8–14) work, which provides the basic framework of these principles.

Principle 1: Assess Actuarial Risk/Needs

Develop and maintain a complete system of ongoing offender risk screening/triage and needs assessments. Assessing offenders in a reliable and valid manner is a prerequisite for the effective management (i.e., supervision and treatment) of offenders. Timely, relevant measures of offender risk and need at the individual and aggregate levels are essential for the implementation of numerous principles of best practice in corrections, (e.g., risk, need, and responsivity). Offender assessments are most reliable and valid when staff are formally trained to administer tools. Screening and assessment tools that focus on dynamic and static risk factors, profile criminogenic needs, and have been validated on similar populations are preferred. They should also be supported by sufficiently detailed and accurately written procedures. Offender assessment is as much an ongoing function as it is a formal event. Case information that is gathered informally through routine interactions and observations with offenders is just as important as formal assessment guided by instruments. Formal and informal offender assessments should reinforce one another. They should combine to enhance formal reassessments, case decisions, and working relations between practitioners and offenders throughout the jurisdiction of supervision.

Principle 2: Enhance Intrinsic Motivation

Staff should relate to offenders in interpersonally sensitive and constructive ways to enhance intrinsic motivation in offenders. Behavioral change is an *inside job*; for lasting change to occur, a level of intrinsic motivation is needed. Motivation to change is dynamic, and the probability that change may occur is strongly influenced by interpersonal interactions, such as those with probation officers, treatment providers, and institution staff.

Feelings of ambivalence that usually accompany change can be explored through motivational interviewing, a style and method of communication used to help people overcome their ambivalence regarding behavior changes. Research strongly suggests that motivational interviewing techniques, rather than persuasion tactics, effectively enhance motivation for initiating and maintaining behavior changes.

Principle 3: Target Interventions

3a: Risk Principle

Prioritize primary supervision and treatment resources for offenders who are at higher risk to reoffend. Research indicates that supervision and treatment resources that are focused on lower-risk offenders tend to produce little if any net positive effect on recidivism rates. Shifting these resources to higher-risk offenders promotes harm reduction and public safety because these offenders have greater need for prosocial skills and thinking and are more likely to be frequent offenders. Reducing the recidivism rates of these higher risk offenders reaps a much larger bang for the buck. Successfully addressing this population requires smaller caseloads, the application of well-developed case plans, and the placement of offenders into sufficiently intense cognitive behavioral interventions that target their specific criminogenic needs.

3b: Criminogenic Need Principle

Address offenders' greatest criminogenic needs. Offenders have a variety of needs, some of which are directly linked to criminal behavior. These criminogenic needs are dynamic risk factors that, when addressed or changed, affect the offender's risk for recidivism. Examples of criminogenic needs are criminal personality; antisocial attitudes, values, and beliefs; low self-control; criminal peers; substance abuse; and a dysfunctional family. Based on an assessment of the offender, these criminogenic needs can be prioritized so that services are focused on the greatest criminogenic needs.

3c: Responsivity Principle

Responsivity requires that we consider individual characteristics when matching offenders to services. These characteristics include but are not limited to culture, gender, motivational stages, developmental stages, and learning styles. These factors influence an offender's responsiveness to different types of treatment. The principle of responsivity also requires that offenders be provided with treatment that is proven to be effective with the offender population. Certain treatment strategies, such as cognitive–behavioral methodologies, have consistently produced reductions in recidivism with offenders under rigorous research conditions. Providing appropriate responsivity to offenders involves selecting services in accordance with these factors, including—

1. matching treatment type to offender; and
2. matching style and methods of communication with offender's stage of change readiness.

3d: Dosage

Providing appropriate doses of services, prosocial structure, and supervision is a strategic application of resources. Higher-risk offenders require significantly more initial structure and services than lower-risk offenders. Services and supervision should be more intensive during the first 3 to 9 months postrelease. During that critical time period, 40% to 70% of an offender's free time should be clearly occupied with delineated routine and appropriate services, (e.g., outpatient treatment, employment assistance, education). Certain offender subpopulations (e.g., severely mentally ill, chronic dual diagnosed) commonly require strategic, extensive, and extended services. However, too often, individuals within these subpopulations are neither explicitly identified nor provided a coordinated package of supervision and services. The evidence indicates that incomplete or uncoordinated approaches can have negative effects, often wasting resources.

3e: Treatment Principle

Treatment, particularly cognitive–behavioral types, should be applied as an integral part of the sentence/sanction process. A proactive and strategic approach to supervision and case planning that delivers targeted and timely treatment interventions and ensures that appropriate dosage is delivered will provide the greatest long-term benefit to the community, the victim, and the offender. This does not necessarily apply to lower-risk offenders, who should be diverted from the criminal justice and corrections systems whenever possible.

Principle 4: Provide Skills Training Using Cognitive–Behavioral Treatment Methods

Provide evidence-based programming that emphasizes cognitive–behavioral strategies and is delivered by well-trained staff. To successfully deliver this treatment to offenders, staff must understand antisocial thinking, social learning, and appropriate communication techniques. Skills are not only taught to the offender but are also practiced or role-played, and the resulting prosocial attitudes and behaviors are positively reinforced by staff. Correctional agencies should prioritize, plan, and budget to predominantly implement programs that have been scientifically proven to reduce recidivism.

Principle 5: Increase Positive Reinforcement

When learning new skills and making behavioral changes, individuals respond better and maintain learned behaviors for longer periods of time when approached with *carrots* rather than *sticks*. Sustained behavioral change is better achieved when an individual receives a higher ratio of positive to negative reinforcements. Research indicates that a reinforcement ratio of *four positive to every one negative* is optimal for promoting behavior changes. These rewards do not have to be applied consistently to be effective (as negative reinforcement does) but can be applied randomly.

Increasing positive reinforcement should not be done at the expense of or interfere with the administration of swift, certain, and real responses for negative and unacceptable behavior. Offenders having problems with responsible self-regulation generally respond positively to reasonable and reliable additional structure and boundaries. Offenders may initially overreact to new demands for accountability, seek to evade detection or consequences, and fail to recognize any personal responsibility. However, with exposure to clear rules that are consistently (and swiftly) enforced with appropriate and graduated consequences, offenders will tend to comply in the direction of the most rewards and least punishments. This type of extrinsic motivation can often be useful for beginning the process of behavior change.

Principle 6: Engage Ongoing Support in Natural Communities

Realign and actively engage prosocial supports for offenders in their communities. Offender relapse issues (e.g., high-risk situations, triggers) potentially *come to life* when offenders return to their natural communities and neighborhoods. It is therefore incumbent on supervising officers to have a good understanding of the general and particular assets and liabilities of various communities. Research indicates that many successful interventions with high-risk populations (e.g., inner-city substance abusers, homeless, dual diagnosed) actively recruit and use family members, spouses, and supportive others in the offender's immediate environment to positively reinforce desired new behaviors. This community reinforcement approach (CRA) has been found effective for a variety of behaviors (e.g., unemployment, alcoholism, substance abuse, and marital conflicts); and research also indicates the efficacy of twelve-step programs, religious activities, and restorative justice initiatives geared toward improving bonds and ties to prosocial community members.

Principle 7: Measure Relevant Processes/Practices

Accurate and detailed documentation of case information, along with a formal and valid mechanism for measuring outcomes, is the foundation of EBP. Agencies must routinely assess changes in offenders' cognitive and skill development and recidivism if services are to remain effective.

In addition to routinely measuring and documenting offender changes, staff performance should also be regularly assessed. Staff that are periodically evaluated for performance achieve greater fidelity to program design, service delivery principles, and outcomes. Staff whose performance is not consistently monitored, measured, and subsequently reinforced work less cohesively, more frequently at cross-purposes, and provide less support to the agency mission.

Principle 8: Provide Measurement Feedback

After a method for measuring relevant processes and practices is in place (Principle 7), this information must be used to monitor progress and change. Providing feedback to offenders regarding their progress builds accountability and is associated with enhanced motivation for change, lower treatment attrition, and improved outcomes (e.g., reduced drink/drug days, treatment engagement, goal achievement).

The same is true within an organization. Monitoring delivery of services and fidelity to procedures helps build accountability and maintain integrity to the agency's mission. Regular performance audits and case reviews, with an eye toward improved outcomes, keep staff focused on the ultimate goal of reduced recidivism through the use of evidence-based principles.

Turning Research into Practice

Translating these evidence-based principles into practice can be challenging (Latessa 2004; Rhine and Mawhorr 2006). According to Weiss (1998) translating research into practice is easier when the evidence is noncontroversial, if the changes required to implement the change are small scale, if the environment is stable, or when

BOX 6.1 SUPERVISORS, LINE STAFF, AND PROGRAM PROVIDERS

REQUIRED KNOWLEDGE AND SKILLS

- Knowledge of criminogenic needs and risk factors.
- Knowledge of evidence-based supervision and treatment interventions.
- Knowledge of the process of criminal thinking.
- Knowledge of the stages of individual change.
- Knowledge of social learning theory and behavior management principles.
- Knowledge of graduated responses to noncompliance.
- Knowledge of relapse prevention strategies.
- Skills in conducting risk and needs assessments.
- Skills in developing probationer case plans and behavioral contracts.
- Skills in motivational enhancement techniques and motivational interviewing.
- Skills in cognitive–behavioral therapy.
- Skills in staff supervision and leading change (supervisors).

Source: Adapted from White, T. F. 2005, Court Support Services: CT, p. 24.

BOX 6.2 SUPERVISOR RESPONSIBILITIES

- Learn the principles of recidivism reduction and EBP.
- Ensure that staff are well trained in and understand agency policy and procedures, as well as the skills and principles of EBP.
- Help staff adapt to change by doing the following:
  - When possible, seek staff input and promote collaboration.
  - Clearly communicate expectations and allow for discussion and feedback.
  - Provide training and coaching as needed.
  - Demonstrate supportive modeling.
  - Give timely performance feedback.
  - Provide positive reinforcement.
  - Recognize individual contributions and celebrate team accomplishments.
- Model the skills and principles of EBP and the behaviors that you want staff to exhibit.
- Create an office culture that values honesty and ensures fair, equitable, and respectful treatment of staff, probationers, and community members.
- Provide staff with feedback and positive reinforcement for behavior that supports EBP.
- Periodically observe staff when interacting with a probationer during an office visit, and provide them with feedback, reinforcement, and instruction.
- Meet with staff at least monthly and respond to staff questions, provide performance feedback, and assist them in developing strategies for handling difficult cases.
- Conduct periodic random reviews of each probation officer's completed risk/needs assessments and case plans and give feedback to the officer.
- Review staff responses to probationer noncompliance to ensure that the actions taken are appropriate.
- Periodically visit referral programs and talk to program providers.

Source: Adapted from White, T. F. 2005, Court Support Services: CT, p. 21.

BOX 6.3 ADMINISTRATOR'S RESPONSIBILITIES

- Provide leadership that will facilitate the successful implementation of EBP by doing the following:
  - Create and articulate the vision, mission, and goals.
  - Identify external and internal stakeholders.
  - Collaborate with stakeholders to develop strategies and initiatives for achieving the vision.
  - Determine intermediate process measures and outcome measures to evaluate goal achievement.
  - Monitor the implementation of the strategies and initiatives, and make modifications or changes as indicated.
  - Evaluate mission and goal achievement.
- Enhance staff support and facilitate the management of change through staff involvement, open and honest communication, positive role modeling, performance feedback, and positive reinforcement.
- Create an office culture that fosters and values honesty and ensures fair, equitable, and respectful treatment of staff, probationers, and community members.
- Model the skills and principles of EBP and the behaviors that you want staff to exhibit.
- Practice the principles of collaborative leadership:
  - Focus less on roles and more on functions.
  - Promote the importance of process as well as goal and task accomplishment.
  - Create opportunities for shared power and responsibility.
  - Foster participative decision making.
  - Utilize conflict-resolution strategies based on problem-solving models rather than authoritarian or political models.
- Ensure operational alignment with the principles of EBP by modifying and developing supportive policy, procedures, and performance standards.
- Provide agency staff with the tools, knowledge, and skills needed to implement and support EBPs.

nobody knows what to do. Bogue et al. (2004) have reported that implementation of EBP at its most basic level requires correctional organizations to begin:

1. Developing staff knowledge, skills, and attitudes congruent with current research-supported practice (Principles 1–8).
2. Implementing offender programming consistent with research recommendations (Principles 2–6).

Table 6.2 Examples of Evidence-Based Implementation of Principles

Elements	*Responsible Individuals*	*Probation Model*[a]	*Prison Model*[b]
Offender risk and needs assessment	Line staff	To conduct an accurate risk and needs assessment.	To conduct effective inmate classification procedures that assign inmates to appropriate levels of security and placement within a prison according predictors of misconduct and escape.
Supervision conditions	Line staff	To match the term of supervision and the conditions to the levels of offender risk, and to require treatment interventions congruent with criminogenic needs.	To match prison term conditions to level of risk and require participation in prison programs that address criminogenic needs.
Offender case plan	Line staff	To develop a case plan that delineates the offender's criminogenic needs, appropriate programmatic interventions, offender's motivation to address identified needs, offender responsibilities, and probation officer case activities. To make appropriate program referrals.	To develop a case plan that delineates the offender's criminogenic needs, appropriate programmatic interventions, offender's motivation to address identified needs, offender responsibilities, and prison environment.

Offender supervision activities	Line staff	To monitor compliance with probation conditions and to facilitate the implementation of the case plan. To decrease the offender's ambivalence, defensiveness, and resistance to stopping his/her procriminal and antisocial behavior.	To monitor compliance with prison conditions and to facilitate the implementation of the case plan. To decrease the offender's ambivalence, defensiveness, and resistance to stopping his/her procriminal and antisocial behavior.
Offender treatment	Program provider	To provide the appropriate type of evidence-based treatment that focuses on the offender's criminogenic needs, to enhance offender motivation, and to provide positive reinforcement and relapse prevention.	To provide treatment that addresses criminogenic needs. To provide treatment that varies according to prison security level; is structured; and is matched to temperament, learning style, motivation, culture, and gender of inmates. To increase the use of positive reinforcement and skills training with directed practice.
Quality assurance	Supervisors and administrators	To model and facilitate organizational alignment with the principles of evidence-based supervision. To provide staff training that increases their knowledge and skills in EBP, and to support and reinforce knowledge and skill application.	To measure relevant processes and practices for impact. To provide measurement feedback that provides staff with information that their efforts are appreciated. To use results from measuring processes and practice to guide decision making.

[a] White, T. F., 2005, Court Support Services Division, Connecticut.
[b] Serrin, R. C., 2005, National Institute of Corrections, Washington, DC.

3. Sufficiently monitoring staff and offender programming to identify discrepancies or fidelity issues (Principle 7).
4. Routinely obtaining verifiable outcome evidence (Principle 8) associated with staff performance and offender programming. (Bogue et al. 2004, p. 11)

Just what does this mean in terms of changing organizational policies, procedures, and actions for implementing EBP? Campbell (2008, p. 28) states that for EBPs to be implemented in corrections, "organizational development must focus primarily on ensuring that the organizational culture and structures can effect change and support the implementation of evidence-based practices." The process begins with leaders who establish a vision, mission, and measurable goals that "create a culture that supports the use of EBP" (p. 42).

White (2005) provides an implementation framework for changing daily practice to reflect EBP. He argues that in order to effectively implement EBP, correctional organizations must clearly define the responsibilities of administrators, program providers, supervisors, and line staff in a manner consistent with the Eight Evidence-Based Principles. Carrying out their responsibilities requires that each actor possess working knowledge of EBP and the skills to carry out their duties (see Boxes, 6.1, 6.2, and 6.3, for lists of skills and abilities).

Table 6.2 presents two descriptions of how EBPs could be implemented in a correctional setting and delineates the types of activities that administrators, supervisors, and line staff would engage in to support the evidence-based approach.

Conclusion

Correctional administrators planning to implement changes within the organization or in programs providing services to offender populations should consider taking an evidence-based approach. EBP is a data-driven approach that stresses evaluating what we do to and for correctional populations. More importantly, tools are readily available from organizations such as the National Institute of Corrections, the Crime and Justice Institute, and others to help administrators move through this process. The National Institute of Corrections, for example, has made available an implementation checklist (see Appendix A) for agencies. Correctional agencies implementing this framework effectively have seen significant reductions in negative correctional outcomes, significant cost savings, and greater levels of commitment to the organization and job satisfaction from staff.

Learning Objectives

After completing this chapter, you should be able to—

Define *evidence-based practice*
Define *evidence-based policy*
Discuss the advantages and disadvantages of EBPs in corrections

Explain staff resistance to EBP
Recognize the key steps to implementing EBP
Explain "what works" to reduce crime
Explain "what works" to prevent crime
Discuss the principles of EBP
Provide examples of how to implement EBP

Key Terms

Evidence-based policy
Evidence-based practice
Principles of effective interventions
"What works" to prevent crime
"What works" to reduce crime

Discussion Questions

1. Why has EBP received so much attention?
2. Select an evidence-based correctional treatment modality, then discuss what steps would need to be taken to implement the program.
3. Describe five features of correctional organizations that might make implementing EBPs challenging.

Suggested Reading

Andrews, D. A. 1994. *An overview of treatment effectiveness: Research and clinical principles.* Longmont, CO: National Institute of Corrections.

Andrews, D. A., I. Zinger, D. Hoge, J. Bonta, P. Gendreau, and F. T. Cullen. 1990. Does correctional treatment work? A clinically relevant and psychologically informed meta-analysis. *Criminology* 28: 369–404.

Aos, S., J. Mayfield, and W. Yen. 2006. *Evidence-based treatment of alcohol, drug, and mental health disorders: Potential benefits, costs, and fiscal impacts for Washington State.* Olympia, WA: Washington State Institute for Public Policy.

Aos, S., M. Miller, and E. Drake. 2006. *Evidence-based adult corrections programs: What works and what does not.* Olympia, WA: Washington State Institute of Public Policy.

Corrigan, P. W., S. G. McCracken, and C. McNeilly. 2005. Evidence-based practices for individuals with serious mental illnesses and substance use disorders. In *The handbook of evidence-based clinical practices in behavioral healthcare: Applications and new directions,* edited by C. Stoutand, H. Hayes. New York: John Wiley & Sons.

Lowencamp, C. T., E. Latessa, and P. Smith. 2006. Does correctional program quality really matter? The impact of adhering to the principles of effective intervention. *Criminology and Public Policy* 5(3): 201–220.

Web Sites

The Center on Evidence-Based Interventions for Crime and Addiction (CEICA)
http://www.tresearch.org/headlines/2005Oct_BelenkoCenter.htm

Centre for Evidence-Based Social Services
http://www.cebss.org/index.html

Practice Improvement Collaboratives
http://csat.samhsa.gov/pic/index.html
SAMHSA Model Programs
http://modelprograms.samhsa.gov
Treatment Research Institute
http://www.tresearch.org/homepage.htm

References

AMH (Oregon Addictions and Mental Health Division). 2007. Operational definitions for evidence-based practice. Available at: www.oregon.gov/DHS/mentalhealth/ebp/ebp-defintion.pdf (accessed November 2008).

Aos, S., M. Miller, and E. Drake. 2006. *Evidence-based public policy options to reduce future prison construction, criminal justice costs, and crime rates.* Olympia: Washington State Institute for Public Policy.

Berman, E. M. 1998. *Productivity in public and nonprofit organizations.* Thousands Oaks, CA: Sage Publications.

Bogue, B., N. Campbell, and E. Clawson. 2004. *Implementing evidence-based practice in community corrections.* Washington, DC: National Institute of Corrections.

Borduin, C.M., B. Man, L. T. Cone, S. Henggeler, B. Fucci, D. Blaske, and R. Williams. 1995. Multisystemic treatment of serious juvenile offenders: Long-term prevention of criminality and violence. *Journal of Consulting and Clinical Psychology* 3: 569–587.

Braga, A. A., D. M. Kennedy, E. J. Waring, and A. M. Piehl. 2001. Problem oriented policing, deterrence, and youth violence: An evaluation of Boston's Operation Ceasefire. *Journal of Research in Crime and Delinquency* 38: 195–225.

Campbell, N. 2008. Comprehensive framework for paroling authorities in an era of evidence-based practices. National Institute of Corrections. Available at: http://nicic.org/Downloads/PDF/Library/022906.pdf (accessed July 12, 2009).

Center for Substance Abuse Treatment. 2006. Treatment Vol. 1: Understanding evidence-based practices for co-occurring disorders.

Clawson, E., B. Bogue, and L. Joplin. 2005. Implementing evidence-based practices in corrections. http://www.cjinstitute.org/files/AmericanStudiesJrnlArticle091504.pdf.

Davidson J. T., R. Crawford, and E. Kerwood. 2009. Constructing an EBP post-conviction model of supervision in U.S. Probation, District of Hawaii: A case study. Available at: http://www.uscourts.gov/fedprob/September_2008/04_constructing_EBP.html (accessed August 15, 2009).

Dollaghan, C. 2004. Evidence-based practice in communication disorders: What do we know and when do we know it? *Journal of Communication Disorders* 37: 391–400.

Gibbs, L., E. Armstrong, D. Raleigh, and J. Jones. 2007. Evidence-based practice for the helping professions. Available at: www.evidence.brookscole.com (accessed).

Hurley, M., and D. Hanley. 2006. Planning for quality: A strategy for reentry initiatives. *Western Criminology Review* 7: 62–78

Joplin, L., B. Bogue, N. Campbell, M. Carey, E. Clawson, D. Faust, K. Florio, B. Wasson, and W. Woodward. 2004. Using an integrated model to implement evidence-based practices in corrections. Wasington, DC. Publication of the International Community Corrections Association and American Correctional Association.

Latessa, E. 2004. The challenge of change: Correctional programs and evidence-based practices. *Criminology and Public Policy* 3(4):47–560.

Latessa, E. J., F. T. Cullen, and P. Gendreau. 2002. Beyond correctional quackery—Professionalism and the possibility of effective treatment. *Federal Probation* 66: 43–49.

Lipsey, M. W., and D. B. Wilson. 1998. Effective intervention for serious juvenile offenders: A synthesis of research. In *Serious and violent juvenile offenders: Risk factors and successful interventions,* edited by R. Loeber, D. P. Farrington, pp. 313–345. Thousand Oaks, CA: Sage Publications.

Petersilia, J. 2005. Center for evidence-based corrections: Proposal to California's Youth and Adult Correctional Agency (YACA). Department of Criminology, Law and Society: University of California, Irvine.

Prendergast, M., S. Schinke, and J. Sachwald. 2006. Issues in defining and applying evidence-based practices criteria. Paper presented at the Treatment Research Institute Conference. Philadelphia, PA.

Rhine, E., T. Mawhorr, and E. Parks. 2006. Implementation: The bane of effective correctional programs. *Criminology and Public Policy* 5(2): 347–358.

Sackett, D. L., W. Rosenberg, J. Muir Gray, R. B. Haynes, and W. S. Richardson. 1996. Evidence-based medicine: What it is and what it isn't. *British Medical Journal* 312: 71–72.

Serrin, R. C. 2005. *Evidence-based practice: Principles for enhancing correctional results in prisons.* Washington, DC: National Institute of Corrections.

Sherman, L. W., D. P. Farrington, B. C. Welsh, and D. L. MacKenzie (Editors). 2006. *Evidence-based crime prevention* (Revised edition). New York: Routledge.

Sperber, K. G., M. Henderson-Hurley, and D. Hanley. 2005. Bridging the gap between theory and practice: A call to action. *Federal Probation* 69 (1). Available at: http://www.uscourts.gov/fedprob/jun2005/gap.html.

Spring, B. 2007. Evidence-based behavioral practice. Available at: http://www.ebbp.org/ebbp.html.

Warren, T. 2007. *Evidence-based practices to reduce recidivism: Implications for state judiciaries.* Crime and Justice Institute. Available at: www.cjinstitute.org and www.nicic.org.

Weiss, C. H. 1998. Have we learned anything new about the use of evaluation? *American Journal of Evaluation* 19: 21–33.

Welsh, B. 2007. Evidence-based crime prevention: Scientific basis, trends, results and implications for Canada. Research Report 2007-1. Final Report. Prepared for the National Crime Prevention Centre, Department of Public Safety and Emergency Preparedness Canada. Available at: http://www.publicsafety.gc.ca/prg/cp/_fl/ebcp-eng.pdf.

White, T. F. 2005. Re-engineering probation towards greater public safety: A framework for recidivism reduction through evidence-based practice. Connecticut: Court Support Services Division. Available at: http://www.nicic.org/Library/021046.

Chapter 7

Evaluations and Outcomes

Most funding sources are now requiring agencies to produce results that are *outcome* based. In other words, agencies must show that what they do is effective in producing changes in the clients and/or offenders that they serve. One of the most significant landmarks in this relatively new position is the passing of the Government Performance and Results Act (GPRA) legislation in 1993. With this legislation, the U.S. federal government began holding all agencies that receive federal funding responsible for producing results, not just for meeting certain process goals. Specifically, GPRA requires that agencies develop long-term strategic plans, that agencies identify measurable goals and objectives, and that links between program activities are geared toward reaching those goals and budgets (GPRA 1993). While GPRA was the federal government's ambitious effort to increase outcome-based accountability among all of its agencies, its effects have been more widespread. Many organizations and agencies are taking the initiative, even if not required by specific funding sources, to demonstrate effectiveness through evaluations and outcome monitoring. In this chapter, evaluations and outcome monitoring will be jointly referred to as *outcome-based evidence.*

Disadvantages and Advantages to Outcome-Based Evidence

Although valuable, most agencies view evaluations and outcome monitoring as many people view going to the dentist. It has to be done, but no one wants to do it. There are many reasons for the reluctance toward evaluations. First, many practitioners do not understand the "science" behind evaluations and outcome monitoring. It is true that evaluations can be complex, but they can also be quite simple, particularly in the form of outcome monitoring (McNamera nd). Second, many view evaluations as adding new or different tasks to already stressed staff and work environments. Often, evaluations and outcome monitoring include the same supervision and management activities currently in place (McNamera nd). Another reason evaluations and outcome measures are frowned upon is that many who have been working in the field (especially those who have been working in the field for some time) believe that they "just know" what the client needs. Much like risk and needs assessments changed the way in which staff "just knew" what the offender needed by providing a list of direct questions and commonly streamlining the process of client intake, evaluations and outcome monitoring also have a strong impact on the types of programs utilized by the organization (McNamera nd). Outcomes, regardless of how they are obtained, provide the organization with evidence of its success and give clues as to what types of improvements can be made. Despite these issues and hesitations, evaluations and outcome monitoring are powerful tools toward self-efficacy and efficiency of the organization.

There are several benefits to conducting evaluations and establishing outcome monitoring processes within a correctional organization. First, correctional agencies have experienced an increased demand in services, while resources have been reduced. Second, results can significantly assist agencies and organizations in improving their programs. Constructive criticism may be a difficult pill to swallow but, like most medicine, once taken, it can make things a lot better. Just as risk and needs assessments offer a prescription for the types of treatment needed by clients and offenders, outcome monitoring offers organizations a prescription for the areas that need improvement. Another reason is that historically, evaluations have focused primarily on process measures, such as the number of times contact was made with a client, the number of drug tests taken, and so forth. Outcomes (i.e., the impact these activities have on the client) have not traditionally been the focus of many organizations. Due to the current climate of funding sources and many stakeholders (discussed earlier), the demand for evidence of outcomes has increased significantly.

In this chapter, the differences between evaluations and outcome monitoring will be briefly discussed. There are many books written on both subjects, and the goal here is not to provide the reader with a comprehensive understanding of the subject but rather to introduce the reader to the basic concepts of obtaining outcome-based evidence.

Difference between Evaluation and Outcome Monitoring

Often, the terms *evaluation*, *assessment*, and *outcome monitoring* are used synonymously. These activities all utilize numbers and measure the performance of the agency, but the process of obtaining the numbers and purpose of each of these activities is very different. Evaluations, assessments, and outcome monitoring are used for different reasons.

Evaluations

Evaluation has a long history in corrections. Evaluations, very simply, measure the success or failure of a specific program or intervention (Yang nd). Historically, evaluations have been used to determine whether an intervention has produced a desired outcome or change for the people who participate in the program. However, evaluations can be used for much more than answering the yes-or-no question of success.

When a program or initiative is developed, there are certain expectations associated with that initiative or program. There is a reason that organizations develop specific programs or modify existing efforts. For example, the most commonly desired outcome of any correctional program is to increase public safety by reducing or eliminating recidivism. An evaluation can determine whether the program has achieved its desired outcome and to what extent the intervention was successful. Further, it can also uncover barriers to success, as well as provide solutions to those barriers (Guerra-Lopez 2008). Consulting previous evaluations of similar types of programs can also assist agencies in avoiding some of the pitfalls, obstacles, and issues associated with the development and implementation of that initiative or program.

Evaluation is a broad term, implying and encompassing several different activities. Evaluations can suggest needs assessment, process evaluation, impact and outcome evaluations, or any combination of these.

Needs Assessments

Needs assessments are typically conducted prior to or at the initial stage of implementation of a new program or initiative. The needs assessment process can identify both risk and protective factors of the organization, community, or program itself. It can also examine the current practices and resources of the organization to identify whether duplication of efforts exists and where resources are low or nonexistent. Essentially, the needs assessment process examines the current status of the agency and the community. This effort can provide valuable information that forms a baseline from which the agency can begin to make changes. Without knowing where the agency currently stands, it is very difficult to know how to move forward or even where "forward" is.

Most importantly, the needs assessment process focuses the organization's attention on the current context in which the program is operating (Yang nd). No agency exists in a vacuum. Change and influences are always present from both inside and outside of the organization. Redirecting attention toward the current context (both internal and external) allows the agency to identify specific influences and to prioritize these influences. No agency can make everyone happy all of the time. Therefore, it is important to understand the demands that are crucial to the organization's success and survival.

Process Evaluations

Process evaluations highlight how the organization functions on a daily basis. Specifically, process evaluations examine the implementation of policies and procedures, management functions, tasks of employees, the target population of those being served, and the needs (either of offenders or the community) that the agency addresses. These evaluations can show changes in programs, but they cannot demonstrate whether these activities actually make a difference in the lives of community members or offenders.

Once an organization has defined its optimum operating standards, the process evaluation can show how well the organization is meeting those targets. Additionally, the process evaluation can provide the organization with information on making changes and modifications to improve its performance (Yang nd), according to how the agency itself has *defined* performance. For example, a probation agency that has outlined contact standards for its low-, medium-, and high-risk offenders can determine, using a process evaluation, the extent to which these standards are being met. Further, the process evaluation can offer the agency information regarding benchmarks or the status of desired changes to or improvements in these standards. If the contact standard for medium-risk offenders is two face-to-face contacts per month and the agency has a determined that meeting this standard will require that 85% of officers have two face-to-face contacts with medium-risk offenders each month, the process evaluation will shed light on the status of this standard. Process evaluations are applicable to all efforts, regardless of their focus, duration, or target population. However, they cannot and do not show whether the number of contacts has any impact on the recidivism of those offenders.

Outcome Evaluations

Outcome evaluations are also called *impact* evaluations. Since the purpose of outcome evaluations is to show the impact or success of agency processes (for example, efforts), these are the evaluations that are most commonly thought of when the term *evaluation* is used. Agencies can choose a variety of outcomes as indicators of whether its process produces changes in clients. Once the outcome or impact is defined, the actual evaluation can begin.

The primary difference between evaluations and outcome monitoring is that evaluations require rigorous research methodologies (CDC 2007). The most common type of research design used for impact or outcome evaluations is experimental or quasi-experimental designs. Simply stated, these designs require two groups of offenders to be involved in the study. One group participates in the program or initiative and the other group does not. In research, these groups are called the treatment group and the control group, respectively. There are many variations of this basic concept. Although it is often difficult to provide one group with treatment and not another, this is the only way the organization can be sure the changes in the offender are due to (i.e., caused by) the offender's participation in the program.

While evaluations may seem daunting and complex, agencies and organizations cannot afford to be complacent in demonstrating productivity, regardless of how it is defined. Productivity is essential to any organization, and the correctional field is no different. Therefore, a discussion of outcome monitoring is also pertinent.

Outcome Monitoring

Outcome monitoring (also called *outcomes-based evaluation* or OBE) is designed to establish a correlation or attribution between changes in the client and participation in the program. Often, outcome monitoring can be a large portion of an impact evaluation. OBE provides management with a solid tool to continually measure how the program performs in relation to its initial goals (Motylewski and Horn 2002). However, an impact or outcomes evaluation will focus on whether the program was success in achieving the goals set (such as those detailed in the strategic plan) by the agency or program, while outcome monitoring typically examines whether the client has changed since coming to the program.

There are several purposes to outcome monitoring. First, an agency can recognize progress toward goals and objectives (CDC 2007). Organizations need to understand where they stand in progressing toward their goals, as well as to identify strengths, weaknesses, and areas where improvements or modifications need to be made to advance further. Second, outcome monitoring can provide the organization with information regarding how subgroups (e.g., males, females, sex offenders, mentally ill) develop while in the program (CDC 2007). Identifying and addressing different needs of subgroups can increase the agency's effectiveness with these individuals, as well as increase the agency's effectiveness as a whole. Finally, outcome monitoring can provide the agency with information regarding the quality of implementation of a particular program or initiative and how the implementation impacts client change (CDC 2007). Often, once a program has been designed, organizations put it in place without considering the implementation of that process. The failure to consider how a program is implemented can be detrimental to the success of that program (McGuire 2004). Factors such as staff attitudes, organizational culture, and community context can all impact the implementation of a program or initiative (McGuire 2004; Tubman and Vento 2001).

BOX 7.1 WASHINGTON STATE EXAMPLE OF RESULTS FROM A QUALITY OUTCOME EVALUATION

The Washington State Institute for Public Policy conducted an outcome evaluation of the Department of Corrections Dangerous Mentally Ill Offender (DMIO) program. This program was designed to better address the needs of dangerous mentally ill offenders released from prison. The program serves offenders for 3 years after release.

The goals of the project were as follows:

- To transition offenders back into the community by referring them to resources.
- To prepare communities to receive offenders from institutions.
- To increase communication among DOC staff.
- To reduce recidivism.

CHARACTERISTICS OF DMIO

Target population: Inmates with at least 18 months left to serve
Community advisor responsibilities: Prepare neighborhoods for return of offenders, develop list of resources, and train Neighborhood Readiness Teams

EVALUATION DESIGN

Sample size: 172 participants in the program
Comparison group: Statistically matched comparison group of offenders with mental health problems
Recidivism: Measured as any new offense, overall felony, and violent-only felony
Follow-up: 3 years postrelease

RESULTS

Exhibit 2
Overall Felony Recidivism Rates
DMIO Participants versus Comparison Group*
(Three-Year Follow-up)

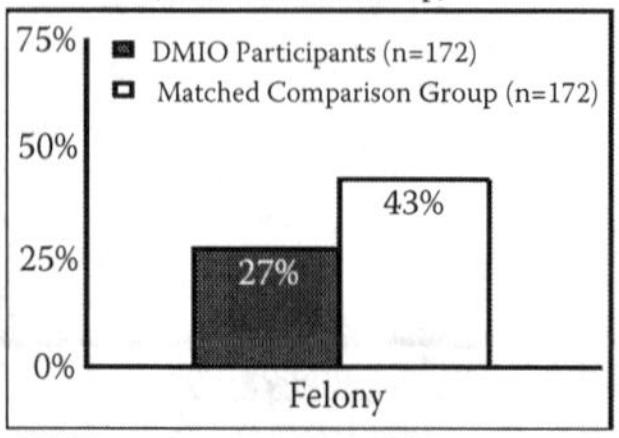

* McNemar test, x2-11.458. p–.0004

Exhibit 3
DMIO Program Benefits and Costs
(In 2007 Dollars)

	Taxpayers and Victims	Taxpayers Only
Benefits (lifetime)	$33,548	$15,247
Costs (over 3 years)	$26,982	$26,982
Benefit/Cost Radio	$1.24	$0.57
Net Benefits	$6,566	–$11,735

Source: Adapted from Mayfield, J. and D. Lovell, 2008, Washington State Institute for Public Policy, Olympia, WA.

Simply stated, outcome monitoring involves utilizing pre- and posttest measures to assess changes in the participants of a program. With this type of focus, the agency is always aware of the current situation of offenders and the community (McNamera nd). This type of evaluation can be used in conjunction with or as a part of daily management activities. However, it is essential that the outcomes are effective. Outcomes are effective if they reflect the program's goals and represent the organization's desired impact on participants. Outcomes must also be realistic in terms of the types of behaviors the program can effect. Too often, organizations and programs set goals too high and have no control over the factors that may impact the achievement of these goals. An example of this overreaching is an employment program. Employment programs provide clients with skills to assist in obtaining and retaining employment. An expectation of this program to eliminate recidivism is unrealistic. Other issues may impact an offender's ability to abstain from criminal behavior. The program only targets employment and, therefore, only employment outcomes should be used to measure its success. Finally, effective outcomes must have measureable indicators (Motylewski and Horn 2002). Outcome indicators include those tasks that can be observed and measured (McNamera nd), such as changes between pre- and posttests, reductions in risk scores, length of time to obtain employment, and so forth. Table 7.1 outlines some of the indicators that could be used for an employment program.

Utilizing Results

Regardless of how progress is measured, organizations need to focus attention on demonstrating achievements of outcomes to funding sources, stakeholders, clients, and staff. These outcomes can be measured in the short-term (0 to 6 months), intermediate (3 to 9 months), or long-term (6 to 12 months). One of the most important benefits of evaluation for organizations and programs is the ability to use these results as a guide for improvement.

Carter (1994) suggests that evaluation results be examined through a five-step process. First, the results should be used to develop recommendations for improvement that are realistic. This means not only accepting the results as they are but critically analyzing the results and what they mean for the program. Negative results can be viewed as constructive criticism, and plans can be developed to rectify the problems that have led to the negative outcomes. Second, results can be used in multiple ways. Other programs could benefit from the results, or the results could be viewed within a larger context of other evaluations of similar programs. This information could shed light on a larger problem with the program design itself. Third, constantly reminding stakeholders of the results can actually assist programs in averting disaster. When funding sources (in particular) question a program's success, corrective actions based on results from evaluations could alleviate some of the pressure placed on a program. Fourth, the results should be shared with all stakeholders, not just with administrators. Although the findings

Table 7.1 Outcome Indicators

Type of Outcome	*Definition*	*Example of Question*	*Example of Measure*
Attitude	What someone feels or thinks.	Since your involvement in this program, do you believe that it is important to maintain a job?	85% of clients will believe that employment is important.
Skill	What someone can do.	N/A	85% of clients will be able to complete job applications online.
Knowledge	What someone knows.	What types of information would you use to look for a job?	85% of clients will identify at least two employment resources.
Behavior	How someone acts.	N/A	85% of clients will maintain employment for a minimum of 3 months.
Status	Someone's social or professional situation.	N/A	20% of clients will receive raises and/or promotions within the first 6 months of employment.
Life Condition	Someone's physical condition.	N/A	20% of clients will obtain physical exams as a result of having health insurance provided by their employers.

Source: Adapted from Motylewski and Horn, 2002, Institute of Museum and Library Services.

may have to be rewritten for specific audiences, the benefits could be immense. Staff, as well as participants, may have different perspectives and suggestions for program improvement. Finally, the recommendations made by all stakeholders should be implemented into the program. Further, staff should be assigned the responsibility of ensuring that the recommendations and suggestions made are properly implemented.

Evaluability: A Major Concern

Administrators might struggle over the decision to conduct an evaluation or outcome assessment. Part of that struggle might be a result of their inability to answer basic questions prior to conducting the assessment. At a minimum, administrators need to decide the following:

1. What questions will be answered?
2. Who will conduct the evaluation?
3. What evaluation criteria will be used?
4. What data will be collected?
5. What analyses will be conducted?
6. How much will this evaluation cost?
7. How will the results of this evaluation be used?

Administrators must weigh the feasibility and cost of the evaluation against the benefits. Evaluability assessment is a process that helps administrators and evaluators "…identify evaluations that might be useful, explore what evaluations would be feasible, and design useful evaluations" Wholey (2004, p. 33).

Administrators often view evaluations as tools that will ultimately lead to enhanced service delivery and improved organizational functioning. It is worth noting that evaluations can and do go wrong. There is ample evidence of programs reported to be ineffective but which in reality achieved organizational goals (Henderson Hurley, Humphrey, and McDermott 2008). There are five possible explanations for situations where evaluations did not lead to improvements in program performance*:

1. When program evaluations are conducted too soon. (Box 7.2 from the Washington State Institute for Public Policy provides an example of negative results from an evaluation conducted too soon.)
2. Evaluators and administrators fail to agree on the goals and performance criteria to be used in evaluating the program. The result is that the evaluation answers questions that are not relevant to policy and management decisions.
3. Program goals are unrealistic given the program design, the resources committed to the program, and program activities currently under way.
4. Relevant performance information cannot be obtained. The result is that there may be insufficient data to conduct statistical analyses. If such data is used, then results may misrepresent actual program performance.
5. Policymakers and managers are unable or unwilling to change the program on the basis of evaluation information. The result here is "throwing the baby out with the bath water."

* The five explanations of why evaluations may not lead to improved practice were modified from Wholey's discussion (Wholey 2004, pp. 33–34).

BOX 7.2 WASHINGTON STATE: EXAMPLE OF RESULTS WHEN OUTCOME EVALUATION IS CONDUCTED TOO SOON

The Washington State Institute for Public Policy conducted an outcome evaluation of the Department of Corrections "Going Home Project." This program was a federally funded reentry program designed to help transition high-risk offenders from incarceration to the community through various community partnerships. The project began in 2003 and the last offenders to participate in the program were released back into the community by June 2007. The goals of the project were as follows:

- To transition offenders back into the community by referring them to resources.
- To prepare communities to receive offenders from institutions.
- To increase communication among DOC staff.
- To reduce recidivism.

CHARACTERISTICS OF "GOING HOME"

Target population: Inmates with at least 18 months left to serve
Community advisor responsibilities: Prepare neighborhoods for return of offenders, develop list of resources, and train Neighborhood Readiness Teams

EVALUATION DESIGN

Sample size: 131 offenders
Recidivism: Measured as violent felony convictions, general felony convictions, and total recidivism including felonies and misdemeanors
Follow-up: 18 months

RESULTS

Eighteen months after offenders had been released from the "Going Home Project":

- 15% had been reconvicted of a violent felony
- 43% had been reconvicted of a felony
- 62% had be reconvicted of a felony or misdemeanor

(*Continued*)

BOX 7.2 (Continued)

DISCUSSION

If given a cursory review the data suggests that that the program should not be considered effective. However, there are several problems with such a conclusion. First, the literature suggests that a minimum of 36-months follow-up is necessary to fully account for recidivism. Second, no comparison group is utilized. We have no idea whether these results are atypical when compared with a similar group of offenders. For example, the 15% and 43% reconviction figures could in fact represent an improvement over similar groups of offenders who did not participate in the program.

Source: Adapted from Drake, E., 2009, Washington State Institute for Public Policy, Olympia, WA.

Table 7.2 Key Steps in Evaluability Assessment

1.	Involve all stakeholders.
2.	Describe the program mission, vision, and goals from the perspectives of policymakers, executives, managers, line staff, and other stakeholders.
3.	Examine the measurability of program goals.
4.	Agree on needed changes in program activities or goals.
5.	Explore all possible evaluation designs that may be used to address your issues.
6.	Determine priorities for data and analyses.
7.	Determine how information will be used.

Source: Mayfield, J., 2009, Washington State Institute for Public Policy, Olympia, WA.

If an administrator proceeds with an evaluation under these circumstances, the results of the evaluation may be inconclusive or inaccurate and generally provide little direction for change. Thus, evaluability assessment addresses these concerns by the following (Wholey 2004, p. 35):

1. Comparing and contrasting the expectations and assumptions of those who influence the program and engage in direct service delivery.
2. Comparing such expectations with the reality of program activities under way and program outcomes that are occurring or are likely to occur.

3. Determining whether relevant program performance information is likely to be obtained at a reasonable cost.
4. Exploring which of the evaluations that could be conducted would be most useful.

As a result of this process, correctional administrators can clarify program designs, explore program reality, and, if necessary, redesign the program to increase the likelihood of successful outcomes for correctional populations; and therefore organizational functional improvements will occur. An in-depth discussion of all of the procedures necessary to conduct an evaluabilty analysis is beyond the scope of this book, Table 7.2 presents the reader with the basic steps for implementation.

Conclusion

Instituting any change in an organization or program is time-consuming. Program evaluation is no exception. However, the benefits far exceed the disadvantages. By identifying a program's success and understanding why the successes (and failures) are occurring, programs can begin to herald achievements to stakeholders, as well as make improvements to the process. Investing time and energy into evaluations can change both internal and external attitudes and beliefs about the program itself. Additionally, program improvements benefit the client in many ways, which is the ultimate goal of any correctional effort.

Learning Objectives

After completing this chapter, you should be able to—

- Explain why correctional organizations are focusing on evaluations and outcomes now more than ever before
- Describe the advantages and disadvantages of evaluation and outcome monitoring
- Define *evaluation*
- Know the types of evaluations relevant for correctional organizations
- Define *needs assessment*
- Explain the role of needs assessments
- Define *process evaluation*
- Explain the importance of process evaluations
- Define *outcome evaluation*
- Explain the importance of outcome evaluations
- Define *outcome monitoring*
- Describe evaluability assessment
- Explain how to use results from evaluation

Discussion Questions

1. Develop a plan to implement an outcome evaluation for a correctional treatment program. Describe the program to be evaluated, the outcome to be assessed, the population to be examined, and the methodology to be used; and explain how the results could be used to improve practice.
2. What problems might a correctional agency experience when using external consultants to conduct program evaluations?
3. Why is monitoring important when discussion evaluation and outcomes?

References

Carter, R. 1994. Managing evaluation projects step by step. In *Handbook of practical program evaluation*, edited by J. S. Wholey, H. P. Hatry, K. E. Newcomer. San Francisco: Jossey-Bass.

CDC (Center for Disease Control). 2007. Evaluating CDC HIV prevention programs. Volume 2: Supplemental Handbook. Chapter 6: Monitoring outcomes of HE/RR interventions. http://www.imls.gov/applicants/faqs.shtm (accessed March 5, 2009).

GPRA. 1993. *Government Performance and Results Act of 1993*. 103rd U.S. Congress.

Guerra-Lopez, I. J. 2008. *Performance evaluation: Proven approaches for improving program and organizational performance.* San Francisco: Jossey-Bass.

Henderson Hurley, M., A. Mathias-Humphrey, and M. J. McDermott. 2008. Barriers to effective program implementation: Rural school-based probation. *Federal Probation* 72(1): 28–36.

Mayfield, J. 2009. The dangerous mentally ill offender program: Four-year felony recidivism and cost effectiveness. Washington State Institute for Public Policy, Olympia. Available at: http://www.wsipp.wa.gov/pub.asp?docid=09-02-1901 (accessed August 1, 2009).

McGuire, J. 2004. Commentary: Promising answers, and the next generation of questions. *Psychology, Crime and Law* 10: 335–345.

McGuire, J. 2005. In *What works and why: Effective approaches to Reentry.* Laurel, MD: American Correctional Association.

McNamera, C. nd. Basic guide to outcomes-based evaluation for nonprofit organization with very limited resources. Free Management Library. Available at: http://www.managementhelp.org/evaluatn/outcomes.htm (accessed February 21, 2009).

Motylewski, K., and C. Horn. 2002. Grant applications: Outcome based evaluation. Institute of Museum and Library Services. Available at: http://www.imls.gov/applicants/faqs.shtm (accessed March 15, 2009).

Tubman, J., and M. K. Vento. 2001. Ifs, maybes, and buts: Influencing staff enforcement of pupil smoking restrictions. *Health Education Research* 1: 329–340.

Wholey, J. 2004. Evaluability assessment. In *Handbook of practical program evaluation*, editied by J. S. Wholey, H. P. Hatry, K. E. Newcomer, pp. 33–62. San Francisco: Jossey-Bass.

Yang, E. n.d. Needs assessment, process and outcome evaluation: What do they mean? Available at: http://www.coalitioninstitute.org/Evaluation-Research/EvaluationArticles/Needs_Assessment_and_Evaluation.htm (accessed March 10, 2009).

Chapter 8

Conclusion

Institutions and correctional agencies exist in environments that are significantly influenced by internal and external stakeholders, politics, legislative changes, as well as a plethora of other factors. These influences force correctional organizations to constantly change and adapt to meet requirements and expectations. While the primary expectation of correctional agencies and institutions is to make differences in the offenders in their care and under their supervision (Applegate, Cullen, and Fisher 1997), other requirements and expectations are, at best, very broad, and at worst, unknown. Regardless of the source, constant changes within the organization leave the organization, as well as its members, in a perpetual cycle of confusion (see Figure 1.1).

The result of these unrealistic demands and unspoken expectations is a state of constant change and confusion. It is unreasonable to assume that all parties will be satisfied; however, correctional organizations are dependent upon outside influences to survive and staff to succeed.

Compounding these issues, correctional environments, by their nature, are strained. Inmates and correctional officers are codependent upon reach other to maintain control and order of the institution (Stojkovic and Farkas 2003). Dealing with unpredictable human behavior is challenging and often discouraging. Individuals typically embark on a career in corrections with the best of intentions—the desire to make a difference—either to make the community safer or to help the offender become a productive member of society or both. However, success rates for offenders are not typically considered "high" (e.g., Ulmer 2001), which constantly wears on a staff member's ability to have a positive attitude. All of this leaves the correctional administrator in an awkward position, asking the question, "What can I do now?" Further, this information leaves the correctional field with the question, "What can *we* do now?"

Attempts to institute the latest fad or "magic bullet" are not new to corrections—nor are these attempts often successful. All too often, a policy or initiative is hailed as *the* answer to offender behavior. It is almost an attitude of "If you do this, they will be fixed." Rarely are these policies and initiatives successful in other jurisdictions. Failure to implement the primary elements or to devote the necessary resources into an initiative are common reasons why these replications fail (e.g., Petersilia 1990). Correctional organizations often are not consciously aware of the resources and effort required to make a major policy change, or even a smaller change. More problematic, these organizations do not know what resources and capital exist within their own structures. In other words, they do not know where they are, so designing a plan to go somewhere else is doomed for failure.

Research has shown that organizations, regardless of their purpose or focus, can be successful when specific elements are in place. This text highlights some of the research that has been conducted regarding organizational capacity and the six domains contained therein. However, no research is worth a grain of salt unless it is put into practice. This final chapter presents an outline of activities that can be utilized by any correctional organization to begin the process of establishing the capacity to adapt to change.

One of the ways in which difficulties and disruptions of change can be reduced is to invest in the organizational capacity of the organization. There are many components included in organizational capacity. Simply, *organizational capacity* refers to an organization having qualified, motivated leaders who engage in effective communication strategies with both internal and external stakeholders, innovative and comprehensive technology, evidence-based practice in daily operations, and effective monitoring and evaluation practices. Organizational capacity is a necessary condition for organizations to produce effective outcomes at every level (Ting 2009).

There are six domains in our conceptualization of organizational capacity: administration and guidance, communication, information technology, human resource capital, evidence-based practice, and evaluation and outcomes. These domains are not mutually exclusive. None of them exists in a vacuum. Each of these areas impacts another area. Therefore, failure or inadequacy in one will eventually hamper the effectiveness of another.

Step 1: Assessment

The very first step in the process of instituting organizational capacity in a correctional setting is to assess the organization in its *current* state. Although the assessment may only provide a snapshot of the organization at one time and place, it provides a starting point for the organization to begin. There are many elements, many of them hidden or unknown to administrators, that can hamper the change process. Staff attitudes, communication difficulties, lack of understanding about policies and procedures, middle management's lack of commitment, as well as many other issues may reduce the success of any change in the organization. Identifying problems *before* making changes prevents these issues from becoming overwhelming and potential landmines.

Consultants may be a resource for correctional administrators in this process, particularly at the assessment stage. However, correctional administrators must be realistic about what a consultant can and cannot do, as well as the particular services a consultant offers. The consultant or outside expert provides a list or series of prescriptions for the agency to follow. Although this prescription may seem innovative, this "must do" list does not take into consideration the vast array of correctional contexts, neglects the role of external and internal stakeholders in the change management process, and leaves out an assessment of current organizational functioning (Bertram 1991). Outside consultants cannot consider idiosyncrasies of institutions because these individual characteristics are unknown to them. Consultant input is useful for providing guidance, but the organization itself must do the work. Only those internal to the organization have a comprehensive, practical understanding of that institution's environment, culture, and purpose. Depending on consultants alone to navigate the change process can lead to disaster.

Consultants can conduct assessments and provide the organization with valuable baseline knowledge. The type of assessment conducted, however, will provide knowledge for different times. For example, one of the most widely used program assessments has been the Correctional Program Assessment Inventory (CPAI) (Gendreau and Andrews 1994). The CPAI (Gendreau and Andrews 1992) assesses how closely a particular program adheres to the known principles of effective treatment. One of the stated limitations to the CPAI is that it "does not address the reasons that a problem exists within a program. Rather, the process is designed to determine the integrity of the program, not necessarily the reasons that certain practices do or do not take place" (Yates 2003, p. 3). Althoug the CPAI has been found to be correlated with program quality (e.g., Lowenkamp and Latessa 2005), it is difficult to determine, as Yates stated, why certain problems arise. An initial assessment of organizational capacity can provide some of these answers prior to the organization's investment in a significant amount of training, programming, or both that will fail because the organization is ill-equipped to implement any change.

The concept of organizational capacity in corrections is a relatively new concept. Examining the structure of an organization rather than the provision of services may be foreign to many in the field. However, it is impractical to expect positive results in service delivery when the organization is striving to stay alive. Only stable, well-equipped, and prepared organizations can embark on such endeavors as implementing the principles of effective intervention. There are several assessments that address some of the issues presented in this work. The Institute of Behavioral Research at Texas Christian University has compiled some of the most noted assessments in this area. Additionally, Quest Consulting

Network has developed the Standardized Organizational Assessment for Results (SOAR).* SOAR addresses each of the six domains for the organization and highlights areas that are in need of improvement. SOAR also compares perceptions of line staff, middle managers, and administrators in terms of current practices versus desired practices. This information is reported to the organization. It is then recommended that the organization embark on a 12-month plan of targeted change and a reassessment be conducted to determine the progress made in the previously identified need areas. The purpose of this endeavor is to allow the organization to build the capacity to make changes prior to the changes being made.

Step 2: Identify Mission, Goals, and Objectives

Regardless of the assessment used,† once the initial results are received the organization can begin to specify mission, goals, and objectives. If the organization already has a mission statement with related goals and objectives, these can be reviewed to determine whether they are still applicable for the direction in which the organization is headed. If these are still applicable, the next steps can be employed. If not, these statements need to be modified to reflect the newly selected directions of the organization.

It is important to remember that members of external stakeholder groups, as well as representatives from all levels of staff, be included in the decision-making process. Including these individuals can assist in communicating the new direction for the organization. Moreover, the participation of various representatives promotes acceptance from external stakeholders and commitment from all staff.

Step 3: Effectively Communicate

Effective communication can be a difficult task, particularly in large organizations. Simply stated, the larger the number of staff, the more opportunity there is for messages to get distorted. The selection of communication techniques must consider the target audience as well as the context of the message being communicated. Too often, messages do not reach the intended target with the intended content. Information is susceptible to individual interpretation. Forming small teams or workgroups can assist in the transfer of information from administrators through the organization to line staff. However, forming rapport among team members can take time and effort. The organization must be prepared for obstacles that may transpire during the communication process. The culture of the organization, if negative, may be one of the largest obstacles to overcome. Organizational culture is

* In the interest of full disclosure, the authors are also the developers and authors of SOAR.

† It is strongly recommended that the assessment utilized for this purpose specifically addresses organizational capacity and its components.

typically formed over a period of time and can be very difficult to change. However, changes are possible if other steps are taken.

Step 4: Enhance Technology

Technology can be a large asset or a huge hindrance to an organization. Outdated, complicated, and inefficient technological systems only complicate the line staff's daily responsibilities. For example, computer systems that are not streamlined force line staff to double or triple enter information into multiple systems. Rectifying this situation can give the administration credibility and encourage appreciation by line staff. Also, simplifying this situation can increase efficiency throughout the entire organization.

Step 5: Invest in Human Resources

In effective organizations, staff are considered to be the organization's most valuable asset. From the beginning of this process, staff must be of central concern. Without line staff, there are no services provided to offenders. Without line staff support, the services that are provided may not be of the utmost quality. Providing training, providing opportunities for professional development, and increasing opportunities for upward mobility within the organization demonstrate to the staff that the organization does value them. In return, staff begin to build a commitment to the organization and identify with its mission.

At this point, the organization can begin to implement new service-delivery strategies and evidence-based practice. Implementing change in correctional organizations does not happen overnight. Organizations that are most effective at changing operations have invested heavily in strategic implementation planning. Such organizations modify implementation plans as new information is gathered, resulting in a more time-consuming process. Thus, real change in corrections can take months or years to fully implement. However, the payoff is worth it. An organization that is flexible and adaptable can survive most any blow. For an organization to succeed, it must survive. This is a time of constant change, when all correctional organizations must be ready to transform themselves into the next requirement. Research has produced a lot of information regarding what is effective in treating offenders. It is now time we invest in research that states how organizations adapt in support of those offenders.

Learning Objective

After completing this chapter, you should be able to discuss the steps for implementing change in correctional organizations.

Key Term

Organizational capacity

Discussion Questions

1. For each step in the process of implementing organizational capacity, what types of activities are necessary? List and describe each activity.
2. For each activity described above, describe and define appropriate measures that could be used to evaluate effectiveness.

References

Applegate, B. K., F. T. Cullen, and B. S. Fisher. 1997. Public support for the correctional treatment: The continuing appeal of the rehabilitative ideal. *The Prison Journal* 77(3): 237–258.

Bertram, D. 1991. Getting started in total quality management. *Total Quality Management* 2(3): 279–282.

Gendreau, P., and D. Andrews. 1994. *The correctional program assessment inventory*. Saint John: University of New Brunswick.

Lowenkamp, C. T., and E. J. Latessa. 2005. Does correctional program quality really matter? The impact of adhering to the principles of effective interventions. Available at: http://www.cjonline.uc.edu/system/Correctional_Program_Quality.pdf.

Petersilia, J. 1990. Conditions that permit intensive supervision programs to survive. *Crime and Delinquency* 36: 125–145.

Rickett, D. 2000. Capacity building. Global Mapping International. Available at: http://www.gmi.org/research/capbuild.htm.

Stojkovic, S., and M. A. Farkas. 2003. *Correctional leadership: A cultural perspective*. Belmont, CA: Wadsworth Publishing.

Ulmer, R. R. 2001. Effective crisis management through established stakeholder relationships: Malden Mills as a case study. *Management Communication Quarterly* 14(4): 590–615.

Yates, H. M. 2003. Correctional program assessment inventory conducted on the Forensic Reentry Development Program (FRED). State Correctional Institution, Muncy, Pennsylvania. PA Department of Corrections. Available at: http://www.cor.state.pa.us/stats/lib/stats/CPAIResultsonFRED.pdf.

Appendix A

Implementing Effective Correctional Management of Offenders in the Community Implementation Checklist

Revised August 22, 2005

This checklist is a tool to guide organizations in their self-assessment and planning for implementation of evidence-based practices for community corrections. It is built on the integrated model of implementation which focuses equally on evidence-based practices, organizational development, and collaboration. The model components are identified throughout the checklist by the following symbols:

An Integrated Model for Implementation

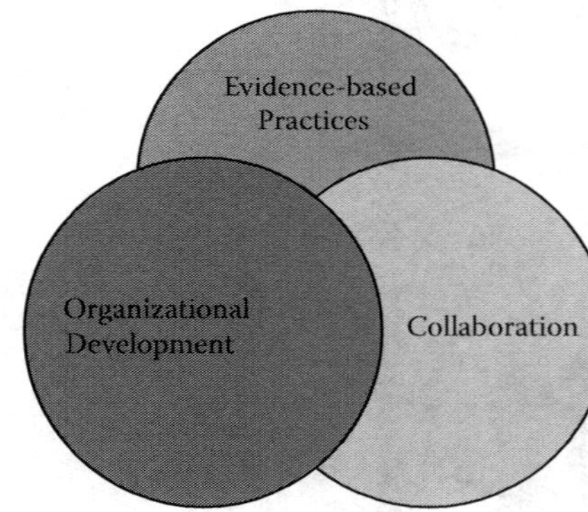

Evidence-Based Practices

Organizational Development

Collaboration

Instructions

1. Bring together a cross-representational group of organizational members, including management, supervisors, and line staff, to complete this checklist.
2. Using a scale of 1 = *We haven't yet begun working on this* through 5 = *We have accomplished this task*, ask the group to rate how much work has been completed in each of the identified areas.
3. Use the ratings to help prioritize your organization's areas of focus for implementing evidence-based practices. Rerating the organization over time (annually, for example) will highlight changes and accomplishments achieved in the ongoing implementation process.

Evidence-Based Practices Implementation Checklist	*Rate These Items Based on the Level of Completion:* *1 = We haven't yet begun.* *2 = We have started work on this.* *3 = We are about halfway complete.* *4 = We are almost finished.* *5 = We have accomplished this!*					*Comments*
	1	*2*	*3*	*4*	*5*	
Administration and Planning						
1) Leadership A) Identify organizational leadership that is committed to implementing EBP and has the leadership, change management, and coaching skills necessary to do so.						
B) Identify champions throughout the organization who are committed to EBP and willing to assist in coordinating implementation.						

(*Continued*)

(Continued)

	Evidence-Based Practices Implementation Checklist	*Rate These Items Based on the Level of Completion: 1 = We haven't yet begun. 2 = We have started work on this. 3 = We are about halfway complete. 4 = We are almost finished. 5 = We have accomplished this!*					*Comments*
		1	*2*	*3*	*4*	*5*	
	2) Vision / Mission Statement A) Redefine vision, mission, and values statement to reflect a commitment to EBP.						
	B) Use an inclusive process that elicits agency-wide and stakeholder participation.						
	C) Post throughout organization.						
	D) Consistently reference statements in decision making and day-to-day operations.						
	3) Policies and Procedures A) Write or revise policies and procedures to reflect the principles of EBP.						

	B) Use an inclusive process that elicits agency-wide and stakeholder participation.						
	4) Policy and Implementation Teams A) Develop an implementation structure that identifies what work will occur at the state level versus the local level.						
	B) Establish statewide and local policy teams of system policy makers and decision makers to guide implementation at a systemic level.						
	C) Establish implementation and work teams that both staff the policy teams and focus on the logistics of implementation.						
	D) Using a chartering process, establish working agreements for teams to clarify roles, reporting and communication structures, membership and attendance expectations, decision-making processes, and information-sharing and input-gathering structure.						

(Continued)

(Continued)

	Evidence-Based Practices Implementation Checklist	*Rate These Items Based on the Level of Completion:* *1 = We haven't yet begun.* *2 = We have started work on this.* *3 = We are about halfway complete.* *4 = We are almost finished.* *5 = We have accomplished this!*					*Comments*
		1	*2*	*3*	*4*	*5*	
	E) Establish the following during the first one or two meetings: i) A chair, lead worker, and/or coordinator						
	ii) Vision, mission, and goal statements						
	iii) Resource needs, i.e., staffing and facilitation						
	iv) Action plans with timelines and assignments						
	5) System Stakeholders / Collaboration A) Involve external stakeholders, such as other public safety partners, community-based providers, and local business representatives in the planning and implementation processes.						

	B) System Stakeholders and Policy Makers i) Involve local government officials as partners and champions in the planning and implementation process.						
	ii) Provide brief educational presentations / training sessions to these officials regarding EBP.						
	iii) Meet regularly with and involve system stakeholders in the planning and implementation process. Provide regular implementation updates and share successes and challenges.						
	C) Media i) Develop a media policy and identify an internal spokesperson.						
	ii) Educate the media about what EBP means in and to the field of corrections.						
	iii) Cultivate relationships with local media and invite them to visit facilities and offices, conduct ride-alongs, and hear about the work of the agency.						

(Continued)

(Continued)

Evidence-Based Practices Implementation Checklist	*Rate These Items Based on the Level of Completion:* *1 = We haven't yet begun.* *2 = We have started work on this.* *3 = We are about halfway complete.* *4 = We are almost finished.* *5 = We have accomplished this!*					*Comments*
	1	*2*	*3*	*4*	*5*	
D) Community-Based Service Providers i) Involve community-based service providers in the planning and implementation of EBP.						
ii) Provide EBP-related training slots or sessions to community-based providers.						
iii) Incorporate requirements including the use of EBP, use of social learning theory and cognitive behavioral techniques, and measurable performance indicators into provider contracts.						

	iv) Develop a system for monitoring and providing feedback regarding contract measurements and hold providers accountable for contract requirements.						
	6) Planning A) Develop a strategic action plan for implementing EBP.						
	B) Include cross-agency and stakeholder representation in the planning process.						
	C) Address operations, organizational development issues, and collaboration.						
	D) Include measurable and time-limited goals and objectives, and assign individuals responsibility for completion of each objective.						
	E) Complete regular updates of the strategic action plan indicating implementation status and timeline for each objective.						
	F) When possible, maintain a balanced workload by eliminating existing tasks when new tasks are adopted.						

(Continued)

(Continued)

Evidence-Based Practices Implementation Checklist	*Rate These Items Based on the Level of Completion:* *1 = We haven't yet begun.* *2 = We have started work on this.* *3 = We are about halfway complete.* *4 = We are almost finished.* *5 = We have accomplished this!*					*Comments*
	1	*2*	*3*	*4*	*5*	
7) Communication A) Develop a plan/strategy for communicating information regarding planning and implementation throughout the organization and to external stakeholders.						
B) Establish a communication subcommittee responsible for ensuring communication flow.						
C) Celebrate successes, even small wins!						
8) Resources / Budget A) Align budget structure with EBP priorities.						

	i) Focus funding on programs that serve medium- and high-risk offenders.						
	ii) Focus funding on programs that are based on EBP.						
	iii) Focus funding on programs that provide evidence of recidivism reduction.						
	iv) Redesign or eliminate programs that are in conflict with EBP.						
Human Resources and Training							
	9) Recruitment and Hiring A) Develop recruiting strategies and literature that focus on the knowledge, skills, and attitude necessary to deliver EBP.						
	B) Rewrite job descriptions to emphasize the knowledge, skills, and attitude necessary to deliver EBP.						
	C) Develop interview and hiring processes that emphasize the knowledge, skills, and attitude necessary to delivery EBP.						

(Continued)

(Continued)

	Evidence-Based Practices Implementation Checklist	*Rate These Items Based on the Level of Completion:* *1 = We haven't yet begun.* *2 = We have started work on this.* *3 = We are about halfway complete.* *4 = We are almost finished.* *5 = We have accomplished this!*					*Comments*
		1	*2*	*3*	*4*	*5*	
	D) Develop a succession planning strategy. i) Provide leadership-skill building opportunities to staff whose behavior and attitude are in alignment with EBP.						
	ii) Build on staff strengths.						
	iii) Balance internal promotional opportunities and external hiring as appropriate.						
	10) Training A) Review current training curriculum and identify training needs.						

	B) Incorporate experiential teaching techniques and adaptations for participant learning styles into trainings.						
	C) Develop a training plan that incorporates training all agency staff in the principles, philosophy, and implementation of EBP. i) Include EBP training in staff orientation sessions.						
	ii) Include EBP training in officer academy / initial training.						
	iii) Train staff in motivational interviewing, social learning theory, and cognitive behavioral techniques.						
	iv) Train staff to administer assessment tools using motivational interviewing techniques.						
	v) Train staff / supervisors / management in the interpretation of data and other reporting mechanisms.						
	D) Train supervisors to conduct performance evaluations and ongoing performance monitoring and EBP.						

(*Continued*)

(Continued)

	Evidence-Based Practices Implementation Checklist	*Rate These Items Based on the Level of Completion:* *1 = We haven't yet begun.* *2 = We have started work on this.* *3 = We are about halfway complete.* *4 = We are almost finished.* *5 = We have accomplished this!*					*Comments*
		1	*2*	*3*	*4*	*5*	
	E) Train management and supervisors in leadership skills and change management.						
	11) Performance Management A) Develop performance evaluation forms that reflect the principles of EBP i) Use of positive reinforcements (4 to 1) with each other and offenders						
	ii) Contact with community supports during case planning						
	B) Develop a system of performance evaluation and monitoring that is ongoing (not limited to once a year).						
	C) Develop methods of feedback for performance information for all staff on a regular basis.						

	D) Develop methods of providing 360-degree feedback, especially for supervisor, middle management, and executive-level staff.						
	E) Conduct random video / audio / observation review of staff performance.						
	F) Conduct periodic and random reviews of assessments and case plans.						
	G) Develop methods of rewarding staff for aligning their behavior with EBP.						
	H) Promote staff based on their knowledge, skills, ability, and attitude related to EBP.						
	I) Measure supervisor performance based on the following:						
	i) Ability to teach and model EBP with staff and others.						
	ii) Ability to observe officer–offender interaction and provide feedback, reinforcement, and instruction in support of EBP.						
	J) Observe and/or provide clinical supervision for cognitive behavioral treatment groups.						

(Continued)

(Continued)

Evidence-Based Practices Implementation Checklist	*Rate These Items Based on the Level of Completion:* *1 = We haven't yet begun.* *2 = We have started work on this.* *3 = We are about halfway complete.* *4 = We are almost finished.* *5 = We have accomplished this!*					*Comments*
	1	*2*	*3*	*4*	*5*	
Information Systems, Measurement, and Evaluation						
12) Measurement A) Develop outcome measures to track progress toward strategic goals. (Incorporate data identified in measurement matrix.)						
B) Develop process and intermediate measures that can be tracked on a regular basis to monitor progress toward strategic goals. (Incorporate measures identified in measurement matrix.)						
13) Information Management A) Develop or adjust information system to provide data required by measurement matrix.						

	B) Develop reporting mechanisms that allow for regular feedback of identified data to managers, supervisors, and staff.						
	C) Collect data regarding offender assessment and case management and provide regular reports back to managers, supervisors, and staff.						
	D) Measure incremental offender change and provide regular reports back to managers, supervisors, and staff.						
	E) Develop mechanisms to measure treatment dosage at individual and aggregate levels as identified in measurement matrix.						
	14) Research and Evaluation A) Develop research and evaluation capacity (hire well-trained staff or partner with a local university or contractor).						
	B) Use the intermediate and outcome measures to measure the effectiveness of internal and contracted programs, treatment, and general supervision.						

(*Continued*)

(Continued)

	Evidence-Based Practices Implementation Checklist	*Rate These Items Based on the Level of Completion:* *1 = We haven't yet begun.* *2 = We have started work on this.* *3 = We are about halfway complete.* *4 = We are almost finished.* *5 = We have accomplished this!*					*Comments*
		1	*2*	*3*	*4*	*5*	
	C) Evaluate implementation to ensure fidelity to implementation model.						
	D) Conduct regular, random case audits to ensure that officers are implementing assessments, developing case plans, following-through on case plans, and utilizing sanctions appropriately.						
Assessment, Case Planning, Interventions, and Supervision							
(icon)	**15) Assessment and Classification** A) Use a preliminary screening tool to assess risk on all offenders at intake.						
	B) Place low-risk offenders on administrative caseloads.						

	C) Implement a third-generation assessment tool for all offenders that score as medium- and high-risk on preliminary screening tool.						
	D) Implement specialized instruments / trailers for special populations.						
	E) Implement a system of regular reassessments and reflect changes in case plans.						
	F) Implement a quality assurance system to ensure that officers are correctly administering assessment instruments and using motivational interviewing techniques. Involve line staff in identifying what is and what is not working well.						
	16) Case Planning A) Develop personalized case plans for all offenders.						
	B) Use the case plan to appropriately target interventions based on EBP:						
	i) Prioritize supervision and treatment resources for offenders assessed as higher risk.						

(Continued)

(Continued)

Evidence-Based Practices Implementation Checklist	*Rate These Items Based on the Level of Completion:* *1 = We haven't yet begun.* *2 = We have started work on this.* *3 = We are about halfway complete.* *4 = We are almost finished.* *5 = We have accomplished this!*					*Comments*
	1	*2*	*3*	*4*	*5*	
ii) Address at least the top four criminogenic needs as identified by the assessment.						
iii) Be responsive to temperament, learning style, motivation, gender, and culture when referring to programs.						
iv) Incorporate appropriate doses of services, prosocial structure, and supervision based on risk level, i.e., structure 40% to 70% of high-risk offenders' time during the initial three to nine months.						
C) Incorporate treatment into the full sentence/sanction requirements, ensuring that treatment interventions are delivered in a targeted and timely manner.						

	D) Incorporate engagement of natural and community supports in offenders' lives.						
	17) Treatment / Programs A) Review current in-house treatment / programs for adherence to EBP, including the use of cognitive behavioral techniques, motivational interviewing, skill training with directed practice, and positive reinforcement.						
	B) Assess strengths and gaps using a program assessment tool, such as the Correctional Program Assessment Inventory (CPAI).						
	C) Develop a plan for strengthening, eliminating, or adding programs in alignment with EBP.						
	18) Intermediate Sanctions A) Assess availability of intermediate sanctions, identify gaps, and develop a plan for increasing or adjusting availability.						
	B) Use a multidisciplinary team to develop guidelines for sanctions/revocations.						

(*Continued*)

(Continued)

	Evidence-Based Practices Implementation Checklist	*Rate These Items Based on the Level of Completion:* *1 = We haven't yet begun.* *2 = We have started work on this.* *3 = We are about halfway complete.* *4 = We are almost finished.* *5 = We have accomplished this!*					*Comments*
		1	*2*	*3*	*4*	*5*	
	C) Consider the use of administrative sanctions in lieu of formal revocations, keeping the length of sanctions short, as timeliness of response is more important than duration.						

Contributors: Brad Bogue, Nancy Campbell, Mark Carey, Elyse Clawson, Dot Faust, Kate Florio, Lore Joplin, Billy Wasson, and William Woodward.

Project Contact Information		
		Dot Faust, Correctional Program Specialist National Institute of Corrections, Community Corrections Division dfaust@bop.gov (202) 514-3001 www.nicic.org
		Elyse Clawson, Executive Director Crime and Justice Institute eclawson@crjustice.org (617) 482-2520 www.cjinstitute.org

Appendix B: Citations to the Studies Used in the Meta-Analyses*

(Some studies contributed independent effect sizes from more than one location.)

Adolescent Diversion Project

Blakely, C. H. (1981). The diversion of juvenile delinquents: A first step toward the dissemination of a successful innovation. Doctoral dissertation, Michigan State University.

Davidson, W. S. II, and Redner, R. (1988). The prevention of juvenile delinquency: Diversion from the juvenile justice system. In R. H. Price, E. L. Cowen, R. P. Lorion, and J. Ramos-McKay (eds.), *14 ounces of prevention: A casebook for practitioners* (pp. 123–127). Washington, DC: American Psychological Association.

Emshoff, J. G., and Blakely, C. H. (1983). The diversion of delinquent youth: Family-focused intervention. *Children and Youth Services Review* 5: 343–356.

Adult Boot Camps

Austin, J., Jones, M., and Bolyard, M. (1993). Assessing the impact of a county operated boot camp: Evaluation of the Los Angeles County regimented inmate diversion program. San Francisco: National Council on Crime and Delinquency.

Burns, J. C., and Vito, G. F. (1995). An impact analysis of the Alabama boot camp program. *Federal Probation* 59(1): 63–67.

* The Washington State Institute for Public Policy has compiled the most complete list of available research on evidence-based correctional practices. This appendix provides the reader with citations for the evidence available for adult and juvenile correctional programs. (Adapted from Aos, S., M. Miller, and E. Drake, 2006, Evidence-Based Public Policy Options to Reduce Future Prison Construction, Criminal Justice Costs, and Crime Rates. Olympia, WA. Available at: http://www.wsipp.wa.gov/pub.asp?docid=06-10-1201, accessed August 1, 2009.)

Camp, D. A., and Sandhu, H. S. (1995). Evaluation of female offender regimented treatment program (FORT). *Journal of the Oklahoma Criminal Justice Research Consortium* 2: 50–77.
Colorado Department of Corrections. (1993). Colorado regimented inmate training program: A legislative report.
Farrington, D. P., Ditchfield, J., Hancock, G., Howard, P., Jolliffe, D., Livingston, M. S., and Painter, K. (2002). Evaluation of two intensive regimes for young offenders. London, UK: Home Office Research Study 239.
Gransky, L. A., and Jones, R. J. (1995). Evaluation of the post-release status of substance abuse program participants. Illinois Criminal Justice Authority Report.
Harer, M. D., and Klein-Saffran, J. (1996). Lewisburg ICC evaluation. Washington, DC: Bureau of Prisons, Office of Research and Evaluation. Memo.
Jones, M., and Ross, D. L. (1997). Is less better? Boot camp, regular probation and rearrest in North Carolina. *American Journal of Criminal Justice* 21(2): 147–161.
Kempinen, C. A., and Kurlychek, M. C. (2003). An outcome evaluation of Pennsylvania's boot camp: Does rehabilitative programming within a disciplinary setting reduce recidivism? *Crime and Delinquency* 49(4): 581–602.
MacKenzie, D. L., and Souryal, C. (1994). Multisite evaluation of shock incarceration: Executive summary. Washington, DC: U.S. Department of Justice/NIJ.
Smith, R. P. (1998). Evaluation of the work ethic camp. Olympia: Washington State Department of Corrections.
Stinchcomb, J. B., and Terry, W. C. (2001). Predicting the likelihood of rearrest among shock incarceration graduates: Moving beyond another nail in the boot camp coffin. *Crime and Delinquency* 47(2): 221–242.
Wright, D. T., and Mays, G. L. (1998). Correctional boot camps, attitudes, and recidivism: The Oklahoma experience. *Journal of Offender Rehabilitation* 28(1/2): 71–87.

Adult Drug Courts

Barnoski, R., and Aos, S. (2003), Washington State's drug courts for adult defendants: Outcome evaluation and cost-benefit analysis. Washington State Institute for Public Policy, 03–03–1201.
Bavon, A. (2001). The effect of the Tarrant County drug court project on recidivism. *Evaluation and Program Planning* 24: 13–24.
Bell, M. M. (1998). King County drug court evaluation: Final report. Seattle: M. M. Bell, Inc.
Breckenridge, J. F., Winfree, Jr., L. T., Maupin, J. R., and Clason, D. L. (2000). Drunk drivers, DWI 'drug court' treatment, and recidivism: Who fails? *Justice Research and Policy* 2(1): 87.
Brewster, M. P. (2001). An evaluation of the Chester County (PA) drug court program. *Journal of Drug Issues* 31(1): 177–206.
Carey, S. M., and Finigan, M. W. (2004). A detailed cost-analysis in a mature drug court setting: A cost-benefit evaluation of the Multnomah County drug court. *Journal of Contemporary Criminal Justice* 20(3): 315–338.
Craddock, A. (2002). North Carolina drug treatment court evaluation: Final report. Raleigh: North Carolina Court System.
Crumpton, D., Brekhus, J., Weller, J., and Finigan, M. (2003). Cost analysis of Baltimore City, Maryland Drug Treatment Court. Portland, OR: NPC Research, Inc.

Deschenes, E. P., Cresswell, L., Emami, V., Moreno, K., Klein, Z., and Condon, C. 2001. Success of drug courts: Process and outcome evaluations in Orange County, California. Final Report. Submitted to the Superior Court of Orange County, CA, September 20, 2001.

Ericson, R., Welter, S., and Johnson, T. L. (1999). Evaluation of the Hennepin County drug court. Minneapolis: Minnesota Citizens Council on Crime and Justice.

Evaluation: Spokane County drug court program. (1999). Spokane, WA: Spokane County Drug Court.

Fielding, J. E., Tye, G., Ogawa, P. L., Imam, I. J., and Long, A. M. (2002). Los Angeles County drug court programs: Initial results. *Journal of Substance Abuse Treatment* 23(3): 217–224.

Finigan, M. W. (1998). An outcome program evaluation of the Multnomah County S.T.O.P. drug diversion program. Portland, OR: NPC Research, Inc.

Godley, M. D., Dennis, M. L., Funk, R., Siekmann, M., and Weisheit, R. (1998). An evaluation of the Madison County assessment and treatment alternative court. Chicago: Illinois Criminal Justice Information Authority.

Goldkamp, J. S., and Weiland, D. (1993). Assessing the impact of Dade County's felony drug court. Final Report. Philadelphia: Crime and Justice Research Institute.

Goldkamp, J. S., Weiland, D., and Moore, J. (2001). The Philadelphia treatment court, its development and impact: The second phase (1998–2000). Philadelphia: Crime and Justice Research Institute.

Goldkamp, J. S., White, M. D., and Robinson, J. B. (2001). Do drug courts work? Getting inside the drug court black box. *Journal of Drug Issues* 31(1): 27–72.

Gottfredson, D. C., Coblentz, K., and Harmon, M. A. (1997). A short-term outcome evaluation of the Baltimore City drug treatment court program. Perspectives, Winter: 33–38.

Gottfredson, D. C., Najaka, S. S., Kearley, B. (2002, November). A randomized study of the Baltimore City drug treatment court: Results from the three-year follow-up. Paper presented at the annual meeting of the American Society of Criminology, Chicago.

Granfield, R., Eby, C., and Brewster, T. (1998). An examination of the Denver drug court: The impact of a treatment-oriented drug-offender system. *Law and Policy* 20: 183–202.

Harrell, A., Roman, J., and Sack, E. (2001). Drug court services for female offenders, 1996–1999: Evaluation of the Brooklyn treatment court. Washington, DC: The Urban Institute.

Johnson, G. D., Formichella, C. M., and Bowers, D. J. (1998). Do drug courts work? An outcome evaluation of a promising program. *Journal of Applied Sociology* 15(1): 44–62.

Latessa, E. J., Shaffer, D. K., and Lowenkamp, C. (2002). Outcome evaluation of Ohio's drug court efforts: Final Report. Cincinnati: Center for Criminal Justice Research, Division of Criminal Justice, University of Cincinnati.

Listwan, S. J., and Latessa, E. J. (2003). The Kootenai and Ada County drug courts: Outcome evaluation findings. Cincinnati, OH: Center for Criminal Justice Research, University of Cincinnati.

Listwan, S. J., Shaffer, D. K., and Latessa, E. J. (2001). The Akron municipal drug court: Outcome evaluation findings. Cincinnati: Center for Criminal Justice Research, University of Cincinnati.

Listwan, S. J., Sundt, J. L., Holsinger, A. M., and Latessa, E. J. (2003). The effect of drug court programming on recidivism: The Cincinnati experience. *Crime and Delinquency* 49(3): 389–411.

Listwan. S. J., Shaffer, D. K., and Latessa, E. J. (2001). The Erie County drug court: Outcome evaluation findings. Cincinnati: Center for Criminal Justice Research, University of Cincinnati.

Logan, T., Hoyt, W., and Leukefeld, C. (2001). Kentucky drug court outcome evaluation: Behaviors, costs, and avoided costs to society. Lexington: Center on Drug and Alcohol Research, University of Kentucky.

Martin, T. J., Spohn, C. C., Piper, R. K., and Frenzel-Davis, E. (2001). Phase III Douglas County drug court evaluation: Final Report. Institute for Social and Economic Development.

Martinez, A. I., and Eisenberg, M. (2003). Initial process and outcome evaluation of drug courts in Texas. Austin, Texas: Criminal Justice Policy Council.

McNeece, C. A., and Byers, J. B. (1995). Hillsborough County drug court: Two-year (1995) follow-up study. Tallahassee: Institute for Health and Human Services Research, School of Social Work, Florida State University.

Miethe, T. D., Lu, H., and Reese, E. (2000). Reintegrative shaming and recidivism risks in drug court: Explanations for some unexpected findings. *Crime and Delinquency* 46(4): 522–541.

Peters, R. H., and Murrin, M. R. (2000). Effectiveness of treatment-based drug courts in reducing criminal recidivism. *Criminal Justice and Behavior* 27(1): 72–96.

Rempel, M., Fox-Kralstein, D., Cissner, A., Cohen, R., Labriola, M., Farole, D., Bader, A., and Magnani, M. (2003). The New York State adult drug court evaluation: Policies, participants and impacts. New York: Center for Court Innovation.

Shanahan, M., Lancsar, E., Haas, M., Lind, B., Weatherburn, D., and Chen, S. (2004). Cost-effectiveness analysis of the New South Wales adult drug court program. *Evaluation Review* 28(1): 3–27.

Spohn, C., Piper, R. K., Martin, T., and Frenzel, E. D. (2001). Drug courts and recidivism: The results of an evaluation using two comparison groups and multiple indicators of recidivism. *Journal of Drug Issues* 31(1): 149–176.

Stageberg, P., Wilson, B., and Moore, R. G. (2001). Final report on the Polk County adult drug court. Iowa Department of Human Rights, Division of Criminal and Juvenile Justice Planning.

Tjaden, C. D., Diana, A., Feldman, D., Dietrich, W., and Jackson, K. (2002). Denver drug court: Second year report, outcome evaluation. Vail, CO: Toucan Research and Computer Solutions.

Truitt, L., Rhodes, W. M., Seeherman, A. M., Carrigan, K., and Finn, P. (2000). Phase I: Case studies and impact evaluations of Escambia County, Florida and Jackson County, Missouri drug courts. Cambridge, MA: Abt Associates. Some results also reported in Belenko, S. (2001). Research on drug courts: A critical review, 2001 update. New York: The National Center on Addiction and Substance Abuse at Columbia University.

Turner, S., Greenwood, P., Fain, T., and Deschenes, E. (1999). Perceptions of drug court: How offenders view ease of program completion, strengths and weaknesses, and the impact on their lives. *National Drug Court Institute Review* 2(1): 61–86.

Utah Substance Abuse and Anti-Violence Coordinating Council. (2001). Salt Lake County drug court outcome evaluation. Salt Lake City: Utah Substance Abuse and Anti-Violence Coordinating Council.

Vito, G. F., and Tewksbury, R. A. (1998). The impact of treatment: The Jefferson County (Kentucky) drug court program. *Federal Probation* 62(2): 46–51.

Wolfe E., Guydish J., and Termondt J. (2002). A drug court outcome evaluation comparing arrests in a two year follow-up period. *Journal of Drug Issues* 32(4): 1155–1171.

Adult Intensive Supervision Probation or Parole Surveillance

Bagdon, W., and Ryan, J. E. (1993). Intensive supervision of offenders on prerelease furlough: An evaluation of the Vermont experience. FORUM on Corrections Research, Volume 5(2). Available at: http://www.csc-scc.gc.ca/text/pblct/forum/e052/e052j_e.shtml.

Brown, K. (1999). Intensive supervision probation: The effects of supervision philosophy on intensive probationer recidivism. Dissertation, University of Cincinnati. Available at: http://www.uc.edu/criminaljustice/graduate/Dissertations/KBrown.PDF.

Byrne, J. M., and Kelly, L. (1989). Executive summary: Restructuring probation as an intermediate sanction: An evaluation of the Massachusetts intensive probation supervision program. Final Report to the National Institute of Justice, Research Program on the Punishment and Control of Offenders. Washington, DC: National Institute of Justice.

Deschenes, E. P., Turner, S., and Petersilia, J. (1995). A dual experiment in intensive community supervision: Minnesota's prison diversion and enhanced supervised release programs. *Prison Journal* 75(3): 330–357.

Erwin, B. S., Bennett, L. A. (1987). New dimensions in probation: Georgia's experience with intensive probation supervision. Research Brief, National Institute of Justice, January.

Fulton, B., Stichman, A., Latessa, E., and Lawrence, T. (1998). Evaluating the prototypical ISP, Iowa correctional services second judicial district. Final Report. Division of Criminal Justice, University of Cincinnati.

Johnson, G., and Hunter, R. M. (1995). Evaluation of the specialized drug offender program, In Ross, R. R. and Ross, R. D. (eds.), *Thinking straight: The reasoning and rehabilitation program for delinquency prevention and offender rehabilitation* (pp. 214–234). Ottawa: Air Training and Publications.

Lichtman, C. M., and Smock, S. M. (1981). The effects of social services on probationer recidivism: A field experiment. *Journal of Research in Crime and Delinquency* January: 81–100.

Petersilia, J., Turner, S., and Deschenes, E. P. (1992). Intensive supervision programs for drug offenders. In Byrne, J. M., Lurigio, A. J., and Petersilia, J. (eds.), *Smart sentencing: The emergency of intermediate sanction* (pp. 18–37). Sage: Newbury Park.

Petersilia, J., and Turner, S. (1990). *Intensive supervision for high-risk probationers: Findings from three California experiments.* Santa Monica, CA: RAND.

Smith, L. G., and Akers, R. L. (1993). A comparison of recidivism of Florida's community control and prison: A five-year survival analysis. *Journal of Research in Crime and Delinquency* 30(3): 267–292.

Stichman, A., Fulton, B., Latessa, E., and Lawrence, T. (1998). Evaluating the prototypical ISP, Hartford intensive supervision unit Connecticut office of adult probation administrative office of the courts. Final Report. Division of Criminal Justice, University of Cincinnati.

Turner, S., and Petersilia, J. (1992). Focusing on high-risk parolees: Experiment to reduce commitments to the Texas Department of Corrections. *Journal of Research on Crime and Delinquency* 29(1): 34–61.

Adult Intensive Supervision Probation or Parole Treatment

Deschenes, E. P., Turner, S., and Petersilia, J. (1995). A dual experiment in intensive community supervision: Minnesota's prison diversion and enhanced supervised release programs. *Prison Journal* 75(3): 330–357.

Hanley, D. (2002). Risk differentiation and intensive supervision: A meaningful union? Dissertation. University of Cincinnati.

Harrell, A., Mitchell, O., Hirst, A., Marlow, D., and Merrill, J. C. (2002). Breaking the cycle of drugs and crime: Findings from the Birmingham BTC demonstration. *Criminology and Public Policy* 1(2): 189–216.

Harrell, A., Mitchell, O., Merrill J. C. and Marlowe, D. B. (2003). Evaluation of breaking the cycle. Washington, DC: The Urban Institute.

Harrell, A., Roman, J., Bhati, A., and Parthasarathy, B. (2003). Evaluation of breaking the cycle. Washington, DC: The Urban Institute.

Paparozzi, M. A. (1994). A comparison of the effectiveness of an intensive parole supervision program with traditional parole supervision. Unpublished Doctoral Dissertation. Rutgers, The State University of New Jersey.

Pearson, F. S. (1988). Evaluation of New Jersey's intensive supervision program. *Crime and Delinquency* 34(4): 437–448.

Petersilia, J., and Turner, S. (1990). *Intensive supervision for high-risk probationers: Findings from three California experiments*. Santa Monica, CA: RAND.

Aggression Replacement Training (ART) (Including Washington Studies)

Barnoski, R. (2004). Outcome evaluation of Washington State's research-based programs for juvenile offenders. Washington State Institute for Public Policy.

Gibbs, J. C. (1995). EQUIP: A peer-group treatment program for delinquents. In Ross, R. R., Antonowicz, D. H., and Dhaliwal, G. K., *Going straight, effective delinquency prevention and offender rehabilitation* (Chapter 8). Ottawa: AIR Training Publications.

Goldstein, A. P., and Glick, B. (1995). Aggression replacement training for delinquents. In Ross, R. R., Antonowicz, D. H., Dhaliwal, G. K., (eds), *Going straight, effective delinquency prevention and offender rehabilitation* (Chapter 6). Ottawa: AIR Training Publications.

Behavioral Therapy for Sex Offenders

Davidson, P. R. (1984). Behavioral treatment for incarcerated sex offenders: Post-release outcome. Paper presented at Conference at Kingston, Ontario, Canada, March.

Rice, M. E., Quinsey, V. L., and Harris, G. T. (1991). Sexual recidivism among child molesters released from a maximum security psychiatric institution. *Journal of Consulting and Clinical Psychology* 59: 381–386.

Case Management in the Community for Drug-Involved Offenders

Anglin, M. D., Longshore, D., and Turner, S. (1999). Treatment alternatives to street crime: An evaluation of five programs. *Criminal Justice and Behavior* 26(2): 168–195.

California Department of Corrections. (1996). Parolee partnership program: A parole outcome evaluation. Sacramento: California Department of Corrections.

Hanlon, T. E., Nurco, D. N., Bateman, R. W., and O'Grady, K. E. (1999). The relative effects of three approaches to the parole supervision of narcotic addicts and cocaine abusers. *The Prison Journal* 79(2): 163–181.

Longshore, D., Turner, S., and Fain, T. (2005). Effects of case management on parolee misconduct. *Criminal Justice and Behavior* 32(2): 205–222.

Owens, S., Klebe, K., Arens, S., Durham, R., Hughes, J., Moor, C., O'Keefe, M., Phillips, J., Sarno, J., and Stommel, J. (1997). The effectiveness of Colorado's TASC programs. *Journal of Offender Rehabilitation* 26: 161–176.

Rhodes, W., and Gross, M. (1997). Case management reduces drug use and criminality among drug-involved arrestees: An experimental study of an HIV prevention intervention. Final report to the National Institute of Justice/National Institute on Drug Abuse.

Circles of Support and Accountability (Faith-Based Supervision of Sex Offenders)

Wilson, R. J., Picheca, J. E., and Prinzo, M. (2005). Circles of support and accountability: An evaluation of the pilot project in south central Ontario. Draft Report to Correctional Service of Canada, R168, e-mailed to M. Miller, October 20, 2005.

Cognitive–Behavioral Therapy for the General Population, in Prison

Armstrong, T. (2003). The effect of moral reconation therapy on the recidivism of youthful offenders. *Criminal Justice and Behavior* 30(6): 668–687.

Burnett, W. (1997). Treating post-incarcerated offenders with moral reconation therapy: A one-year recidivism study. *Cognitive Behavioral Treatment Review* 6(3/4): 2.

Culver, H. E. (1993). Intentional skill development as an intervention tool. Doctoral Dissertation, University of Massachusetts. UMI 9329590.

Falshaw, L., Friendship, C., Travers, R., and Nugent, F. (2004). Searching for what works: HM Prison Service accredited cognitive skills programmes. *British Journal of Forensic Practice* 6(2): 3–13.

Friendship, C., Blud, L., Erikson, M., Travers, R., and Thornton, D. (2003). Cognitive-behavioural treatment for imprisoned offenders: An evaluation of HM Prison Service's cognitive skills programmes. *Legal and Criminological Psychology* 8: 103–114.

Golden, L. (2002). Evaluation of the efficacy of a cognitive behavioral program for offenders on probation: Thinking for a change. University of Texas Southwestern Medical Center at Dallas. Available at: www.nicic.org/pubs/2002/018190.pdf.

Grandberry, G. (1998). Moral reconation therapy evaluation. Final Report. Olympia: Washington State Department of Corrections.

Henning, K. R., and Frueh, B. C. (1996). Cognitive-behavioral treatment of incarcerated offenders: An evaluation of the Vermont Department of Corrections' cognitive self-change program. *Criminal Justice and Behavior* 23(4): 523–541.

Hubbard, D. J., and Latessa, E. J. (2004). Evaluation of cognitive-behavioral programs for offenders: A look at outcome and responsivity in five treatment programs. Final Report. Division of Criminal Justice, University of Cincinnati.

Johnson, G., and Hunter, R. M. (1995). Evaluation of the specialized drug offender program. In Ross, R. R., and Ross, R. D. (eds.), *Thinking straight: The reasoning and rehabilitation program for delinquency prevention and offender rehabilitation* (pp. 214–234). Ottawa: Air Training and Publications.

Larson, K. A. (1989). Problem-solving training and parole adjustment in high-/risk young adult offenders. *The Yearbook of Correctional Education* (1989): 279–299.

Little, G. L., Robinson, K. D., and Burnette, K. D. (1993). Cognitive behavioral treatment of felony drug offenders: A five-year recidivism report. *Psychological Reports* 73: 1089–1090.

Little, G. L., Robinson, K. D., and Burnette, K. D. (1993). 5 recidivism results on MRT-treated DWI offenders released. *Cognitive Behavioral Treatment Review* 2(4): 2.

Little, G. L., Robinson, K. D., Burnette, K. D., and Swan, E. S. (1998). Nine-year reincarceration study on MRT-treated felony offenders: Treated offenders show significantly lower reincarceration. *Cognitive Behavioral Treatment Review* 7(1): 2–3.

Ortmann, R. (2000). The effectiveness of social therapy in prison: A randomized experiment. *Crime and Delinquency* 46(2): 214–232.

Porporino, F. J., and Robinson, D. (1995). An evaluation of the reasoning and rehabilitation program with Canadian federal offenders. In Ross, R. R. and Ross, R. D. (eds.), *Thinking straight: The reasoning and rehabilitation program for delinquency prevention and offender rehabilitation* (Chapter 8). Ottawa: Air Training and Publications.

Raynor, P., and Vanstone, M. (1996). Reasoning and rehabilitation in Britain: The results of the Straight Thinking on Probation (STOP) Programme. *International Journal of Offender Therapy and Comparative Criminology* 40(4): 272–284.

Robinson, D. (1995). The impact of cognitive skills training on post-release recidivism among Canadian federal offenders. Research Report, Correctional Research and Development, Correctional Service Canada.

Ross, R. R., Fabiano, E. A., and Ewles, C. D. (1988). Reasoning and rehabilitation. *International Journal of Offender Therapy and Comparative Criminology* 32: 29–36.

Van Voorhis, P., Spruance, L. M., Ritchey, P. N., Listwan, S. J., and Seabrook, R. (2004). The Georgia cognitive skills experiment: A replication of reasoning and rehabilitation. *Criminal Justice and Behavior* 31(3): 282–305.

Van Voorhis, P., Spruance, L. M., Ritchie, P. N., Johnson-Listwan, S., Seabrook, R., and Pealer, J. (2002). The Georgia cognitive skills experiment outcome evaluation, Phase II. Cincinnati, OH: University of Cincinnati, Center for Criminal Justice Research. Available at: http://www.uc.ed/criminaljustice/ProjectReports/Georgia_Phase_II_final.report.pdf.

Wilkinson, J. (2005). Evaluating evidence for the effectiveness of the Reasoning and Rehabilitation Programme. *The Howard Journal of Criminal Justice* 44(1): 70–85.

Yessine, A. K., and Kroner, D. G. (2004). Altering antisocial attitudes among federal male offenders on release: A preliminary analysis of the counter-point community program. Research Report No. R-152, Correctional Research and Development, Correctional Service Canada.

Cognitive–Behavioral Therapy in Prison for Drug-Involved Offenders

Aos, S., Phipps, P., and Barnoski, R. (2004). Washington's drug offender sentencing alternative: An evaluation of benefits and costs. Olympia: Washington State Institute for Public Policy.

Daley, M., Love, C. T., Shepard, D. S., Petersen, C. B., White, K. L., and Hall, F. B. (2004). Cost-effectiveness of Connecticut's in-prison substance abuse treatment. *Journal of Offender Rehabilitation* 39(3): 69–92.

Hall, E. A., Prendergast, M. L., Wellisch, J., Patten, M., and Cao, Y. (2004). Treating drug-abusing women prisoners: An outcome evaluation of the Forever Free program. *The Prison Journal* 84(1): 81–105.

Hanson, G. (2000). Pine Lodge intensive inpatient treatment program. Washington State Department of Corrections.

Pelissier, B., Rhodes, W., Saylor, W., Gaes, G., Camp, S. D., Vanyur, S. D., and Wallace, S. (2000). TRIAD drug treatment evaluation project: Final report of three-year outcomes: Part 1 Federal Bureau of Prisons, Office of Research and Evaluation. Available at: http://www.bop.gov/news/PDFs/TRIAD/TRIAD_pref.pdf.

Porporino, F. J., Robinson, D., Millson, B., and Weekes, J. R. (2002). An outcome evaluation of prison-based treatment programming for substance users. *Substance Use and Misuse* 37(8–10): 1047–1077.

Washington State Department of Corrections, Division of Management and Budget, Planning and Research Section (April 1998). Substance abuse treatment program evaluation of outcomes and management report.

Wexler, H. K., Falkin, G. P., Lipton, D. S., and Rosenblum, A. B. (1992). Outcome evaluation of a prison therapeutic community for substance abuse treatment. In C. G. Leukefeld and F. M. Tims (eds.), *Drug abuse treatment in prisons and jails* (pp. 156–174). NIDA research Monograph 118, Rockville, MD: NIDA.

Cognitive–Behavioral Treatment in Prison, Sex Offenders

Bakker, L., Hudson, S., Wales, D., and Riley, D. (1999). And there was light: An evaluation of the Kia Marama treatment programme for New Zealand sex offenders against children. Unpublished Report.

Barnoski, R. (2006). Sex offender sentencing in Washington State: Does the prison treatment program reduce recidivism? Olympia: Washington State Institute for Public Policy. Available at: http://www.wsipp.wa.gov/rptfiles/06-06-1205.pdf.

Looman, J., Abracen, J., and Nicholaichuk, T. P. (2000). Recidivism among treated sexual offenders and matched controls: Data from the regional treatment centre (Ontario). *Journal of Interpersonal Violence* 15(3): 279–290.

Marques, J. K. (1999). How to answer the question 'does sex offender treatment work?' *Journal of Interpersonal Violence* 14(4): 437–451.

Robinson, D. (1995). The impact of cognitive skills training on post-release recidivism among Canadian federal offenders. Research Report No. R-41, Correctional Research and Development, Correctional Service Canada.

Song, L., and Lieb, R. (1995). Washington State sex offenders: Overview of recidivism studies. Olympia: Washington State Institute for Public Policy.

Cognitive–Behavioral Treatment in the Community, Sex Offenders

Allam, J. (1999). Sex offender re-conviction–treated vs. untreated offenders. West Midlands Probation Service Sex Offender Treatment Programme.

Baird, C., Wagner, D., Decomo, B., Aleman, T. (1994). Evaluation of the effectiveness of supervision and community rehabilitation programs in Oregon. National Council on Crime and Delinquency.

Marshall, W. L., Eccles, A., and Barbaree, H. E. (1991). The treatment of exhibitionists: A focus on sexual deviance versus cognitive and relationship features. *Behaviour Research and Therapy* 29(2): 129–135.

McGrath, R. J., Hoke, S. E., and Vojtisek, J. E. (1998). Cognitive-behavioral treatment of sex offenders: A treatment comparison and long-term follow-up study. *Criminal Justice and Behavior* 25: 203–225.

Procter, E. (1996). A five-year outcome evaluation of a community-based treatment programme for convicted sexual offenders run by the probations service. (England) *The Journal of Sexual Aggression* 2(1): 3–16.

Education in Prison (Basic Education or Postsecondary)

Batiuk, M., Lahm, K., McKeever, M. Wilcox, N., and Wilcox, P. (2005). Disentangling the effects of correctional education: Are current policies misguided? An event history analysis. *Criminology and Criminal Justice* 5: 55–74.

Batiuk, M. E., Moke, P., and Rountree, P. W. (1997). Crime and rehabilitation: Correctional education as an agent of change. *Justice Quarterly* 14: 167–180.

Blackburn, F. S. (1981). The relationship between recidivism and participation in a community college program for incarcerated offenders. *Journal of Correctional Education* 32(3): 23–25.

Burke, L. O., and Vivian, J. E. (2001). The effect of college programming on recidivism rates at the Hampden County House of Correction: A 5-year study. *Journal of Correctional Education* 52: 160–162.

Drake, E. K. (2005). Correctional education and its impacts on post-prison employment patterns and recidivism (unpublished). Olympia, WA: Washington State Department of Corrections.

Duguid, S., Hawkey, C., and Knights, W. (1998). Measuring the impact of post-secondary education in prison: A report from British Columbia. *Journal of Offender Rehabilitation* 27(1/2): 87–106.
Harer, M. D. (1995). Prison education program participation and recidivism: A test of the normalization hypotheses. Washington, DC: Federal Bureau of Prisons, Office of Research and Evaluation.
Holloway, J., and Moke, P. (1986). Post-secondary correctional education: An evaluation of parolee performance. Unpublished manuscript, Wilmington College, Ohio.
Linden, R., Perry, L., Ayers, D., and Parlett, T. A. (1984). An evaluation of a prison education program. Canadian *Journal of Criminology* 26: 65–73.
O'Neil, M. (1990). Correctional higher education: Reduced recidivism? *Journal of Correctional Education* 41: 28–31.
Mitchell, O. (2002). Statistical analysis of the three state CEA data. Unpublished.
Piehl, A. M. (1994). Learning while doing time. Kennedy School Working Paper #R94-25. Cambridge, MA: John F. Kennedy School of Government, Harvard University.
Walsh, A. (1985). An evaluation of the effects of adult basic education on rearrest rates among probationers. *Journal of Offender Counseling, Services, and Rehabilitation* 9(4): 69–76.

Correctional Industries

Drake, E. (2003). Class I impacts: Work during incarceration and its effects on post-prison employment patterns and recidivism. Olympia: Washington State Department of Corrections.
Maguire, K. E., Flanagan, T. J., and Thornberry, T. P. (1988). Prison labor and recidivism. *Journal of Quantitative Criminology* 4(1): 3–18.
Saylor, W. G., and Gaes, G. G. (1996). PREP: A study of rehabilitating inmates through industrial work participation, and vocational and apprenticeship training. Washington, DC: Federal Bureau of Prisons.
Smith, C. J., Bechtel, J., Patricky, A., and Wilson-Gentry, L. (2005). Correctional Industries preparing inmates for re-entry: Recidivism and post-release employment. Final Draft Report (e-mail from author).

Counseling / Psychotherapy for Juvenile Offenders

Lee, R., and Olejnik, S. (1981). Professional outreach counseling can help the juvenile probationer: A two-year follow-up study. *Personnel and Guidance Journal* 59: 445–449.
Persons, R. W. (1967). Relationship between psychotherapy with institutionalized boys and subsequent community adjustment. *Journal of Consulting Psychology* 31(2): 137–141.
Shivrattan, J. L. (1988). Social interactional training and incarcerated juvenile delinquents. *Canadian Journal of Criminology* 30: 145–163.
Sowles, R. C., and Gill, J. H. (1970). Institutional and community adjustment of delinquents following counseling. *Journal of Consulting and Clinical Psychology* 34(3): 398–402.
Thambidurai, G. (1980). A comparative outcome study of a contract parole program for individuals committed to the youth correctional complex in the State of New Jersey. Unpublished Ph.D. Thesis. Rutgers University of the State of New Jersey, New Brunswick, New Jersey.

Court Supervision (Compared to Simple Release without Services)

Davidson, W. S. II., and Redner, R. (1988). The prevention of juvenile delinquency: Diversion from the juvenile justice system. In R. H. Price, E. L. Cowen, R. P. Lorion, and J. Ramos-McKay (eds.), *14 ounces of prevention: A casebook for practitioners* (pp. 123–137). Washington, DC: American Psychological Association.

Dunford, F. W., Osgood, D. W., and Weichselbaum, H. F. (1982). National evaluation of diversion projects, executive summary and microfiche. U.S. Department of Justice.

Koch, J. R. (1986). Community service and outright release as alternatives to juvenile court: An experimental evaluation. Doctoral Dissertation, Michigan State University, 1985. *Dissertation Abstracts International,* 46(07), 2081A. (University Microfilms No. 85-20537).

National Council on Crime and Delinquency. (1987). The impact of juvenile court intervention. San Francisco: NCCD.

Patrick, S., and Marsh, R. (2005). Juvenile diversion: results of a 3-year experimental study. *Criminal Justice Policy Review* 16(1): 59–73.

Severy, L. J., and Whitaker, J. M. (1982). Juvenile diversion: An experimental analysis of effectiveness. *Evaluation Review* 6(6): 753–774.

Day Fines (Compared to Standard Probation)

Turner, S., and Greene, J. (1999). The FARE probation experiment: implementation and outcomes of day fines for felony offenders in Maricopa County. *The Justice System Journal* 21(1): 1–21.

Diversion with Services (Compared to Regular Juvenile Court Processing)

Baron, R., Feeney, F., and Thornton, W. (1973). Preventing delinquency through diversion: The Sacramento County 601 diversion project. *Federal Probation* 37(1): 13–18.

Crofoot, J. A. (1987). A juvenile diversion program's effectiveness with varying levels of offender severity. Doctoral Dissertation, United States International University. Dissertation Abstracts International No. 8713047.

Davidson, W. S. II., and Redner, R. (1988). The prevention of juvenile delinquency: Diversion from the juvenile justice system. In R. H. Price, E. L. Cowen, R. P. Lorion, and J. Ramos-McKay (eds.), *14 ounces of prevention: A casebook for practitioners* (pp. 123–137). Washington, DC: American Psychological Association.

Dunford, F. W., Osgood, D. W, and Weichselbaum, H. F. (1982). National evaluation of diversion projects, executive summary and microfiche. U.S. Department of Justice.

Howard, W. L. (1997). The effects of tutoring, counseling and mentoring on altering the behavior of African American males in a juvenile diversion program. Dissertation: UMI 9717719.

Kelley, T. M., Schulman, J. L., and Lynch, K. (1976). Decentralized intake and diversion: The juvenile court's link to the youth service bureau. *Juvenile Justice* 27(1): 3–11.

King, W. R., Holmes, S. T., Henderson, M. L., and Latessa, E. J. (2001). The community corrections partnership: Examining the long-term effects of youth participation in an Afrocentric Diversion Program. *Crime and Delinquency* 47(4): 558–572.

Koch, J. R. (1986). Community service and outright release as alternatives to juvenile court: An experimental evaluation. Doctoral dissertation, Michigan State University, 1985. *Dissertation Abstracts International,* 46(07), 2081A. (University Microfilms No. 85-20537).

Lipsey, M. W., Cordray, D. S., and Berger, D. E. (1981). Evaluation of a juvenile diversion program using multiple lines of evidence. *Evaluation Review* 5(3): 283–306.

Myers, W., Burton, P., Sanders, P., Donat, K., Cheney, J., Fitzpatrick, T., and Monaco, L. (2000). Project Back-on-Track at 1 year: A delinquency treatment program for early-career juvenile offenders. *Journal of the American Academy of Child and Adolescent Psychiatry* 39(9): 1127–1134.

Palmer, T., and Lewis, R. V. (1980). *An evaluation of juvenile diversion.* Cambridge: Oelgeschlager, Gunn and Hain.

Quay, H. C., and Love, C. T. (1977). The effect of a juvenile diversion program on rearrests. *Criminal Justice and Behavior* 4: 377–396.

Rausch, S. (1983). Court processing versus diversion of status offenders: A test of deterrence and labeling theories. *Journal of Research in Crime and Delinquency* 20: 39–54.

Regoli, R., Wilderman, E., and Pogrebin, M. (1985). Using an alternative evaluation measure for assessing juvenile diversion programs. *Children and Youth Services Review* 7: 21–38.

Severy, L. J., and Whitaker, J. M. (1982). Juvenile diversion: An experimental analysis of effectiveness. *Evaluation Review* 6(6): 753–774.

Stratton, J. G. (1975). Effects of crisis intervention counseling on predelinquent and misdemeanor juvenile offenders. *Juvenile Justice* 26(4): 7–18.

Wiebush, R. G. (1985). Recidivism in the juvenile diversion project of the young volunteers in action program. Final Report.

Wooldredge, J., Hartman, I., Latessa, E., and Holmes, S. (1994). Effectiveness of culturally specific community treatment for African American juvenile felons. *Crime and Delinquency* 40(4): 589–598.

Diversion with Services (Compared to Simple Release)

Davidson, W. S. II., and Redner, R. (1988). The prevention of juvenile delinquency: Diversion from the juvenile justice system. In R. H. Price, E. L. Cowen, R. P. Lorion, and J. Ramos-McKay (eds.), *14 ounces of prevention: A casebook for practitioners* (pp. 123–137). Washington, DC: American Psychological Association.

Dunford, F. W., Osgood, D. W, and Weichselbaum, H. F. (1982). National evaluation of diversion projects, executive summary and microfiche. U.S. Department of Justice.

Koch, J. R. (1986). Community service and outright release as alternatives to juvenile court: An experimental evaluation. Doctoral dissertation, Michigan State University, 1985. *Dissertation Abstracts International,* 46(07), 2081A. (University Microfilms No. 85-20537).

Lipsey, M. W., Cordray, D. S., and Berger, D. E. (1981). Evaluation of a juvenile diversion program using multiple lines of evidence. *Evaluation Review* 5(3): 283–306.

Severy, L. J., and Whitaker, J. M. (1982). Juvenile diversion: An experimental analysis of effectiveness. *Evaluation Review* 6(6): 753–774.

Dangerous Mentally Ill Offenders

Lovell, D., Gagliardi, G. J., and Phipps, P. (2005). Washington's dangerous mentally ill offender law: Was community safety increased? Olympia, WA: Washington State Institute for Public Policy.

Domestic Violence Courts

Grover, A. R., MacDonald, J. M., Alpert, G. P., and Geary, I. A. Jr. (2003). The Lexington County domestic violence courts: A partnership and evaluation. National Institute of Justice Grant 2000-WT-VX-0015.

Newmark, L., Rempel, L., Diffily, K., and Kane, K. M. (2001). Specialized felony domestic violence courts: Lessons on implementations and impacts from the kings county experience. Washington, DC: Urban Institute. Available at: http://www.urban.org/Uploaded PDF/410381_DomViolCourts.pdf.

Drug Treatment in Jail

Dugan, J. R., and Everett, R. S. (1998). An experimental test of chemical dependency therapy for jail inmates. *International Journal of Offender Therapy and Comparative Criminology* 42(4): 360–368.

Knight, K., Simpson, D. D., and Hiller, M. L. (2003). Outcome Assessment of Correctional Treatment (OACT). Internet retrieval.

Peters, R. H., Kearns, W. D. Murrin, M. R., Dolente, A. S., and May, R. L. (1993). Examining the effectiveness of in-jail substance abuse treatment. *Journal of Offender Rehabilitation* 19: 1–39.

Taxman, F. S., and Spinner, D. L. (1997). Jail Addiction Services (JAS) demonstration project in Montgomery County, Maryland: Jail and community based substance abuse treatment program model. University of Maryland, College Park.

Tunis, S., Austin, J., Morris, M., Hardyman, P., and Bolyard, M. (1996). Evaluation of drug treatment in local corrections. Washington, DC: National Institute of Justice (May).

Drug Treatment in the Community

Aos, S., Phipps, P., and Barnoski, R. (2004).Washington's drug offender sentencing alternative: An evaluation of benefits and costs. Olympia: Washington State Institute for Public Policy.

Baird, C., Wagner, D., Decomo, B., and Aleman, T. (1994). Evaluation of the effectiveness of supervision and community rehabilitation programs in Oregon. National Council on Crime and Delinquency.

California Department of Corrections. (1997). Los Angeles prison parole network: An evaluation report. State of California.

Hepburn, J. R. (2005). Recidivism among drug offenders following exposure to treatment. *Criminal Justice Policy Review* 16: 237–259.

Lattimore, P. K., Krebs, C. P., Koeste, W., Lindquist, C., and Cowell, A. J. (2004). Predicting the effect of substance abuse treatment on probationer recidivism. *Journal of Experimental Criminology* 1(2): 159–189.

Early Childhood Education for Low-Income Three- and Four-Year-Olds

Campbell, F. A., Ramey, C. T., Pungello, E. P., Sparling, J., and Miller-Johnson, S. (2002). Early childhood education: young adult outcomes from the Abecedarian Project. *Applied Developmental Science* 6:42–57.

Garces, E., Thomas, D., and Currie, J. (2002). Long-term effects of Head Start. *American Economic Review* 92(4): 999–1012.

Lally, J. R., Mangione, P. I., and Honig, A. S. (1987). Long-range impact of an early intervention with low-income children and their families. San Francisco: Far West Laboratory for Educational Research and Development. The Center for Child and Family Studies.

Oden, S., Schweinhart, L., Welkart, D., Marcus, S., and Xie, Y. (2000). Into adulthood: A study of the effects of Head Start. Ypsilanti, MI: High/Scope Press.

Pagani, L, Tremplay, R. E., Vitaro, F., and Parent, S. (1998). Does preschool help prevent delinquency in boys with a history of perinatal complications? *Criminology* 36(2): 245–267.

Reynolds, A. J., Temple, J. A., Robertson, D. L., and Mann, E. A. (2002). Age 21 cost-benefit analysis of the Title I Chicago child-parent centers. *Educational Evaluation and Policy Analysis* 24(4): 267–303.

Schweinhart, L. J., Barnes, H. V., and Weikart, D. P. (1993). Significant benefits: The High/Scope Perry Preschool Study through age 27. Ypsilanti, MI: High/Scope Press.

Education/Cognitive–Behavioral Treatment, Domestic Violence

Chen, H., Bersani, C., Myers, S. C., and Denton, R. (1989). Evaluating the effectiveness of a court sponsored abuser treatment program. *Journal of Family Violence* 4(4): 309–322.

Davis, R. C., Taylor, B. G., and Maxwell, C. D. (2000). Does batterer treatment reduce violence? A randomized experiment in Brooklyn. Washington, DC: National Institute of Justice. Available at: http://www.ncjrs.gov/pdffiles1/nij/grants/180772.pdf.

Dunford, F. W. (2000). The San Diego navy experiment: An assessment of interventions for men who assault their wives. *Journal of Consulting and Clinical Psychology* 68:3): 468–476.

Feder, L., and Forde, D. R. (2000). A test of the efficacy of court-mandated counseling for domestic violence offenders: The Broward experiment. National Institute of Justice Grant NIJ96-WT-NX-0008. Final Report.

Gordon, J. A., and Moriarty, L. J. (2003). The effects of domestic violence batterer treatment on domestic violence recidivism: The Chesterfield County experience. *Criminal Justice and Behavior* 30(1): 118–134.

Harrell, A. (1991). *Evaluation of court-ordered treatment for domestic violence offenders.* Washington DC: The Urban Institute.

Labriola, M., Rempel, M., and Davies, R. C. (2005). Testing the effectiveness of batterer programs and judicial monitoring: Results from a randomized trial at the Bronx misdemeanor domestic violence court. Center for Court Innovation. Draft sent to M. Miller by M. Rempel.

Electronic Monitoring

Baird, C. Wagner, D., Decomo, B., and Aleman, T. (1994). Evaluation of the effectiveness of supervision and community rehabilitation programs in Oregon. National Council on Crime and Delinquency.

Bonta, J., Wallace-Capretta, S., and Rooney, J. (2000). Can electronic monitoring make a difference? An evaluation of three Canadian programs. *Crime and Delinquency* 46(1): 61–75.

Dodgson, K., Goodwin, P., Howard, P., Llewellyn-Thomas, S., Mortimer, E., Russell, N. et al. (2001). Electronic monitoring of released prisoners: An evaluation of the home detention curfew scheme (No. Home Office Research Study 222). London Home Office Research Development and Statistics Directorate.

Finn, M. A., and Muirhead-Stevens, S. (2002). The effectiveness of electronic monitoring with violent male parolees. *Justice Quarterly* 19(2): 293–312.

Jolin, A., and Stipak, B. (1992). Drug treatment and electronically monitored home confinement: An evaluation of a community-based sentencing option. *Crime and Delinquency* 38:158–170.

Jones, M., and Ross, D. L. (1997). Electronic house arrest and boot camp in North Carolina: Comparing recidivism. *Criminal Justice Policy Review* 8(4): 383–404.

Klien-Saffran, J. (1992). Electronic monitoring versus halfway houses: A study of federal offenders. Dissertation, obtained from UMI Dissertation Services.

Petersilia, J., and Turner, S. (1990). *Intensive supervision for high-risk probationers: Findings from three California experiments.* Santa Monica, CA: Rand.

Sugg, D., Moore, L., and Howard, P. (2001). Electronic monitoring and offending behaviour—reconviction results for the second year of trials of curfew orders. Findings #141. London Research, Development and Statistics Directorate, Home Office.

Employment Training and Job Assistance Programs in the Community

Anderson, D. B., and Schumacker, R. E. (1986). Assessment of job training programs. *Journal of Offender Counseling, Services, and Rehabilitation* 10: 41–49.

Beck, J. (1981). Employment, community treatment center placement and recidivism: A study of released federal offenders. *Federal Probation* (45): 3–8.

Beck, L. (1979). An evaluation of federal community treatment centers. *Federal Probation* (43): 36–40.

Berk, R. A., Lenihan, K. J., and Rossi, P. H. (1980). Crime and poverty: Some experimental evidence from ex-offenders. *American Sociological Review* 45: 766–786.

Bloom, H., Orr, L. O., Cave, G., Bell, S. H., Doolittle, F., and Lin, W. (1994). The National JTPA Study overview: Impacts, benefits and costs of Title II-A. Cambridge, MA: Abt Associates, Inc.

Cave, G., Bos, H., Doolittle, F., and Toussaint, C. (1993). Jobstart: Final report on a program for school dropouts. New York: Manpower Demonstration and Research Corporation.

Mallar, C. D., and Thornton, C. (1978). Transitional aid for released prisoners: Evidence from the life experiment. *The Journal of Human Resources* XIII(2): 208–236.

Menon, R., Blakely, C., Carmichael, D., and Snow, D. (1995). Making a dent in recidivism rates: Impact of employment on minority ex-offenders. In Thomas, G. E., (ed.), *Race and ethnicity in America: Meeting the challenge in the 21st century* (pp. 279–293). Washington, DC: Taylor & Francis. See also Finn, P. (1998). Texas' Project RIO (re-integration of offenders). Washington, DC: U.S. Department of Justice, June 1998.

Milkman, R. H. (1985). *Employment services for ex-offenders field test—Detailed research results*. McLean, VA: Lazar Institute.

Rossman, S., Sridharan, S., Gouvis, C., Buck, J., and Morley, E. (1999). Impact of the Opportunity to Succeed (OPTS) Aftercare Program for substance-abusing felons: Comprehensive final report. Washington, DC: The Urban Institute.

Schochet, P. Z., Burghardt, J., and Glazerman, S. (2001). National Job Corps study: The impacts of Job Corps on participants' employment and related outcomes. Mathematics Policy Research, Inc., Washington, DC: U.S. Department of Labor.

Uggen, C. (2000). Work as a turning point in the life course of criminals: A duration model of age, employment, and recidivism. *American Sociological Review* 67:529–546.

Faith-Based Programs for General Offenders

Burnside, J., Adler, J., Loucks, N., and Rose, G. (2001). Kainos community in prisons: Report of an evaluation RDS OLR 11/01. Presented to Research Development and Statistics Directorate, Home Office, HM Prison Service England and Wales and Kainos Community. Available at: http://www.homeoffice.gov.uk/rds/pdf/kainos_finalrep.pdf.

Johnson, B. R. (2004). Religious programs and recidivism among former inmates in prison fellowship programs: A long-term follow-up study. *Justice Quarterly* 21(2) 329–354.

O'Connor, T., Su, Y., Ryan, P., Parikh, C., and Alexander, E. (1997). Detroit transition of prisoners: Final evaluation report. Center for Social Research, MD.

Trusty, B., and Eisenberg, M. (2003). Initial process and outcome evaluation of the InnerChange Freedom Initiative: The faith-based prison program in TDCJ. Austin, TX: Criminal Justice Policy Council. Available at: http://www.cjpc.state.tx.us/reports/adltrehat/IFIInitiative.pdf.

Wilson, L. C., Wilson, C. Drummond, S. R., and Kelso, K. (2005). Promising effects on the reduction of criminal recidivism: an evaluation of the Detroit transition of prisoner's faith based initiative. Draft e-mailed to Marna Miller by Joe Williams.

Functional Family Therapy (Including Washington)

Alexander, J. F., and Parsons, B. F. (1973). Short-term behavioral intervention with delinquent families: Impact on family process and recidivism. *Journal of Abnormal Psychology* 81(3): 219–225.

Barnoski, R. (2004). Outcome evaluation of Washington State's research-based programs for juvenile offenders. Washington State Institute for Public Policy.

Barton, C., Alexander, J. F., Waldron, H., Turner, C. W., and Warburton, J. (1985). Generalizing treatment effects of functional family therapy: Three replications. *American Journal of Family Therapy* 13: 16–26.

Gordon, D. A. (1995). Functional family therapy for delinquents. In Ross, R. R., Antonowics, D., H., Dhaliwal, G. K., (eds.), *Going straight: Effective delinquency prevention and offender rehabilitation* (pp. 163–178). Ottawa, Ontario: Air training and Publications.

Gordon, D., Graves, K., and Arbuthnot, J. (1995). The effect of functional family therapy for delinquents on adult criminal behavior. *Criminal Justice and Behavior* 22(1): 60–73.

Hannson, K. (1998). Functional family therapy replication in Sweden: Treatment outcome with juvenile delinquents. Paper presented to the Eighth International Conference on Treating Addictive Behaviors. Santa Fe, NM, February 1998, as reported in: Alexander, J., Barton, C., Gordon, D., Grotpeter, J., Hansson, K., Harrison, R., Mears, S., Mihalic, S., Parsons, B., Pugh, C., Schulman, S., Waldron, H., and Sexton, T. (1998). *Blueprints for violence prevention, Book Three: Functional family therapy*. Boulder, CO: Center for the Study and Prevention of Violence.

Klein, N. C., Alexander, J. F., and Parsons, B. V. (1977). Impact of family systems intervention on recidivism and sibling delinquency: A model of primary prevention and program evaluation. *Journal of Consulting and Clinical Psychology* 45: 469–474.

Family Integrated Transitions (FIT)

Aos, S. (2004). Washington State's Family Integrated Transitions Program for juvenile offenders: Outcome evaluation and benefit-cost analysis. Olympia WA: Washington State Institute for Public Policy.

Guided Group Interaction

Allen, R. F., Dubin, H. N., Pilnick, S., and Youtz, A. C. (1970). Collegefields: From delinquency to freedom. Seattle: Special Child Publications, Inc.

Empey, L. T., and Erickson, M. L. (1972). *The Provo experiment: Evaluating community control of delinquency.* Lexington, MA: Lexington.

Empey, L. T., and Lubeck, S. G. (1971). *The Silverlake experiment: Testing delinquency theory and community intervention.* Chicago: Adine Publishing Company.

Stephenson, R. M., and Scarpitti, F. R. (1974). *Group interaction as therapy: The use of the small group in corrections contributions in sociology*, Number 13. Westport, CT: Greenwood Press.

Guiding Good Choices (Formerly PDFY)

Mason, W. A., Kosterman, R., Hawkins, J. D., Haggerty, K. P., and Spoth, R. L. (2003). Reducing adolescents' growth in substance use and delinquency: Randomized trial effects of a parent-training prevention intervention. *Prevention Science* 4(3): 203–212.

High School Graduation

Lochner, L., and Moretti, E. (2004), The effect of education on crime: Evidence from prison inmates, arrests, and self-reports. *American Economic Review* 94(1): 155–189.

Home Visiting during Pregnancy and Early Childhood

Barth, R. P. (1991). An experimental evaluation of in-home child abuse prevention services. *Child Abuse and Neglect* 15: 363–375.

Barth, R. P., Hacking, S., and Ash, J. R. (1988). Preventing child abuse: An experimental evaluation of the child parent enrichment project. *Journal of Primary Prevention* 8(4) 201–217.

Brayden, R. M., Altemeier, W. A., Dietrich, M. S., Tucker, D. D., Christensen, M. J., McLaughlin, F. J. et al. (1993). A prospective study of secondary prevention of child maltreatment. *Journal of Pediatrics* 122: 511–516.

Caruso, G. L. (1989). Optimum Growth Project: Support for families with young children. *Prevention in Human Services* 6: 123–139.

Center on Child Abuse Prevention Research, National Committee to Prevent Child Abuse. (June 1996). Intensive home visitation: A randomized trial, follow-up and risk assessment study of Hawaii's Healthy Start Program, Executive summary. Washington, DC: National Center on Child Abuse and Neglect, Administration for Children, Youth and Families, U.S. Department of Health and Human Services. NCCAN Grant No. 90-CA-1511.

Chambliss, J. W., and Emshoff, J. G. (1999). The evaluation of Georgia's Healthy Families Program. Results of Phase 1 and 2. EMSTAR Research, unpublished manuscript.

Duggan, A., McFarlane, E., Fuddy, L., Burrell, L., Higman, S. M., Windham, A., and Sia, A. (2004). Randomized trial of a statewide home visiting program: Impact in preventing child abuse and neglect. *Child Abuse and Neglect* 28: 597–622.

DuMont, K., Mitchell-Herzfeld, S., Greene, R., Lee, E., Lowenfels, A., and Rodriguez, M. (2006). Healthy Families New York (HFNY) randomized trial: Impacts on parenting after the first two years.

Earle, R. B. (1995). Helping to prevent child abuse—and future criminal consequences: Hawaii Healthy Start. Program Focus. NCJ 156216. Washington, DC: National Institute of Justice, Office of Justice Programs, U.S. Department of Justice.

Ernst, C. C., Grant, T. M., Streissguth, A. P., and Sampson, P. D. (1999). Intervention with high-risk alcohol and drug-abusing mothers: II. Three-year findings from the Seattle model of paraprofessional advocacy. *Journal of Community Psychology* 27(1): 19–38.

Galano, J., and Huntington, L. (1999). Year VI evaluation of the Hampton, Virginia, Healthy Families Partnership: 1992–1998. Hampton, Virginia, Healthy Families Partnership.

Gray, J. D., Cutler, C. A., Dean, J. G., and Kempe, C. H. (1979). Prediction and prevention of child abuse and neglect. *Journal of Social Issues* 35: 127–139.

Hardy, J. B., and Streett, R. (1989). Family support and parenting education in the home: An effective extension of clinic-based preventive health care services for poor children. *Journal of Pediatrics* 115: 927–931.

Huxley, P., and Warner, R. (1993). Primary prevention of parenting dysfunction in high-risk cases. *American Journal of Orthopsychiatry* 63(4): 582–588.

Landsverk, J., Carrilio, T., Connelly, C. D., Ganger, W. C., Slymen, D. J., Newton, R. R., Leslie, L., and Jones, C. (2002). Healthy Families San Diego clinical trial technical report. Child and Adolescent Services Research Center, San Diego Children's Hospital and Health Center.

Loman, L. A., and Sherburne, D. (2000). Intensive home visitation for mothers of drug-exposed infants: An evaluation of the St. Louis linkages program. St. Louis, MO: Institute of Applied Research.

Mulsow, M. H., and Murray, V. M. (1996). Parenting on edge: Economically stressed, single, African American adolescent mothers. *Journal of Family Issues* 17(5): 704–721.

Stevens-Simon, C., Nelligan, D., and Kelly, L. (2001). Adolescents at risk for mistreating their children Part II: A home-and clinic-based prevention program. *Child Abuse and Neglect* 25(6) 753–769.

Velasquez, J., Christensen, M., and Schommer, B. (1984). Part II: Intensive services help prevent child abuse. *American Journal of Maternity and Child Nursing* 9: 113–117.

Increased Drug Testing on Parole (Compared with Minimal Drug Testing)

Haapanen, R., and Britton, L. (2002). Drug testing for youthful offenders on parole: An experimental evaluation. *Criminology and Public Policy* 1(2): 217–244.

In-Prison Therapeutic Communities with Community Aftercare for Drug-Involved Offenders

Field, G. (1985). The Cornerstone Program: A client outcome study. *Federal Probation* 49: 50–55.

Knight, K., Simpson, D. D., and Hiller, M. L. (1999). Three-year reincarceration outcomes for in-prison therapeutic community treatment in Texas. *The Prison Journal* 79(3): 337–351.

Prendergast, M. L., Hall, E. A., Wexler, H. K., Melnick, G., and Cao, Y. (2004). Amity prison-based therapeutic community: 5-year outcomes. *The Prison Journal* 84(1):36–60.

In-Prison Therapeutic Communities without Community Aftercare for Drug-Involved Offenders

Belenko, S., Foltz, C., Lang, M. A., and Sun, H. (2004). Recidivism among high-risk drug felons: A longitudinal analysis following residential treatment. *Journal of Offender Rehabilitation* 40(1/2): 105–132.

Gransky, L. A., and Jones, R. J. (1995). Evaluation of the post-release status of substance abuse program participants. Illinois Criminal Justice Authority Report.

Klebe, K. J., and O'Keefe, M. (2004). Outcome evaluation of the Crossroads to Freedom House and Peer I therapeutic communities. National Institute of Justice Grant 99-RT-VX-K021.

Mosher, C., and Phillips, D. (2002). Program evaluation of the pine lodge pre-release residential therapeutic community for women offenders in Washington State, Final Report.
Oregon Department of Corrections. (1996). Evaluation of the Powder River and Turning Point Alcohol and Drug Treatment Programs. Salem, OR.
Swartz, J. A., Lurigo, A. J., and Slomka, S. A. (1996). The impact of IMPACT: An assessment of the effectiveness of a jail-based treatment program. *Crime and Delinquency* 42(4): 553–573.
Welsh, W. N. (2003). Evaluation of prison-based therapeutic community drug treatment programs in Pennsylvania. PA: Pennsylvania Commission on Crime and Delinquency.
Wexler, H. K., Falkin, G. H., Lipton, D. S., and Rosenblum, A. B. (1992). Outcome evaluation of a prison therapeutic community for substance abuse treatment. *Criminal Justice and Behavior* 17(1):71–92.
Wilson, R. J., Picheca, J. E., and Prinzo, M. (2005). Circles of support and accountability: An evaluation of the Pilot Project in South Central Ontario. Draft Report to Correctional Service of Canada, R-168, e-mailed to M. Miller, October 20, 2005.

Intensive Supervision of Sex Offenders in the Community

Stalans, L. J., Seng, M., Yarnold, P., Lavery, T., and Swartz, J. (2001). Process and initial evaluation of the Cook County Adult Probation Department's Sex Offender Program: Final and summary report for the period of June 1997 to June 2000. Chicago: Illinois Criminal Justice Information Authority. Available at: http://www.icjia.state.il.us/public/pdf/researchreports/An%20Implementation_Project%20in%20Cook%20County.pdf.
Stalans, L. J., Seng, M., amd Yarnold, P. R. (2002). Long-term impact evaluation of specialized sex offender probation programs in Lake, DuPage and Winnebago Counties. Chicago: Illinois Criminal Justice Information Authority. Available at: http://www.icjia.state.il.us/public/pdf/ResearchReports/Long-termDuPageWinnebago.pdf.

Jail Diversion (Pre- and Postbooking Programs), MICA Offenders

Broner, N., Lattimore, P. K., Cowell, A. J., and Schlenger, W. (2004). Effects of diversion on adults with mental illness co-occurring with substance use: Outcomes from a national multi-site study. *Behavior Sciences and the Law* 21: 1–23.
Christy, A., Poythress, N. G., Boothroyd, R. A., Petrila, J., and Mehra, S. (2005), Evaluating the efficiency and community safety goals of the Broward County Mental Health Court. *Behavioral Sciences and the Law* 23(2): 227–243.
Cosden, M., Ellens, J., Schnell, J., and Yamini-Diouf, J. (2004). Evaluation of the Santa Barbara County Mental Health Treatment Court with Intensive Case Management. University of California, Santa Barbara.
Steadman, H. J., Cocozza, J. J., and Veysey, B. M. (1999). Comparing outcomes for diverted and nondiverted jail detainees with mental illnesses. *Law and Human Behavior* 23(6): 615–627.

Juvenile Justice Other Family-Based Therapy Approaches

Bank, L., Marlowe, J. H., Reid, J. B., Patterson, G. R., and Weinrott, M. R. (1991). A comparative evaluation of parent-training interventions for families of chronic delinquents. *Journal of Abnormal Child Psychology* 19(1): 15–33.

Byles, J. A., and Maurice, A. (1979). The juvenile services project: An experiment in delinquency control. *Canadian Journal of Criminology* 21: 257–262.

Gruher, M. (1979). Family counseling and the status offender. *Juvenile and Family Court Journal* 30: 23–27.

Hinton, W. J. (2004). Examining the impact of a family systems counseling approach for reducing the recidivism rates of first offender juveniles. Unpublished Ph.D. Thesis. Mississippi State University.

McPherson, S. J., McDonald, L. E., and Ryer, C. W. (1983). Intensive counseling with families of juvenile offenders. *Juvenile and Family Court Journal* 34: 27–33.

Metzger, D. S. (1997). School-based probation in Pennsylvania (Final Report). Philadelphia: University of Pennsylvania, Center for Studies of Addiction. As described in Creating a New Criminal Justice System for the 21st Century, Bureau of Justice Assistance.

Moore, R. H. (1987). Effectiveness of citizen volunteers functioning as counselors for high-risk young male offenders. *Psychological Reports* 61: 823–830.

Quinn, W. H., and Van Dyke, D. J. (2004). A multiple family group intervention for first-time juvenile offenders: Comparisons with probation and dropouts on recidivism. *Journal of Community Psychology* 32(2): 177–200.

Schwitzgebel, R., and Kolb, D. A. (1964). Inducing behaviour change in adolescent delinquents. *Behavioural Research Therapy* 1: 297–304.

Shore, M. F., and Massimo, J. L. (1979). Fifteen years after treatment: A follow-up study of comprehensive vocationally oriented psychotherapy. *American Journal of Orthopsychiatry* 49: 240–245.

Spence, S. H., and Marzillier, J. S. (1981). Social skills training with adolescent male offenders: 11. Short-term, long-term and generalized effects. *Behavior Research and Therapy* 19: 349–368.

Stringfield, N. (1977). The impact of family counseling in resocialization adolescent offenders within a positive peer treatment milieu. *Offender Rehabilitation* 1:349–360.

Juvenile Behavior Modification

Jesness, C. F. (1975). Comparative effectiveness of behavior modification and transactional analysis programs for delinquents. *Journal of Consulting and Clinical Psychology* 43(6): 758–779.

Sarason, I. G. (1978). A cognitive social learning approach to juvenile delinquency. In Hare, R. D., and Schalling, D. (eds.), *Psychopathic behaviour: Approaches to research.* Chichester, UK: John Wiley and Sons.

Juvenile Boot Camp

Aloisi, M., and LeBaron, J. (2001). The juvenile justice commission's stabilization and reintegration program: An updated recidivism analysis. New Jersey Dept. of Law and Public Safety.

Barnoski, R. (2004). Washington's juvenile basic training camp: Outcome evaluation, Olympia: Washington State Institute for Public Policy.

Bottcher, J., and Ezell, M. E. (2005). Examining the effectiveness of boot camps: A randomized experiment with a long-term follow up. *Journal of Research in Crime and Delinquency* 42(3): 309–332.

Florida Department of Juvenile Justice. (1996). Leon County Sheriff's Department Boot Camp: A follow-up study of the first five platoons. Prepared by the Bureau of Data and Research, Management Report Number 35.

Florida Department of Juvenile Justice. (1996). Pinellas County Boot Camp: A follow-up study of the first four platoons. Prepared by the Bureau of Data and Research, Management Report Number 33.

Florida Department of Juvenile Justice. (1997). Polk County Juvenile Boot Camp: A follow-up study of the first four platoons. Prepared by the Bureau of Data and Research, Management Report Number 46.

Florida Department of Juvenile Justice. (1996). Manatee County Sheriff's Department Boot Camp: A follow-up study of the first seven platoons. Prepared by the Bureau of Data and Research, Management Report Number 24.

Florida Department of Juvenile Justice. (1997). Bay County Sheriff's Office Juvenile Boot Camp: A follow-up study of the first seven platoons. Prepared by the Bureau of Data and Research, Management Report Number 44.

Florida Department of Juvenile Justice. (1997). Martin County Sheriff's Office Juvenile Boot Camp: A follow-up study of the first four platoons. Prepared by the Bureau of Data and Research, Management Report Number 43.

Peters, M., Thomas, D., and Zamberlan, C. (1997). Boot camps for juvenile offenders. Office of Juvenile Justice and Delinquency Prevention.

Trulson, C., R., Triplett, R., and Snell, C. (2001). Social control in a school setting: Evaluating a school-based boot camp. *Crime and Delinquency* 47(4): 573–609.

Zhang, S. X. (2000). An evaluation of the Los Angeles County juvenile drug treatment boot camp, final report. San Marcos, CA: California State University at San Marcos.

Juvenile Cognitive–Behavioral

Bottcher, J. (1985). The Athena Program: An evaluation of a girl's treatment program at the Fresno County Probation Department's Juvenile Hall. Sacramento: California Youth Authority.

Cann, J., Falshaw, L., Nugent, F., and Friendship, C. (2003). Understanding what works: Accredited cognitive skills programmes for adult men and young offenders. Research Findings No. 226. London: Home Office.

Guerra, N. G., and Slaby, R. G. (1990). Cognitive mediators of aggression in adolescent offenders: 2. Intervention. *Developmental Psychology* 26: 269–277.

Hubbard, D. J., and Latessa, E. J. (2004). Final Report. Evaluation of Cognitive-Behavioral programs for offenders: A look at outcome and responsivity in five treatment programs. Division of Criminal Justice, University of Cincinnati.

Leeman, L. W., Gibbs, J. C., and Fuller, D. (1993). Evaluation of a multi-component group treatment program for juvenile delinquents. *Aggressive Behavior* 19: 281–292.

Mitchell, J., and Palmer, E. J. (2004). Evaluation the Reasoning and Rehabilitation program for young offenders. *Journal of Offender Rehabilitation* 39(4):31–45.

Pullen, S. (1996). Evaluation of the reasoning and rehabilitation cognitive skills development program as implemented in juvenile ISP in Colorado. Denver: Colorado Department of Public Safety, Division of Criminal Justice. Available at: http://dcj.state.co.us/ors/pdf/docs/cog96.pdf.

Robertson, A. A., Grimes, P. W., and Rogers, K. E. (2001). A short-run cost-benefit analysis of community-based interventions for juvenile offenders. *Crime and Delinquency* 47(2): 265–285.

Juvenile Curfews

McDowall, D., Loftin, C., and Wiersema, B. (2000). The impact of youth curfew laws on juvenile crime rates. *Crime and Delinquency* 46(1): 76–91.

Juvenile Day Reporting

Byles, J. A. (1981). Evaluation of an attendance center program for male juvenile probationers. *Canadian Journal of Criminology* 23: 343–355.

Velasquez, J. S., and Lyle, C. G. (1985). Day versus residential treatment for juvenile offenders: The impact of program evaluation. *Child Welfare* 64(2): 145–156.

Juvenile Drug Courts

Anspach, D. F., Ferguson, A. S., and Phillips, L. L. (2003). Evaluation of Maine's statewide juvenile drug treatment court program. Augusta, ME: University of Southern Maine.

Byrnes, E. C., and Hickert, A. O. (2004). Process and outcome evaluation of the third district juvenile drug court in Dona Ana County, New Mexico. Glacier Consulting Inc.

Carey, S. M. (2004). Clackamas County juvenile drug court outcome evaluation: Final report. Portland, OR: NPC Research, Inc.

Gilmore, A. S., Rodriguez, N., and Webb, V. J. (2005). Substance abuse and drug courts: The role of social bonds in juvenile drug courts. *Youth Violence and Juvenile Justice* 3(4): 287–315.

Hartmann, D. J., Rhineberger, G. M., Gregory, P., Mullins, M., Tollini, C., and Williams, Y. (2003). Evaluation of the Kalamazoo County juvenile drug treatment court program: October 1, 2001–September 30, 2002 Year 5. Kalamazoo, Michigan: Kercher Center for Social Research, Western Michigan University.

Henggeler, S. W., Halliday-Boykins, C. A., Cunningham, P. B., Randall, J., Shapiro, S.B, and Chapman, J. E. (2006). Juvenile drug court: Enhancing outcomes by integrating evidence-based treatments. *Journal of Consulting and Clinical Psychology* 74(1): 42–54.

Huff, D., Stageberg, P., Wilson, B. S., and Moore, R. G. (nd). An assessment of the Polk County juvenile drug court. Des Moines: Iowa Department of Human Rights, Division of Criminal and Juvenile Justice Planning and Statistical Analysis Center.

Latessa, E. J., Shaffer, D. K., and Lowenkamp C. (2002, July). Outcome evaluation of Ohio's drug court efforts: Final report. Cincinnati: Center for Criminal Justice Research, Division of Criminal Justice, University of Cincinnati.

LeGrice, L. N. (2003). Effectiveness of juvenile drug court on reducing delinquency. Doctoral dissertation, University of Texas at Arlington.

Nebraska Crime Commission. (2004). Tri-county juvenile drug court evaluation final report (PDF). Available at: http://www.ncc.state.ne.us/pdf/juvenile_justice_materials/2004_DTC_Report.pdf.

O'Connell, J. P., Nestlerode, E., and Miller, M. L. (1999). Evaluation of the juvenile drug court diversion program. State of Delaware Executive Department, Statistical Analysis Center, October 1999.

Parsons, B. V., and Byrnes, E. C. (nd). Byrne evaluation partnership program final report. University of Utah Social Research Institute.

Pitts, W. J., and Guerin, P. (2004). Evaluation of the eleventh judicial district court San Juan County juvenile drug court: Quasi-experimental outcome study using historical information. Institute for Social Research, University of New Mexico.

Juvenile Education Programs

Bednar, R. L., Zelhart, P. F., Greathouse, L., and Weinberg, S. (1970). Operant conditioning principles in the treatment of learning and behavior problems with delinquent boys. *Journal of Counseling Psychology* 17(6): 492–497.

Odell, B. N. (1974). Accelerating entry into the opportunity structure: A sociologically-based treatment for delinquent youth. *Sociology and Social Research* 58(3): 312–317.

Texas Youth Commission. (1993). The relationship between GED attainment and recidivism, an evaluation summary. Texas Youth Commission Department of Research and Planning.

Juvenile Intensive Parole Supervision

Barnoski, R. (2002). Evaluating how juvenile rehabilitation administration's intensive parole program affects recidivism. Olympia: Washington State Institute for Public Policy.

Greenwood, P. W., Deschenes, E. P., and Adams, J. (1993). Chronic juvenile offenders: Final results from the skillman aftercare experiment. Santa Monica: RAND.

Rodriguez-Labarca, J., and O'Connell, J. P., (2004). Delaware's serious juvenile offender program: An evaluation of the first two years of operation. State of Delaware, Statistical Analysis Center, Doc Num: 100208-040204.

Schwitzgebel, R. K., and Baer, D. J. (1967). Intensive supervision by parole officers as a factor in recidivism reduction of male delinquents. *The Journal of Psychology* 67: 75–82.

Sealock, M. D., Gottfredson, D. C., and Gallagher, C. A. (1997). Drug treatment for juvenile offenders: Some good and bad news. *Journal of Research in Crime and Delinquency* 34(2): 210–236.

Sontheimer, H., and Goodstein, L. (1993). Evaluation of juvenile intensive aftercare probation: Aftercare versus system response effects. *Justice Quarterly* 10: 197–227.

Weibush, R. G., Wagner, D., McNultly, B., Wang, Y., and Le, T. (2005). Implementation and outcome evaluation of the intensive aftercare program, final report. Office of Juvenile Justice and Delinquency Prevention. Washington DC: U.S. Department of Justice.

Juvenile Intensive Probation (As an Alternative to Incarceration)

Barton, W. H., and Butts, J. A. (1990). Viable options: Intensive supervision programs for juvenile delinquents. *Crime and Delinquency* 36(2): 238–256.

Deschenes, E. P., and Greenwood, P. (1998). Alternative placements for juvenile offenders: Results from the evaluation of the Nokomis Challenge Program. *The Journal of Research in Crime and Delinquency* 35(3): 267–294.

Gottfredson, D. C., and Barton, W. H. (1993). Deinstitutionalization of juvenile offenders. *Criminology* 31(4): 591–611.

Lerman, P. (1975). *Community treatment and social control.* Chicago: University of Chicago Press.

Weibush, R. G. (1993). Juvenile intensive supervision: the impact on felony offenders diverted from institutional placement. *Crime and Delinquency* 39(1): 68–89.

Juvenile Intensive Probation Supervision

Barnoski, R. (2003). Evaluation of Washington's 1996 Juvenile Court Program (Early Intervention Program) for High-risk, First-time Offenders: Final Report. Olympia: Washington State Institute for Public Policy.

Land, K. C., McCall, P. L., and Parker, K. F. (1994). Logistic versus hazards regression analysis in evaluation research: An exposition and application to the North Carolina Court Counselors' Intensive Protective Supervision Project. *Evaluation Review* 18(4):411–37.

Robertson, A. A., Grimes, P. W., and Rogers, K. E. (2001). A short-run cost-benefit analysis of community-based interventions for juvenile offenders. *Crime and Delinquency* 47(2): 265–285.

Juvenile Jobs Programs

Hackler, J. C., and Hagan, J. L. (1975). Work and teaching machines as delinquency prevention tools: A four-year follow-up. *Social Service Review* 49:92–106.

Minor, K. I. (1988). An evaluation of an intervention program for juvenile probationers. Doctoral dissertation, Western Michigan University. UMI No. 8827331.

Willman, M. T., and Snortum, J. R. (1982). A police program for employment of youth gang members. *International Journal of Offender Therapy and Comparative Criminology* 26: 207–214.

Juvenile Offender Interagency Coordination

Barnoski, R. (2004). Outcome evaluation of Washington State's research-based programs for juvenile offenders, Washington State Institute for Public Policy.

Bottoms, A. E. (1995). *Intensive community supervision for young offenders: outcomes, process and cost.* Cambridge: University of Cambridge Publications.

California Board of Corrections. (2002). Repeat offender prevention program, final report. Sacramento: California Board of Corrections, December 2002.

Carney, M. M., and Buttell, F. (2003). Reducing juvenile recidivism: Evaluating the wrap-around services model. *Research on Social Work Practice* 13(5): 551–568.

Fagan, J., and Reinarman, C. (1991). The social context of intensive supervision: Organizational and ecological influences on community treatment. In T. L. Armstrong, (ed.), *Intensive interventions with high risk youth* (pp. 341–394). New York: Willow Tree Press.

Giblin, M. J. (2002), Using police officers to enhance the supervision of juvenile probationers: An evaluation of the Anchorage CAN program. *Crime and Delinquency* 48(1): 116–137.

Howard, L., Mish, G., Burke, C., and Pennell, S. (2002). San Diego county probation department's repeat offender prevention program final evaluation report. San Diego Regional Planning Agency, October 2002.

King County Juvenile Justice Evaluation Work Group. (2002). New Start: Juvenile justice evaluation report July 1999–March 2002. King County Washington Department of Community and Human Services.

Lane, J., Turner, S., Fain, F., and Sehgal, A. (2005). Evaluating an experimental intensive juvenile probation program: Supervision and official outcomes. *Crime and Delinquency* 51(1): 26–52.

Little, M., Kogan, J., Bullock, R., and Van Der Laan, P. (2004). ISSP: An evaluation in multi-systemic responses to persistent young offenders known to children's services. *British Journal of Criminology* 44(2): 225–240.

National Council on Crime and Delinquency. (1987). The impact of juvenile court intervention. San Francisco: NCCD.

Tolan, P., Perry, H., Shelley, M., and Jones, T. (1987). Delinquency prevention: An example of consultation in rural community mental health. *Journal of Community Psychology* 15: 43–50.

Zhang, S. X., and Zhang, L. (2005). An experimental study of the Los Angeles county repeat offender prevention program: Its implementation and evaluation. *Criminology and Public Policy* 4(2): 205–236.

Juvenile Sex Offender Treatment

Borduin, C. M., Henggeler, S. W., Blaske, D. M., and Stein, R. (1990). Multisystemic treatment of adolescent sexual offenders. *International Journal of Offender Therapy and Comparative Criminology* 35: 105–114.

Borduin, C. M., Schaeffer, C. M., and Heiblum, N. (2000). Multisystemic treatment of aggressive and nonaggressive sexual offending in adolescents: Instrumental and ultimate outcomes. Manuscript in preparation.

Guarino-Ghezzi, G. S., and Kimball, L. M. (1998). Juvenile sex offenders in treatment. *Corrections Management Quarterly* 2: 45–54.

Lab, S. P., Shields, G., and Schondel, C. (1993). Research note: An evaluation of juvenile sexual offender treatment. *Crime and Delinquency* 39(4): 543–553.

Worling, J. R., and Curwen, T. (2000). Adolescent sexual offender recidivism: Success of specialized treatment and implications for risk prediction. *Child Abuse and Neglect* 24(7): 965–982.

Juvenile Therapeutic Community

Pealer, J. A. (2004). A community of peers—Promoting behavior change: The effectiveness of a therapeutic community for juvenile male offenders in reducing recidivism. Unpublished Ph.D. Thesis. University of Cincinnati.

Juvenile Wilderness Challenge

Castellano, T. C., and Soderstrom, I. R. (1992). Therapeutic wilderness programs and juvenile recidivism: A program evaluation. *Journal of Offender Rehabilitation*: 17(3/4): 19–46.

Cytrynbaum, S., and Ken, K. (1975). The Connecticut Wilderness program: A preliminary evaluation report. Hartford, CT: The Council on Human Services.

Deschenes, E. P., and Greenwood, P. (1998). Alternative placements for juvenile offenders: Results from the evaluation of the Nokomis Challenge Program. *The Journal of Research in Crime and Delinquency* 35(3): 267–294.

Elrod, H. P., and Minor, K. (1992). Second wave evaluation of a multi-faceted intervention for juvenile court probationers. *International Journal of Offender Therapy and Comparative Criminology* 36(3): 247–262.

Hileman, M. A. (1979). An evaluation of an environmental stress-challenge program on the social attitudes and recidivism behavior of male delinquent youth. Unpublished master's thesis, Southern Illinois University, Carbondale. Results cited in: West, S. T., and Crompton, J. L. (1999). Do outdoor adventure programs alleviate negative behavior among at-risk youth? A review of the empirical literature. Available at: http://rptsweb.tamu.edu/Faculty/Witt/conpubs/crompt.pdf.

Kelly, F. J., and Baer, D. J. (1971). Physical challenge as a treatment for delinquency. *Crime and Delinquency* 17(4): 437–445.

Metametrics, Inc. (1984). Evaluation of the breakthrough foundation youth at risk program: The 10-day course and follow-up program.

Willman, H. C., and Chun, R. Y. F. (1973). Homeward bound: An alternative to the institutionalization of adjudicated juvenile offenders. *Federal Probation* 37:52–58.

Winterdyk, J., and Roesch, R. (1982). A wilderness experiential program as an alternative for probationers: An evaluation. *Canadian Journal of Criminology* 24: 39–49.

Life Skills Education Programs

Jolin, A., Day, M., Christophersen, K., Friedman, S., Newton, S., and Hooper, R. (1997). An evaluation of the WICSW-Lifeskills Program for women at the Columbia River Correctional Institution: Preliminary results. Portland State University, College of Urban and Public Affairs.

Melton, R., and Pennell, S. (1998). Staying out successfully: An evaluation of an in-custody life skills training program. San Diego, CA: Association of Governments.

Miller, M. L. (1997). Evaluation of the Life Skills Program. Division of Correctional Education, Department of Corrections, Delaware. Wilmington, Delaware.

Life Skills Education Programs for Juvenile Offenders

Department of the Youth Authority, State of California. (1985). Program Research and Review Division. Assessment of Planned Re-Entry Program (PREP).

Josi, D. A., and Sechrest, D. K. (1999). A pragmatic approach to parole aftercare: Evaluation of a community reintegration program for high-risk youthful offenders. *Justice Quarterly* 16(1): 51–80.

Medical Treatment of Sex Offenders

Wille, R., and Beier, K. M. (1989). Castration in Germany. *Annals of Sex Research* 2: 103–133.

Mentoring (Juvenile Justice)

Drake, E., and Barnoski, R. (2006). Recidivism findings for the Juvenile Rehabilitation Administration's mentoring program: Final report. Olympia, WA. Washington State Institute for Public Policy. Available at: http://www.wsipp.wa.gov/rptfiles/06-07-1202.pdf.

Mixed Treatment—Sex Offenders

Hanson, R. K., Broom, I., and Stephenson, M. (2004). Evaluating community sex offender treatment programs: A 12-year follow-up of 724 offenders. *Canadian Journal of Behavioural Science* 36(2): 87–96.

Song, L., and Lieb, R. (1995). Washington state sex offenders: Overview of recidivism studies. Olympia: Washington State Institute for Public Policy.

Multisystemic Therapy

Borduin, C. M., Henggeler, S. W., Blaske, D. M., and Stein, R. (1990). Multisystemic treatment of adolescent sexual offenders. *International Journal of Offender Therapy and Comparative Criminology* 35: 105–114.

Borduin, C. M., and Schaeffer, C. M. (2001). Multisystemic treatment of juvenile sexual offenders: a progress report.

Cunningham, A. (2002). Randomized study of MST in Ontario, Canada. Available at: http://www.lfcc.on.ca/mst_final_results.html.

Henggeler, S. W., Halliday-Boykins, C. A., Cunningham, P. B., Randall, J., Shapiro, S. B., and Chapman, J. E. (2006). Juvenile drug court: Enhancing outcomes by integrating evidence-based treatments. *Journal of Consulting and Clinical Psychology* 74(1): 42–54.

Henggeler, S. W., Clingempeel, W. G., Brondino, M. J., and Pickrel, S. G. (2002). Four-year follow-up of multisystemic therapy with substance-abusing and substance-dependent juvenile offenders. *Journal of the American Academy of Child and Adolescent Psychiatry* 41(7): 868–874.

Henggeler, S. W., Melton, G. B., Brondino, M. J., Scherer, D. G., and Hanley, J. H. (1997). Multisystemic therapy with violent and chronic juvenile offenders and their families: The role of treatment fidelity in successful dissemination. *Journal of Consulting and Clinical Psychology* 65: 821–833.

Henggeler, S. W., Melton, G. B., Smith, L. A., Schoenwald, S. K., and Hanley, J. H. (1993). Family preservation using multisystemic therapy: Long-term follow-up to a clinical trial with serious juvenile offenders. *Journal of Child and Family Studies* 2(4): 283–293.

Ogden, T., and Halliday-Boykins, C. A. (2004). Multisystemic treatment of antisocial adolescents in Norway: Replication of clinical outcomes outside of the U.S. *Child and Adolescent Mental Health* 9(2): 77–83.

Schaeffer, C. M., and Borduin, C. M. (2005). Long-term follow-up to a randomized clinical trial of multisystemic therapy with serious and violent juvenile offenders. *Journal of Consulting and Clinical Psychology* 73(3): 445–453.

Timmons-Mitchell, J., Bender, M. B., Kishna, M. A., and Mitchell, C. C. (2006). An independent effectiveness trial of multisystemic therapy with juvenile justice youth. *Journal of Clinical Child and Adolescent Psychology* 35(2):227–236.

Multidimensional Treatment Foster Care

Chamberlain, P. (1990). Comparative evaluation of specialized foster care for seriously delinquent youths: A first step. Community Alternatives: *International Journal of Family Care* 2: 21–36.

Chamberlain, P., Fisher, P. A., and Moore, K. (2002). Multidimensional treatment foster care: Applications of the OSLC intervention model to high-risk youth and their families. In Reid, J. B., Patterson, G. R., and Snyder, J. J. (eds.), *Antisocial behavior in children and adolescents: Developmental analysis and the Oregon model for intervention.* Washington DC: American Psychological Association.

Leve, L. D., Chamberlain, P., and Reid, J. B. (2005). Intervention outcomes for girls referred from juvenile justice: Effects on delinquency. *Journal of Consulting and Clinical Psychology* 73(6):1181–1185.

Nurse Family Partnership for Low-Income Mothers—Child Outcomes

Olds, D., Henderson, C. R., Cole, R. et al. (1998). Long-term effects of nurse home visitation on children's criminal and antisocial behavior: 15-year follow-up of a randomized trial. *The Journal of the American Medical Association* 280(14): 1238–1244.

Nurse Family Partnership for Low-Income Mothers—Mother Outcomes

Olds, D. L., Eckenrode, J. et al. (1997). Long-term effects of home visitation on maternal life course and child abuse and neglect. *Journal of the American Medical Association* 278(8): 637.

Parole/No Parole

Drake, E., and Barnoski, R. (2006). The effects of parole on recidivism: Juvenile offenders released from Washington State institutions, final report. Olympia: Washington State Institute for Public Policy, Document No. 06-05-1203.

Jackson, P. C. (1983). Some effects of parole supervision on recidivism. *British Journal of Criminology* 23: 17–34.

Parent Child Interaction Therapy (PCIT)

Chaffin, M., Silovsky, J. F., Funderburk, B., Valle, L. A., Brestan, E. V., Balachova, T., Jackson, S., Lensgraf, J., and Bonner, B. L. (2004). Parent–child interaction therapy with physically abusive parents: Efficacy for reducing future abuse reports. *Journal of Consulting and Clinical Psychology* 2(3): 500–510.

Psychotherapy for Sex Offenders

Hanson, R. K., Steffy, R. A., and Gauthier, R. (1993). Long term recidivism of child molesters. *Journal of Consulting and Clinical Psychology* 61: 646–652.

Nutbrown, V., and Stasiak, E. (1987). Research monograph: A retrospective analysis of O.C.I. cost effectiveness 1977–1981. Ontario Correctional Institute.

Romero, J. J., and Williams, L. M. (1983). Group psychotherapy and intensive probation supervision with sex offenders: A comparative study. *Federal Probation* 47: 36–42.

Regular Supervision Compared to No Supervision

Solomon, A. L., Kachnowski, V., Bhati, A. (2005). Does parole work? Analyzing the impact of postprison supervision on rearrest outcomes. Washington, DC: The Urban Institute.

Restorative Justice Programs for Lower Risk Adult Offenders

Bonta, J., Wallace-Capretta, S., and Rooney, J. (2000). A quasi-experimental evaluation of an intensive rehabilitation supervision program. *Criminal Justice and Behavior* 27(3): 312–329.

Dignan, J. (1990). Repairing the damage: An evaluation of an experimental adult reparation scheme in Kettering, Northamptonshire. Sheffield, UK: Centre for Criminological and Legal Research, Faculty of Law, University of Sheffield.

Paulin, J., Kingi, V., and Lash, B. (2005). The rotorua second chance community-managed restorative justice programme: An evaluation. Available at: http://www.justice.govt.nz/pubs/reports/2005/rotorua-second-chance-community-managed-restorative-justice/index.html.

Paulin, J., Kingi, V., and Lash, B. (2005). The Wanganui community-managed Restorative Justice Programme: An evaluation. Available at: http://www.justice.govt.nz/pubs/reports/2005/wanganui-community-managed-restorative-justice/.

Rugge, T., Bonta, J., and Wallace-Capretta, S. (2005). Evaluation of the collaborative justice project: A restorative justice program for serious crime. Public Safety and Emergency Preparedness Canada. Ottawa, Ontario, Canada. Available at: http://www.psepc-sp-pcc.gc.ca/publications/Corrections/cjp/cjp_toc_e.asp.

Triggs, S. (2005). New Zealand court-referred restorative justice pilot: Evaluation. Prepared by the Crime and Justice Research Centre, Victoria University of Wellington, Ministry of Justice.

Restorative Justice—Juveniles

Evje, A., and Cushman, R. (2000). A summary of the evaluations of six California victim offender rehabilitation programs. San Francisco, CA: Judicial Council of California, Administrative Office of the Courts.

Luke, G., and Lind, B. (1998). Reducing juvenile crime: Conferencing versus court. Sydney, Australia: New South Wales Bureau of Crime and Statistics and Research. Available at: http://www.lawlink.nsw.gov.au/lawlink/bocsar/ll_bocsar.nsf/vwFiles/CJB69.pdf/$file/CJB69.pdf.

McCold, P., and Wachtel, B. (1998). Restorative policing experiment: The Bethlehem police family group conferencing project. Community Service Foundation. Pipersville, PA.

McGarrell, E. F. (2001). Restorative justice conferences as an early response to young offenders. Juvenile Justice Bulletin (August). Washington, DC: U.S. Department of Justice, Office of Justice Programs, Office of Juvenile Justice and Delinquency Prevention. Available at: http://www.ncjrs.org/pdffiles1/ojjdp/187769.pdf.

Niemeyer, M., and Shichor, D. (1996). A preliminary study of a large victim/offender reconciliation program. *Federal Probation* 60(3): 30–34.

Nugent, W., and J. B. Paddock. (1996). Evaluating the effects of a victim-offender reconciliation program on reoffense. *Research on Social Work Practice* 6(2): 155–178.

Rowe, W. (2002). A meta-analysis of six Washington state restorative justice projects. Bellingham, WA: Cambie Group International, Inc.

Roy, S. (1993). Two types of juvenile restitution programs in two midwestern counties: A comparative study. *Federal Probation* 57(4): 48–53.

Schneider, A. L. (1986). Restitution and recidivism rates of juvenile offenders: Results from four experimental studies. *Criminology* 24(3): 533–553.

Sherman, L. W., Strang, H., and Woods, D. J. (2000). Recidivism patterns in the Canberra Reintegrative Shaming Experiments (RISE). Canberra, Australia: Centre for Restorative Justice, Research School of Social Sciences, Australian National University. Available at: http://www.aic.gov.au/rjustice/rise/recidivism/report.pdf.

Stone, S., Helms, W., and Edgeworth, P (1998). Cobb County juvenile court mediation program evaluation. State University of West Georgia.

Umbreit, M. S. (1994). *Victim meets offender: The impact of restorative justice and mediation.* Monsey, NY: Willow Tree Press.

Wade, K., Swenson, D., Miller, D., and Sager, S. (2004). An evaluation of restorative justice programs in Milwaukee and Outagamie counties. Madison Wisconsin: Legislative Audit Bureau.

Wiinamaki, L. A. (1997). Victim-offender reconciliation programs: Juvenile property offender recidivism and severity of reoffense in three Tennessee counties. Doctoral dissertation, University of Tennessee, Knoxville. UMI No. 9823140.

Scared Straight

Buckner, J. C., and Chesney-Lind, M. (1983). Dramatic cures for juvenile crime: An evaluation of a prisoner-run delinquency prevention program. *Criminal Justice and Behavior* 10(2): 227–247.

Cook, D. D., and Spirrison, C. L. (1992). Effects of a prisoner-operated delinquency deterrence program: Mississippi's Project Aware. *Journal of Offender Rehabilitation* 17: 89–99.

Finchkenauer, J. O., and Gavin, P. W. (1999). *Scared Straight: The panacea phenomenon revisited.* Prospect Heights, IL: Waveland Press.

Greater Eygpt Regional Planning and Development Commission. (1979). Menard Correctional Center: Juvenile tours impact study. Carbondale, IL.

Lewis, R. V. (1983). Scared straight—California style: Evaluation of the San Quentin Squires program. *Criminal Justice and Behavior* 10(2): 209–226.

Locke, T. P., Johnson, G. M., Kirigin-Ramp, K., Atwater, J. D., and Gerrard, M. (1986). An evaluation of a juvenile education program in a state penitentiary. *Evaluation Review* 10(3): 281–298.

Michigan Department of Corrections. (1967). A six month follow-up of juvenile delinquents visiting the Ionia Reformatory (Research Report No. 4). Lansing: Michigan Department of Corrections, May.

Orchowsky, S., and Taylor, K. (1981). The insiders juvenile crime prevention program: An assessment of a juvenile awareness program. Richmond: Virginia Department of Corrections.

Vreeland, A. D. (1981). Evaluation of Face-to Face: A juvenile aversion program. Unpublished doctoral dissertation, University of Texas, Dallas.

Yarborough, J. C. (1979). Evaluation of JOLT as a deterrence program. Lansing: Michigan Department of Corrections, Program Bureau.

Seattle Social Development Project (SSDP)

Hawkins, J. D., Kosterman, R., Catalano, R. F., Hill, K. G., and Abbott, R. D. (2004). Promoting positive adult functioning through social development intervention in childhood: Long-term effects from the Seattle Social Development Project. Paper presented at Society for Prevention Research annual meeting in Quebec City, used with permission.

Team Child

Ezell, M. (1997). Teamchild: Evaluation of the second year. Unpublished Manuscript.

Norrbin, S. C., Rasmussen, D. W., and Von-Frank, D. M. (2004). Using civil representation to reduce delinquency among troubled youth. *Evaluation Review* 28(3): 201–217.

Teen Courts

Butts J., Buck, J., and Coggeshall, M. (2002). The impact of teen court on young offenders. Washington, DC: The Urban Institute.

Hissong, R. (1991). Teen court: Is it an effective alternative to traditional sanctions? *Journal for Juvenile Justice and Detention Services* 6:14–23.

North Carolina Administrative Office of the Courts. (1995). Report on the Teen Court Programs in North Carolina. Raleigh, NC: North Carolina Administrative Office of the Courts.

Therapeutic Community Programs, MICA Offenders

Sacks, S., Sacks, J. Y., McKendrick, K., Banks, S., and Stommel, J. (2004). Modified TC for MICA offenders: Crime outcomes. *Behavioral Sciences and the Law* 22(4): 477–501.

Van Stelle, K. R., and Moberg, D. P. (2004). Outcome data from MICA clients after participation in an institutional therapeutic community. *Journal of Offender Rehabilitation* 39(1): 37–62.

Vocational Education in Prison

Callen, V., and J. Gardner. (2005). Vocational education and training provision and recidivism in Queensland correctional institutions. National Center for Vocational Education Research (NCVER): Queensland, Australia.

Lattimore, P. K., Witte, A. D., and Baker, J. R. (1990). Experimental assessment of the effect of vocational training on youthful property offenders. *Evaluation Review* 14(2): 115–133.

Saylor, W. G., and Gaes, G. G. (1996). PREP: A study of rehabilitating inmates through industrial work participation, and vocational and apprenticeship training. Federal Bureau of Prisons: Washington, DC.

Washington's Dialectical Behavior Therapy (DBT)

Drake, E., and Barnoski, R. (2006). Recidivism findings for the Juvenile Rehabilitation Administration's dialectical behavior therapy program: Final report. Olympia, WA. Washington State Institute for Public Policy. Available at: http://www.wsipp.wa.gov/rptfiles/06-07-1201.pdf.

Work-Release Programs from Prison

Jeffrey, R., and Woolpert, S. (1974). Work furlough as an alternative to incarceration. *The Journal of Criminology* 65(3): 405–415.

LeClair, D. P., and Guarino-Ghezzi, S. (1991). Does incapacitation guarantee public safety? Lessons from the Massachusetts furlough and prerelease programs. *Justice Quarterly* 8(1): 9–36

Turner, S. M., and Petersilia, J. (1996). Work release in Washington: Effects on recidivism and corrections costs. *Prison Journal* 76(2): 138–164.

Waldo, G. P., and Chiricos, T. G. (1977). Work release and recidivism: An empirical evaluation of a social policy. *Evaluation Quarterly* 1(1): 87–108.

Index

F

G

H

L

M

N

O